# MODERN DOGMA
## and the
# RHETORIC OF ASSENT

*Wayne C. Booth*

THE UNIVERSITY OF CHICAGO PRESS

CHICAGO AND LONDON

THE UNIVERSITY OF CHICAGO PRESS, CHICAGO 60637
THE UNIVERSITY OF CHICAGO PRESS, LTD., LONDON
© 1974 by University of Notre Dame Press
All rights reserved. University of Chicago edition published 1974
Printed in the United States of America
International Standard Book Number: 0-226-06572-3
Library of Congress Catalog Card Number: 73-89786
00 99 98 97 96 95 94 93 92 91          6 7 8 9 10

# MODERN DOGMA
## and the
# RHETORIC OF ASSENT

*University of Notre Dame*
*Ward-Phillips Lectures in*
*English Language and Literature*

VOLUME 5

For Katherine and Alison

It is characteristic of the intellectual life of our culture that, in radical psychology as in radical politics, it fosters a form of assent which does not involve actual credence.

Lionel Trilling

*Nullus quippe credit aliquid, nisi prius cogitaverit esse credendum* [No one, indeed, believes anything, unless he previously knows it to be believable].

Augustine

Only connect the prose and the passion.

E. M. Forster

To have "no doubt" about a thesis is equivalent to one or other of the two remaining acts, either to inferring it or else assenting to it. However, the word [Doubt] is often taken to mean the deliberate recognition of a thesis as being uncertain; in this sense Doubt is nothing else than an assent, viz., an assent to a proposition at variance with the thesis.

Newman, *The Grammar of Assent*

We must address with song every object we meet, because Tira'wa (the supreme spirit) is in all things, everything we come to as we travel can give us help.

Pawnee "informant" to A. C. Fletcher

How miserable were the man's mind, or rather his life, that should be debarred the use of his reason, not only in the matter of argument, but in the main end of his being?

Cicero

# Contents

## Contents

# Introduction

In the late sixties I became puzzled, both as a student of rhetoric and as a harried dean, by the inability of most protest groups to get themselves heard and by the equal failure of what one of my students called "establishment protestees" to make their responses intelligible. But when I tried to analyze competing statements to discover the reasons for these "failures of communication," I could seldom find satisfying answers in the words spoken or written by the combatants. Few of the failures seemed caused by sheer slovenliness or ineptitude—the faults were not the kind I was used to dealing with in my students' papers. Even the most skillful stylists and logicians relied on unspoken assumptions that beclouded every line. And whenever I tried dutifully to trace those assumptions back to a point of agreement from which a meeting of minds might begin, I found that I was finally grappling not simply with political assumptions, though these were met along the line, but with some version of the modernist dogmas about belief and doubt that I have made central here.

This century has often been called an age of doubt, an age of skepticism, and—more recently—an age of unreason. It is not hard to find evidence supporting the epithets. To assert that all assertion is meaningless, once the privilege of an intellectual elite, has become a popular pastime. Attacks on reason and thought abound. Celebrations of madness as superior to reason have become commonplace, as in the works of R. D. Laing, Norman O. Brown, and David Cooper. One popular critic, deploring "the New Cult of Madness," concludes that *reason* and *logic* have, in fact, become dirty words. They have been replaced by the life words *feeling* and *impulse*. Consciousness (the rational) is presumed to be shallow, and unconsciousness (the irrational) to be always interesting, often profound, and usually *true*.[1] In the formula of the late Frederick S. Perls, the way to find your real self is "to lose your mind and become your senses."

Yet it is unlikely that any previous period has produced more declarations of passionate belief, more last-ditch stands based on unshakable conviction, and more defenses of reason and attacks on irrationalists. A determined pursuer of Zeitgeists could easily show that we are an age of faith and credulity, if he chose to look only at the thousands of books, articles, radio talks, and TV shows with titles like

1. Melvin Maddocks, "The New Cult of Madness: Thinking as a Bad Habit," *Time*, March 13, 1972, pp. 51–52.

*Introduction*

"What I Believe," "Credo," or "What I Live By." In one popular monograph series, Credo Perspectives, edited by Ruth Nanda Anshen, we find a score of books by famous men of our time—physical scientists, art critics, a supreme court justice, a smattering of social scientists, and *two* popes—all of them *affirming* and *asserting* with great vigor, revealing on every page that they have managed, in a "time of universal doubt," to find reasons for faith and action.

But somehow our picture of the bleak age of doubt is not much affected by these floods of faith, and a close look shows why. Most of them reveal a tone of desperation suggesting—even in those that explicitly affirm confidence in reason—a fear of the triumph of unreason. It is as if every assertion had to be prefaced with proof that the asserter is really a hard-headed skeptic: "Though I know that nothing can be said by way of *proving* my beliefs, though I know that all assertions of value are mere personal preferences, I am determined to assert some anyway: *I believe . . .*"

The result is often an oracular tone reminiscent of Jehovah and his prophets on a bad day, even when the speaker is pleading for reason. Erich Fromm, in the last chapter of *Beyond the Chains of Illusion: My Encounter with Marx and Freud*[2] offers a series of paragraphs beginning "I believe . . ." But the effect of the chanted credo is not to raise confidence in the validity of the beliefs. Rather it makes them sound like mere wishes. Even the beliefs that could easily be defended with careful argument, or that all readers in fact share without argument, come to sound like hopeless, though courageous, special pleading. A truism like "I believe that reason cannot be effective unless man has hope and belief," one that most of Fromm's readers will take as self-evident in spite of ambiguities, is equated with idiosyncratic and puzzling assertions like "I believe in the perfectibility of man, but I doubt whether he will achieve this goal . . . (p. 182)." The result is that even in saying "I believe that the only force that can save us from self-destruction is reason" (p. 179), Fromm implies that all we can hope for is unreasoned pronouncements. He would not of course say that he believes in this implication, but his chosen tone to some degree diminishes the force of his message.

All of the many allies who might work together to discover what can be legitimately believed are thus encouraged simply to affirm *at* each other. Even in work designed to collect together those who would combat destructive skepticisms, there is often no intellectual encounter: no one contributor tries to understand and perhaps support the

2. New York, 1962.

affirmations of any other contributor. We are left with an image of a vast public square, a kind of international Hyde Park, with scattered platforms on which a few isolated prophets shout, arms raised to the sky, "I believe, brother, I believe." Those standing below are not listening. Why should they, since they can see that the prophets are not listening to each other?

This image of a world of futile babblers strongly resembles the practical world of protest and response as it sometimes feels to participants. In both worlds passionate partisans cannot seem to find convincing ways of talking about their beliefs. The "connection" between "the prose and the passion" that E. M. Forster sought in *Howards End* is lost. Or, as Cicero would have put it, "wisdom" (and action guided by wisdom) no longer seems to have any connection with "eloquence." Arguments for our beliefs or actions have become "mere rhetoric" or propaganda or rationalization. Passionate commitment has lost its connection with the provision of good reasons. And reason has been reduced to logical calculation and proof about whatever does not matter enough to engage commitment.

But this torn picture of the world, with all of our commitments and values on one side and all of our rational capacities on the other, is not what I find when I look at what is being said by the major philosophers, historians, social scientists, linguists, and rhetoricians of our time—not, at least, when they address their colleagues. Despite all the talk about crises of confidence and loss of consensus, experts still argue together effectively, and in every field I know anything about there has recently been fresh questioning of those dogmas from the recent past that would sharply separate values from fact, knowledge, and reason.

In short, we seem to conduct much of our practical controversy on "modern" assumptions that many recent theorists would repudiate. If the assumptions are correct, controversy about values and commitments is essentially nonrational, and rhetoric is simply the art of winning. If they are at best questionable, if in fact the whole modernist edifice has been undermined by its own rhetoric of systematic doubt, we may hope now to construct rhetorics of a kind of assent that cannot be dismissed as "mere faith."

These lectures, originally given in the Ward-Phillips series at the University of Notre Dame in April of 1971, are intended as an introduction to one of many possible directions in which postmodernist rhetoric about values can earn its legitimacy. I am aware that some of the examples drawn from student protests of the late sixties already seem dated, but the reader can easily substitute today's blockade by truckers (December 1973), or tomorrow's sit-in by—shall we predict?—the board members of General Motors.

## II

I would expect some readers to be puzzled about where in the intellectual landscape such rhetorical study lies. When I described the lectures to a professor of philosophical psychology, he said that they "belonged to him," and a professor of sociology told me that what I am doing— in a "popular" way and "unfortunately without proper professional terminology"—is a combination of sociology of knowledge and social psychology. A fellow admirer of Bernard Crick's *In Defense of Politics* claimed that my effort is a long footnote on the implications for public discourse of that brief and powerful book. In fact I can think of no field, even in the hard sciences, to which a revived confidence in rhetoric is not in some way pertinent, and I can think of few that cannot in some way contribute to it. As soon as I ask "When *should* I change my mind?" or "What is a good reason?" I become an intellectual imperialist, and I risk becoming vacuous for the sake of covering the world.

It is not surprising that rhetoric has always had an uneasy relationship with other disciplines, particularly philosophy. *As a discipline* it is said to have no substance of its own. Since it is itself empty—so the claim runs—it leads its practitioners into superficiality and irresponsibility. If you want to know how to demonstrate conclusions— in criticism, in politics, in science, in metaphysics—clearly you should go to specialists who know the grounds of argument in those fields. *As an art,* it has been considered mere trickery or bombast or ornament. The claim made by Hans Morgenthau and others that President Kennedy substituted rhetoric for genuine thought and action can be found paralleled through the centuries, beginning with Socrates' attacks on the sophists' ability to make the worse seem the better cause.

I start out, then, like theologians these days, knowing that many readers will think I have no subject matter, and that those who grant me a subject may consider my way of working in it disreputable as compared with their own. The philosophers worry me most, since they know how much could be said about many of the questions I seem to settle with a twist of the wrist. But it is part of my point that modern philosophy—at least until the last two decades—has saddled us with standards of truth under which no man can live. Even the recent philosophers whom I use as witnesses for part of my case are still, many of them, seeking a certainty that would be of no use to our practical discourse even if it were to be found.

## Introduction

If philosophy is defined as inquiry into certain truth, then what I pursue here is not philosophy but rhetoric: the art of discovering warrantable beliefs and improving those beliefs in shared discourse. But the differences are not sharply definable, and I of course think of the inquiry as in a larger sense philosophical. To talk of improving beliefs implies that we are seeking truth, since some beliefs are "truer" than others. Besides, many philosophers from Cicero to the present have defined what they do precisely as I would define rhetoric.

When Locke began his great *Essay Concerning Human Understanding,* he set out to inquire "into the original, certainty, and extent of *human knowledge,* together with the grounds and degrees of *belief, opinion,* and *assent.*" In what followed he was interested, as a philosopher, mainly in a knowledge that could be called universal, and in what could be said about it that might prove permanently true. He still included a good deal about "the grounds *and degrees* of belief, opinion, and assent," much of which later empiricists, more and more obsessed with certainty and less and less with rhetorical likelihoods, would have ruled out. My business is largely with what they left out—with what might be called the origin, *likelihoods,* and extent of human *convictions,* together with the grounds and degrees of belief, opinion, and assent—an argument for the intellectual validity of a subject which, abandoned by philosophers, has too often fallen into the hands of quacks: preachers of "plain style," of "winning friends and influencing [other?] people," of "writing that sells," to say nothing of various "scientific" modes of changing men's minds.

The rhetoric that concerns us here will be the art of probing what men believe they ought to believe, rather than proving what is true according to abstract methods. It is thus always dirtying its hands in mere opinion, offering its services to both sides of a controversy, and producing results that are at best rather messy. And rhetoric is always tainted, in the view of purer disciplines, by concern for audiences.

This might not be too bad if rhetoric worried only about "what all men believe," but more often than not it alters its conclusions, as it manipulates its devices, to suit the local opinions of special audiences: rhetoric not only uses different arguments when addressing different audiences, but it will prove conflicting conclusions, since it is finally and utterly bound to whatever convictions are shared by a given rhetorical community.

This flexibility—not to say venality—can be made to look like a very serious fault, but it can also be turned into a resource, especially in a time when "everyone believes" that "there are no shared values any more." The commonplace that all eternal verities have been dis-

xiii

credited feels threatening to those who think that without established eternal verities men must degenerate into a life that is nasty, poor, solitary, brutish and short. But it is precisely in the handling of such a commonplace that rhetoric comes into its own. Who believes it? Why do they believe it? Do they *really* believe it? What other commonplaces about values do they share as they deplore together the loss of shared values? What "rhetorical communities" can be discovered that may in fact unite seemingly warring factions, and what are the real conflicts that separate rhetorical communities based on conflicting assumptions?

One thing that we all believe, though many of us believe we have no good grounds for the belief, is that there really is a difference between good reasons and bad—which in my terms means a genuine difference between good rhetoric and bad. "Good rhetoric" can of course mean something very different from this: it often means merely whatever is successful in the sense of winning assent regardless of whether assent is justified. At best, in popular usage, *good rhetoric* will mean rhetoric that is effective, in the sense of doing all that is possible to produce persuasion regardless of whether the audience is pig-headed or not. But I shall be pursuing here the art of discovering good reasons, finding what really warrants assent because any reasonable person ought to be persuaded by what has been said. This latter meaning has disappeared from most discussions of communication in our time,[3] and it is the one I deal with most extensively. *Bad rhetoric* throughout

3. I can of course claim only to have sampled the vast literature produced in various schools of communications, information theory, opinion change, and content analysis in the social sciences. But of what I have read, Milton Rokeach's study *The Open and Closed Mind: Investigations into the Nature of Belief Systems and Personality Systems* (New York, 1960) seems unfortunately typical. In his many studies of whether his subjects have open or closed minds, Rokeach seldom even hints at the simple fact—a fact in my terms—that about some opinions one *ought* to be more malleable than about others. The German who is easily persuaded to become a Nazi can hardly be said to have an open mind in the same sense as the nigger-hater who is easily persuaded to grant equal rights to all races. Should Solzhenitsyn be judged as having a closed mind because he refuses to change his mind about the value of freedom of speech? The subtleties suggested by such a question totally escape any simple scale between the "closed" and the "open," just as distinctions about *the quality of reasons offered* are for the most part ignored. *Should* I change? I can never find an answer on the basis of a desirable personality or character trait, without looking at the quality of the reasons offered. I find the same essential limitations in content analysis—almost always the "content" is inert because the quality of reasons is not taken into the study. See Bernard Berelson, *Content Analysis in Communication Research* (Glencoe, Ill., 1952), and (with Morris Janowitz as coeditor) *Reader in Public Opinion and Communications* (New York, 1953), esp. pp. 5, 64, 66. Philosophical discussions of the impossibility of certainty and the harmfulness of dogmatism

the lectures will not be primarily what is technically clumsy—though that is one kind of badness—but the rhetoric which lacks genuine power to move reasonable auditors, if any should happen along. To say as much should ensure that the lectures are at least controversial, since it is—if many theorists are to be believed—utter nonsense: "Who are you to determine who is 'reasonable'?" To which these lectures reply: "The question is not 'Who am I?' but 'Who are we?' "

In theory what I have to say applies to all symbolic resources of man, not just to our use of language. But for convenience I talk mainly of what we do with words, except for a bit in the fourth lecture about music. Popular rhetorics these days are making a good deal out of things like body rhetoric (see, for example, Julius Fast's *Body Language,* an incredibly superficial best seller), TV pictures, and other nonverbal "media"—the changes of mind and soul produced by a look, by a symphony, by a painting, by a beautiful building, by a flourished gun, by a photograph or TV shot, by a cry of "meaningless" pain. These are inherently part of my subject, and I think that to treat them would require no essential modifications in my claims. In spite of the great technical differences in deciding whether a photograph, for example, has been doctored, or a TV news broadcast unfairly edited, the principles both of defensive rhetoric and affirmative response are the same.

### III

My efforts to reduce the inescapable superficiality of the original lectures have taken two directions: expanding the text and providing extensive documentation. The result is a kind of bifocal book. The first focus is the expanded lectures, to be read as if addressed to that patient assembly at Notre Dame—what I wish I had said, given time and the additional reading and thinking that two years of revision have allowed. It is still in a sense spoken to an audience mainly of students, with some professors of English and philosophy eavesdropping. The second focus is mainly in the footnotes—what might be called hints toward a full scholarly treatment of these issues. The reader who chooses the perhaps dizzying task of shifting from book to book will discover my own surprised discovery that "everybody" is suddenly wrestling with my kind of problem; the notes (abetted by the index) contain an elementary book list leading into perhaps a dozen distinct

---

often make the same kind of mistake; see, for example, Stephen C. Pepper's "The Root Metaphor Theory of Metaphysics," *Journal of Philosophy* 32 (1935): 365–74.

academic fields where the dogmas are being refuted and rhetorics of assent constructed, often with more precision than my general account allows for and often without using the word rhetoric.

The reader who prefers a steadier but less challenging path should be able to listen to the lectures as if the footnotes were not there.

## IV

The belief that the primary mental act of man is to assent to truth rather than to detect error, "to take in" and even "to be taken in," rather than "to resist being taken in," is of course not original with me. Notions of "in-spiration" have been found in every historical period, and regardless of who or what provides the breath, they have always entailed the mysterious process of two becoming one. When I assent to your thought (or symphony or novel or account of your divorce) the line between us grows dim; in the ideal case it in a sense disappears, and it is not surprising that many theologians and rhetoricians have echoed Newman's effort to build a grammar of assent and Kenneth Burke's to build a grammar, rhetoric, and symbolic of identification. I could not possibly define the influence of these men on what I have said, any more than I can distinguish what I have borrowed from the many phenomenologists since Dilthey who have explored how we come to know persons and art works by "dwelling in" them; the many sociologists who have developed George Herbert Mead's inquiries into how selves make themselves in encounter with "significant others"; or the many psychologists from Freud and Jung to Carl Rogers who have developed accounts of how selves are built by taking in other selves. The latter's "psychology of assent"—my term, not his—seems to me especially important. In advocating "unconditional positive regard," Rogers tells us in effect that the supreme *ought* is to pass no judgments until we have thoroughly taken in the point of view of the other man, whether he is a patient or an intellectual opponent. Rogers sees the "whole task of psychotherapy" as "dealing with a failure in communication," a failure both within the patient and between him and the world. And he sees the therapist's essential task as subordinating his own feelings and evaluations in order to listen with understanding. Only when he can prove that he understands the patient's position as well as the patient himself (and this includes his capacity to feel with him) can he hope to give real help in "altering the basic personality structure" of the patient—or of the rhetorical opponent.[4]

4. "Communication: Its Blocking and Its Facilitation," a paper presented in 1951 at Northwestern University's Centennial Conference on Communications,

## Introduction

I am conscious of much more extensive borrowing from a philosopher of science, Michael Polanyi. His *Personal Knowledge* is the most important critique of systematic doubt in the name of what I have called systematic assent; though I can by no means agree with all that he says, his "postcritical philosophy" challenges the dogmas of modernism more thoroughly than any other modern work I know. He appears here again and again, usually unacknowledged and often in forms that he might not himself recognize.

Richard McKeon is also everywhere in these pages. Though they lack his learning and genius and at points ignore his explicit advice, I hope that they reflect his passion for giving every idea a chance before fighting it off. His lifelong effort to develop a pluralistic semantics of philosophies that would do justice to the powers of different views is to me the most important rhetoric of philosophical assent.

I am especially grateful to Kary Wolfe for steady and patient editorial assistance during the last months of revision. Finally, both for detailed rigorous criticism and for teaching me warrants for assent that no words can encompass, I thank Phyllis Booth, my wife.

---

reprinted in *Rhetoric: Discovery and Change,* by Richard E. Young, Alton L. Becker, and Kenneth L. Pike (New York, 1970), pp. 284–89. Rogers seems to me seriously confused in the way he puts his case against evaluation or judgment: his own language reveals that even when he is "listening with understanding" he does not and cannot rid himself of clear judgments about "improving" the patient by "releasing potent forces of change" and establishing "realistic and harmonious relationships." But this quibble does not affect the basic suggestiveness of his brief "rhetoric."

Young, Becker, and Pike are, so far as I know, the only writers on rhetoric who have seen the relevance of Rogers to new rhetorical views.

# MODERN DOGMA
## and the
# RHETORIC OF ASSENT

Only when a new passion for moral progress was fused with modern scientific skepticism did the typical state of the modern mind emerge.

Michael Polanyi

The deepest, the only theme of human history, compared to which all others are of subordinate importance, is the conflict of skepticism with faith.

Goethe

We have been reading some of the *Rhetoric* [Aristotle] in the Sixth Form this half-year, and its immense value struck me again so forcibly that I could not consent to send my son to [a] University where he would lose it altogether.

Thomas Arnold, considering whether
to send his son to Oxford

Now not only is positivism, a movement in *philosophy,* not the same as *science* (of which it gives a systematically distorted picture), but . . . even the most positivistic scientists do not act on the credo they expound in their prefaces; they do just about the opposite of what dogma requires as soon as they turn to the analysis and explanation of experience.

Jean Piaget

Nothing said or done can reach
My fanatic heart.

W. B. Yeats

# ONE | Motivism and the Loss of Good Reasons

## THE CRISIS IN OUR RHETORIC

A few months ago I bought a copy of *Seed,* a curiously anonymous Chicago magazine, and I found, among other testimonials to the healing and liberating powers of pot, a "Letter from Tim Leary." It was a very passionate letter indeed, and it included the following manifesto for the "ancient and holy strategy of organic life":

1. Resist lovingly in the loyalty of underground sisterhoods and brotherhoods.
2. Resist passively, break lock-step . . . drop out.
3. Resist actively, sabotage, jam the computer . . . hijack planes . . . trash every lethal machine in the land.
4. Resist publicly, announce life . . . denounce death.
5. Resist privately, guerrilla invisibility.
6. Resist beautifully, create organic art, music.
7. Resist biologically, be healthy . . . erotic . . . conspire with seed . . . breed.
8. Resist spiritually, stay high . . . praise god . . . love life . . . blow the mechanical mind with Holy Acid . . . dose them . . . dose them.
9. Resist physically, robot agents who threaten life must be disarmed, disabled, disconnected by force. . . . Arm yourselves and shoot to live. . . . Life is never violent. To shoot a genocidal robot policeman in the defense of life is a sacred act. . . .
Listen, the hour is late. Total war is upon us. Fight to live or you'll die. Freedom is life. Freedom will live. . . .
WARNING: I am armed and should be considered dangerous to anyone who threatens my life or my freedom.[1]

I doubted, as I read, that Dr. Timothy Leary had really written it; *Seed* is so full of Letters Nobody Ever Wrote. Then I noticed, in pale pink print lower on the page, two comments. One was from "Dick," saying that he does not think Leary wrote the letter:

Or maybe the FBI wrote it. Or maybe I wrote it. I'm leery of the whole thing.
It really doesn't matter who wrote what. Letters from the underground establish their own reality as soon as the straight media prints or broadcasts the[m], and anyway, the principals are unavailable for comment.

1. *Seed* [October or November, 1970], p. 4.

3

The other, from "Bernie," said,

> I think the letter is genuine. I think that it is a signpost and a guidelight for many of us who will soon have to choose to either really open our eyes to the horror around us (and do something about it), or retreat back into our own heads, awaiting the apocalypse. I can feel and believe in my guts that a man like Leary loves life enough to want to go down fighting. There can and must be flowers for our sisters and brothers, but for those who seek to destroy us there can only be bullets and bombs.

Such statements do indeed establish their reality, as statement, once they are incorporated into a "straight medium" like these lectures. I find it striking that in all this long miscellaneous catalogue of ways to resist there is no hint that one might make use of argument. In fact there is no provision even for words—the medium of the plea itself is not included in the plea. When the mind is mentioned it is something to be "blown," or it is a wicked retreat. And the only activities of mind that are hinted at, except perhaps for "announce life" and "praise God," are "organic art" and music. Though much is affirmed that I might want to affirm (if I could find out what it means) and much resisted that I would want to resist, there is no suggestion that either my affirmations or my resistance could be furthered by learning to use my head to improve the quality of my arguments. On the contrary, concern for good argument is explicitly undermined by the contempt for fact and for the reader who cares about getting things straight. As the headlines for the piece put it, "HEAD AFOOT/BELIEVE IT OR NOT"— what a gas, to think of straight readers like me worrying about whether Leary really wrote that letter.

Well, straight or not, "I feel and believe in *my* gut" that *Seed*'s reduction of all protest to blindly chosen *yeses* or *noes,* and of all men to heroes and villains, is a more serious threat than the references to bullets and bombs. Amateurs of doublethink, the editors of *Seed* are in fact playing a dangerous game, one that may well help to destroy the political society that makes possible their publication and our being here together today.

I also feel and believe in *my* gut that—so I could go on, fulminating against the threat such a statement makes to my professional and personal commitments. It is not exactly clear, however, what such lamentations would accomplish. Though we encounter many who write such passages, and read them uncritically, we know that it does no good to shout back our own commitments. What then do we say to those who write this way and think this way—assuming, of course, that they will give us time to say anything before the bullets start flying in defense of life?

Even to ask for that much time—time for discussion, for thought —is for many people these days a dead giveaway. By setting out to talk about such problems, or to announce in my title that I want to deal with rhetoric instead of urging this or that action program, I have already taken sides, if the choice is between those who believe that "he who hesitates has already sold out" and those who believe that "you should look before you leap and then never leap." How can I stand here trying to *think* about protest when I should be out organizing a bit of it?

The question must seem especially pertinent to those who are convinced that professors and ex-deans are committed to inaction, obfuscation, and equivocation. To which I reply, as student of rhetoric and as a man who wants to make his protests count: What kind of reasons can *you* give, now, for *your* beliefs about *Seed,* about Leary, about protest, about professors and deans and their institutions? What are your reasons for believing what you now believe, whether good or bad, about *me* as I stand before you, about me as professor, as ex-dean, and as lecturer today? Did you, for example, believe me when I said that the quotation came from *Seed?* How naive of you! Obviously this conservative speaker needed an extreme illustration of just how irrational our rhetoric has become these days, and he made up the whole story.

Or did he? As the editor of *Seed* said, "Who wrote that letter? Maybe *I* wrote it."

I now look you in the eye and tell you that the story was true. Do you believe me? If you don't, you presumably have what you think are good reasons. You're sadly mistaken, of course, since I am obviously the most *sincere* speaker you're likely to hear this year. But what reasons do you appeal to in thinking about such matters?

For many, such a question would be at this point meaningless: I have so far offered nothing worth being called a reason; I've given only anecdote, emotional appeal, implied and direct references to my own character. You may even have been taught, as I was, that *to be reasonable* in such a situation means taking an absolutely neutral ground until solid proof is available—which in fact amounts to making the negative decision, to deny credence. Since nothing has been proved, an educated man will wait for real evidence. It is part of my point in these lectures that we were taught wrong.

To swallow the letter in *Seed* requires what has traditionally been called an uncritical mind—a mind that says yes too easily. But it is not hard to think of rhetorical situations in which the failure is better described as not saying yes readily enough. I can remember how doggedly, during the years just preceding World War II, I held to my "critical" refusal to believe the atrocity stories about the Nazis. I had been taught that Americans had been gullible in World War I when they believed atrocity propaganda put out by the Allies. I knew better than to believe that the Nazis were persecuting Jews, and I also knew better than to believe the stories about the purges committed by Stalin: everybody who had a "critical mind" knew that the press was pro-capitalist and anticommunist and that therefore you couldn't believe those stories. But of course I have now decided, like you, for good reasons or bad, that in essence those stories were true. Presumably many a Jew inside Nazi Germany committed the same error of what might be called negative credulity, refusing, with fatal "tough mindedness," to believe the rumors about the truth that came his way.

A more pressing instance is upon us today—an instance so overwhelming that I feel almost guilty about not making it the center of my lectures. For a long time it has been "practically certain" that America made a disastrous and brutal mistake in going into Vietnam and that we must get out; let's say, to be very conservative, that the nature of the disaster has been clear, to anyone willing to read and think about it, at least since it became clear to President Johnson in 1968. The arguments have been complicated, I'll admit, and there are indeed at least two sides to every political question; I'm sure that our failure to understand the opposing case has contributed to the delay. Nevertheless, I must say that the critics of the war have long since earned a resounding yes, the defenders of the policy a resounding no. Those of you who doubt me will, I hope, read the statement published in all the papers yesterday (April 25, 1971) by veteran John F. Kerry, as one of thousands of anguished appeals that to me can only be answered with a yes —which means, of course, a no to U.S. policy.

My point here is not, however, the rights and wrongs of the war. It is that the issue of getting out, though to most of us morally and politically clear, has been obscured by our rhetoric rather than clarified.[2] Much—perhaps most—of what has been said by Mr. Nixon

2. "One is embarrassed to add new words on Vietnam. Already there have been millions, and despite the good sense so many of them have shown, they have as yet, after all these years, been unable to sway the American government, through three successive administrations, to desist from a disastrous policy which can only be carried out . . . by cruel and inhuman methods. Yet some of us try to convince ourselves that words can still—must still—play a role in persuading. . . ." (Nathan Glazer, "Vietnam: The Case for Immediate Withdrawal," *Commentary* 51 [May 1971]: 33).

*Note, May 1973:* It took nearly two more years of words and fighting and

and by his opponents has delayed our getting out; instead of public debate, we are surrounded by "credibility gaps."

In short, no matter what side of any issue we are on, we seem to face a clear rhetorical crisis. As a student said to me last week, nobody listens to anybody any more. Or, to quote a janitor I overheard in the airport at Kansas City a while ago, "I believe only half of what I see, and nothing of what I hear or read." Our problem is partly the ancient one of not knowing when to be skeptical and when not to be, when to say no and when to say yes. But the old problem is made much worse by a relatively new one: like the editors of *Seed,* we have lost our faith in the very possibility of finding a rational path through any thicket that includes what we call value judgments.

Before I move to the task of trying to understand, I'd like to offer one fairly extensive example: the choosing up of sides by large numbers of students and faculty in a major university conflict. A very large proportion of the nine thousand faculty and students at the University of Chicago found themselves two springs ago—like the members of many another university—finally split into two camps. I have since heard some of them say that they feel they were *had*—some students have told me that they were "taken in" to the administration building for the sixteen-day sit-in by arguments with little or no substance; some faculty members who rose against them, including myself, would say that we were scarcely impressive in our various responses.

The sit-in began on the issue of a "non-negotiable" demand to the president that he "rehire Marlene Dixon," an assistant professor of human development and sociology. Her colleagues in the Committee on Human Development had recommended retention; her colleagues in the Department of Sociology had recommended against retention. The various administrators to whom the recommendations went had decided against her. Rhetorically it was an ideal case for those students who had announced long before that they were trying to find an issue with which to blast the university wide open: Marlene Dixon, a woman

---

bombing before the last ground troops left Vietnam, and we are still bombing Cambodia. So much, one might be tempted to say, for what good reasons can do in the real world. Now we are in the thick of the "Watergate scandal," with daily revelations of just how little respect for words and reasons Mr. Nixon and his associates have shown. But it takes no Kenneth Burke to recognize the dialectical truth that a scandal requires at least two parties, the scandalous and the scandalized; so long as so many of us are scandalized when leaders poison the public wells of discourse, all is not lost. Still, we must persist in asking how a nation of "educated men and women" could produce so many at the top who show the same contempt for words as is shown by the editors of *Seed.*

and a self-professed radical who had recently changed her field from computer science to Marxist sociology, said to be a popular teacher, not rehired and for reasons kept secret! The only automatic buttons not pushed were race and personal handicaps.

The students' rhetoric was all based, initially, on the flat assertion that she must have been dropped because of her politics, because she was a woman, because she was liked as a teacher. Otherwise, why were we keeping the reasons secret? Many of us claimed that because of all these suspicions, special care had in fact been taken to make sure that only questions of competence as teacher and scholar figured—though of course no one could swear that nobody had voted from irrelevant political or sexist motives, and we were not prepared to open confidential files and reveal the evidence for our claim.

Within a few days none of this mattered very much, as the issues multiplied, finally covering such demands as a fifty-fifty vote for students on all university committees, day-care centers to be provided by the university, doubled salaries to all unskilled university employees, elimination of all formal academic requirements, and even a vote on all appointments by the nonacademic citizens of surrounding Hyde Park.

More important to me today than this frantic and self-defeating multiplication and discarding of issues (Marlene Dixon was almost forgotten) was the degradation of the rhetoric on all sides. Communication—to use the popular near-synonym for what I mean by rhetoric—was bad from the beginning, with the faculty playing cool and aloof and rational, and thus seeming secretive and hypocritical, the students talking of nonnegotiable demands for concessions which many of them knew to be impossible. As one of them told me afterward, "I guess we wanted to put the university in a bind, but we expected people like you to read behind the lines to what we *really* meant."

As things moved along the faculty began to pour out communiqués about the value of reasonable debate—reasonable arguments, they thought, which the students for some reason thought absurd and ignored. The students' replies in turn sounded more and more wildly irrational to the faculty; many faculty members who had been initially sympathetic to the students were finally driven from the cause by the shrill tone of the mimeographed sheets flowing from the occupied administration building. But it was also true that some students who had not originally been sympathetic to the protestors joined them because of what they thought of as the irrational actions and pronouncements of the faculty.

At one point things got so bad that each side found itself reduplicating broadsides produced by the other side, and distributing them, in thousands of copies, without comment; to each side it seemed as if the other side's rhetoric was self-damning, so absurd had it become![3] At the end of the sixteen days, the students left the building, admitting defeat and threatening to come back and burn it down. "The university" had not called the police, nor had it reversed its decision under pressure: committees appointed to review the case concluded that except for student anger there were no *grounds* for reversal. It had thus in a sense succeeded in resisting the two moves that would most clearly have made it less than a university. But the community found itself left with perhaps two thousand pages of mimeographed broadsides and a terribly bitter sense of division.

When I went through the defaced building, I found scrawled on one desk, "Fuck the life of the mind," and on another, " 'Look before you leap, and look, and look, and look . . .' *Booth*." It made me angry. If ever a group of protestors should have looked a bit longer before they leaped, that group was it. And if anyone wanted to confirm the prejudices of the worst reactionaries about the students' attitudes toward intellectual values, he could not have done better than take a tour of the messages scrawled throughout the building.

Nobody now doubts that this event was disastrous, even though some would argue that it was an experience we had to pass through. For many of the radical students it was disastrous—more than forty were finally expelled by a disciplinary committee.[4] For the university

3. See Appendix A for examples. Long after I gave these lectures, I discovered that Daniel Yankelovich has also explored the view that beneath such surface rhetoric lie issues about the relation of thought and feeling, man and nature, reason and faith (*The Changing Values on Campus* [New York: Washington Square Press, 1972]). For him students represent a new idea: "that we must initiate a new stage in man's relatedness to nature and the natural." His interviews and questionnaires show students embracing meanings that "add up to a new world view, a philosophy of life and of nature capable of transforming man's relationship to himself and his society"; it is in opposition to "dominant modes of thinking in American culture as represented by technology, rationalism, and traditional middle-class sensibility" (pp. 167–71). I think that his book tends too often to confirm and deepen the scientismist/irrationalist split we both deplore, but I should like, quite arbitrarily, to take his book as providing experimental evidence for my conclusion that campus confrontations have been representative of issues raised by modernism.

4. None simply for taking part in the sit-in. Refusal to grant jurisdiction to the committees—at that time consisting wholly of faculty members—was in most cases the additional offense that led to expulsion. Whether expulsion counted as "disastrous" for the students expelled was hard to tell from what was said. Beforehand many said that to be kicked out of such a corrupt institution would be a good thing; afterward Marlene Dixon claimed that a police bust would have been better: "Cracked heads will mend, but a ruined career is ruined forever."

it was disastrously embittering—only now has something like the normal level of tolerable mistrust between faculty and students been restored. If the main purpose of a university is learning and teaching, everyone concerned would say that the real university was diminished for many months. And even the more extreme students who at first claimed that their defeat was a victory, since at least "the university has been *polarized*," found at the end that the sit-in had produced apathy in most other students, not unity and spirit. All later efforts to mount a major protest have failed.

A full history of this one event would require hundreds of pages, especially if the historian tried to do justice to the many causes, national, local, and personal, that made it both strikingly alike and slightly different from the many other confrontations of that troubled year. But I should like to concentrate on the verbal and intellectual failures that our event shared with hundreds of confrontations—and not only in universities—during the past five years. In doing so, I am aware that to abstract any one set of causes is to distort things dangerously. There were forces at work in 1969 which would probably have produced something like our event even if our rhetorical practice had been immeasurably improved. But I am convinced that impoverished notions of rhetoric contributed greatly to our disaster.

Many of the other possible causes are of kinds that are always present in all situations in our time, and we can, without being arbitrary, hold them to one side: psychological instability in the protesters and their opponents; the effects of Spock-designed upbringing on the students or the personal history and class interest of the faculty; ambition in the various leaders; sheer wickedness—I confess that I observed in myself and others, at the height of our encounter, all of the seven deadly sins except sloth—and of course sloth had helped to bring on the troubles by operating powerfully earlier on.

I choose, then, to talk about the whole thing as in part a rhetorical failure, but I should make clear that I don't mean by that simply what people usually mean by a "failure of communication." That phrase seems to suggest that if we could get our words right, all would be well. By using the traditional word rhetoric I want to suggest a

---

Even as late as the spring of 1973, an expelled student produced on campus a "docufantasy" movie "proving" that the students had been right all the while. As one favorable reviewer put it, it was edited in a very "sophisticated" manner, including plausible views of cops, called by the administration, mowing down helpless students. The student paper then reported, to new students in the fall, that cops had been called to end the sit-in!

whole philosophy of how men succeed or fail in discovering together, in discourse, new levels of truth (or at least agreement) that neither side suspected before. In talking of a failure in rhetoric, I am thus taking for granted that substantive issues were at stake in the discourse itself, not mere ornamental failures to choose the right word or trick of presentation. Rhetoric has almost always had a bad press, and it more often than not still carries a sense of trickery or bombastic disguise for a weak case: making the worse appear the better cause. But I am groping toward something far more important, though obviously far too grandiose to be achieved in four lectures: a view of rhetoric as the whole art of discovering and sharing warrantable assertion.[5]

We discovered in our sit-in that most of our protesting students, regardless of many differences among them, believed (a) that the university and society were violating certain values that the students *felt* to be important; (b) that the university offered, in violation of those values, something called reason or knowledge or the life of the mind; (c) that values were not subject to rational determination, not part of the cognitive domain with which the university-trained mind could deal; (d) and that the way to pursue values (or to fight their violation) is thus through action, through sit-ins, demonstrations, violence and the threat of violence. Again and again one heard the refrain, "We have tried reason, and it has once again failed. We had no recourse but . . ."

I should like to argue that these notions show our rhetorical failure as something not invented on the spot: it stemmed from a radically mistaken conception of the nature and possibilities of argument about important matters like crimes and wars and sit-ins, a conception that had been built into academic life and for which the faculty were more responsible than the students. The students made a tragic mistake; the faculty had helped prepare them for it, not by failing to teach them or love them, as they often claimed, but by teaching them error.

---

5. Though it may for some seem to dramatize the absurdity of my project, I should emphasize from the beginning that the bibliography of the subject as thus conceived must include every treatise on the grounds for corrigible or warrantable assertion in any subject. It is thus potentially immense, though even in the loosest interpretation it would still be but a fraction of all the books and articles in any library. What should be clear is that only a small part of it would consist of the thousands of works that specifically mention "rhetoric"—the sort of thing listed in my bibliography below—and that many works ostensibly about rhetoric would not be in the list. I have naturally considered, and reluctantly rejected, the notion of inventing a new term that would include all studies of legitimate suasion and exclude all arts of trickery or of propaganda as lying, and all catalogues of ornament.

### WHEN SHOULD I CHANGE MY MIND?

In these lectures, I am grappling with two very old and very hard questions:

1. *How should men work when they try to change each other's minds, especially about value questions?*

2. *When should you and I change our minds?*—that is, how do we know a good reason when we see one?

We are all aware, in these sophisticated times, that every term in these closely related questions is ambiguous: What is a man? What is a mind? What is a value? What does "should" mean? What is a "change" of mind? Depending on how we choose to resolve these ambiguities, the two questions could lead us into psychology, sociology, anthropology, physiology, political science, law, and on into semantics, semiotics, epistemology, ethics and value theory, and metaphysics.

When I say that we academics have taught error, I mean that for many decades, many serious workers in most academic disciplines took for granted certain half-truths about my two questions. If I am right, it is no longer possible for any informed person to take for granted any of these half-truths which I shall now describe, yet I find them still asserted as dogmas by some professionals and accepted as eternal truths by many of my students—including those who deny that there can be eternal truths.

To see why I stoop to using that smear word, dogma, think for a moment about some predictable reactions to my question, "When *should* I change my mind?" Many of our friends, especially the behaviorist psychologists, can be counted on to reply somewhat as follows:

> The word *should* is a value term and it is therefore meaningless in discussing such matters. There is no point in asking when you should change your so-called mind. Ask only when you in fact *do* change your mind—that is, what will produce change in your behavior. Your mind *is* changed by what happens to it and what you then are conditioned to *do* in response. To stand to one side exhorting it to a *choice* of change is absurd.

A considerably larger group might answer like this:

> There can be no "should" about changing your mind *except* when empirical proofs are available or when correct or incorrect logical calculation is in question. A man ought to change his mind if his views are not in accord with "the facts," with the way things are, as shown by observation. Similarly he ought to change his mind if he has made an error in logic or mathematical calcula-

12

tion. But moral and ethical and aesthetic and political and religious judgments are of course not factual, and there can in consequence be no "ought" about them: we cannot say that a man *should* change his mind about his ethical (and *a fortiori* his religious) views. At most we can say that we would *like* him to or that it would be better for us if he would.

We can leave to one side for a moment the curious internal inconsistency in both of these views—the more or less hidden and unprovable *ought* lying behind these exhortations to think one way and not another. What is most interesting here is the automatic reliance on the distinction between facts and values, and the quality of the reply one often receives if he questions that distinction. If the word dogma is applicable to any general notion that cannot, for the believer, be brought into question, the belief that you cannot and indeed should not allow your values to intrude upon your cognitive life—that thought and knowledge and fact are on one side and affirmations of value on the other—has been until recently a dogma for all right-thinking moderns.

Like most dogmas, this one has a lot to be said for it. Many of the most impressive intellectual achievements of man, especially in the natural sciences, were made possible by the supreme effort of intellect and will enabling inquirers to say: not what I want to believe but what "nature" or "what is the case" requires me to believe! The transition from what came to be called "subjectivity" to an effort at "objectivity" was in one sense a transition from immaturity to wisdom, and it is necessarily reenacted in everyone's life if he wishes to inquire honestly into the way things are. *My* preferences, *my* desires, *my* subjective states must again and again be modified or repudiated as I am dragged, kicking and screaming, out of infantile solipsism into adult membership in an inquiring community. Many men and women in our time, as in every other, seem never to undergo such schooling. As we observe the various irrationalisms that result, it is perhaps natural that we should cling almost desperately to any belief or practice that seems to preserve standards of communal testing as against untested assertion and raging commitment. If allowing values to affect once again our conclusions about the factual meant giving up all the knowledge earned in man's invention of objective inquiry, we might indeed feel driven to a dogmatic struggle to preserve some last vestige of rationality in a world gone mad.

Some of the attacks on reason and objectivity and the fact-value distinction would seem to justify fears that the savages are about to drag us back into the night from which we have so painfully emerged. Instead of pursuing ways of testing values in public discourse, defenders of value have often enough simply accepted the fact-value distinction and then leapt blindly for the value side. Convinced that reason's domain is a tiny little cold corner of man's life—whatever can be proved or disproved by scientific method—these counter-dogmatists feel free to assert any value that "feels" right. Since acceptance of the dichotomy—whether by men of reason or men of faith—is often taken as the key test of modernity, I shall call the whole collection of dogmas that spring from it modernism, even though the term has often meant other things.[6]

The characteristic debate of modernists is a kind of meaningless logomachy between the adherents of reason or knowledge or science and the adherents of values or faith or feeling or wisdom or "true knowledge." Each of these two main sects—what I shall for shorthand call the scientismists and the irrationalists—can easily show the absurdities of the other, but the polemical displays of either side are so far from engaging the real issues that they often seem to confirm, in their demonstration that meaningful argument about such matters is impossible, the very distinction on which the war is based.

But what if the distinction itself is "in fact" only a half-truth, useful in some inquiries, entirely misleading in others? Then we might find grounds for questioning both the desiccated "defenses of reason" —meaning reason about value-free fact—and the "blind leaps of faith" that have been characteristic of so many recent confrontations. Surely the stakes are high enough to justify a closer look.

## The Factual "Is" and the Wishful "Ought"

The distinction between what is and what ought to be, between fact and value, never won total acceptance even at the height of modernism (whenever we take that hypothetical moment to have been). Philosophies which, like Plato's and Aristotle's and Spinoza's, in some sense discover the *ought* in the *is* have always had adherents, and new attempts at harmony have been frequent, as I shall later show. But it is probably accurate to say that from the seventeenth century until quite recently, it grew increasingly unfashionable to see the universe or world or nature or "the facts" as implicating values.

For most of this period, values could still be reasoned about; though more and more theorists came to say that you could not derive normative propositions from descriptive premises, and thus to divide

6. "Modernism" is unfortunate in suggesting many beliefs that do not concern me. It is also misleading if it suggests that most men who hold these beliefs do so only because they are up-to-date: they are opinions which won in early battle because they at least seemed to have reason on their side.

values and facts implacably, they did not at first conclude from the disjunction that reason was helpless in the world of purposes. It never occurred to Hobbes, "the atheist," or to Locke or Kant, that *all* norms are irrational or nonrational. Hume, the skeptic, had no serious trouble establishing the possibility of a rational "standard of taste," both in ethics and in aesthetics. Even the utilitarians, for whom the distinction became more and more important, never suggested that knowledge is impossible about questions of value, though they tried to reduce all value to usefulness. They clearly believed that men *ought* to believe and act in certain ways, and that to do otherwise was to be unreasonable, not just inconvenient or naughty or self-expressive.

It is really only in the last seventy-five years or so that the fact-value split became a truism *and* that the split began to entail the helplessness of reason in dealing with any values but the calculation of means to ends. I cannot trace here the story of the rise and fall of the disjunction, and of various conclusions thought to follow from it. Suffice it to say that by now it has been attacked everywhere, yet it survives everywhere, survives as strongly in the thought of many who defend values as in the thought of those who cling to positivistic notions of scientific knowledge. As Karl Popper summarizes the view, in his eloquent and well-known defense of the values of the open society against its enemies, "It is impossible to derive a sentence stating a norm or a decision from a sentence stating a fact; this is only another way of saying that it is impossible to derive norms or decisions or proposals from facts."[7]

7. *The Open Society and Its Enemies* (London: Routledge and Kegan Paul, 1947), p. 53. See the whole of Popper's chapter 5, and especially section 3. Nearly two decades ago, Maurice Mandelbaum summarized the recent history on this point as follows: "Perhaps the most significant factor which has led to . . . [the] limitation of the scope of ethics has been the attempt to draw a sharp distinction between normative and descriptive disciplines. Among most contemporary philosophers it now passes for an obvious truth that ethics is not to be regarded as having a descriptive or explanatory function; it is held that its task, being normative, is to deal not with 'what is' but with 'what ought to be.' However . . . this distinction between normative and descriptive disciplines has been espoused only in the last decades; in its present form it can scarcely be said to have been current before Sidgwick" (*The Phenomenology of Moral Experience* [Baltimore, 1955; paperback ed., 1969], p. 13).
Nothing could be more pointless, in 1971, than to add one more polemic in the ancient quarrel between science and values (or religion; or "the humanities"). The quarrel has always been largely sterile—one of those prolonged wars in which both sides are at best right only in what they have to say for themselves, largely wrong in what they have to say about the enemy. Even those who claim to be peace-makers, like C. P. Snow in *The Two Cultures*, seem inevitably to deepen the split that they set out to deplore.

## Motivism and the Loss of Good Reasons

Whenever words are used as opposing counters, in word games that allow the counters to be slipped in and out of the slots almost at random, we know that thought is not taking place. And that is what we find in a great deal that is said about the fact-value split. One can easily construct a long column of opposed terms that roughly match the original and entirely misleading split between fact and value: objective

---

The temper has recently been changing, as I shall show, but if anyone thinks that I am beating a dead horse, he has been reading too much professional philosophy or anthropology and not enough of the amateur philosophizing that specialists in other fields employ when they find it convenient. In much of recent literary scholarship, for example, the dogmas of modernism are for the most part accepted: scientism is accepted as what "reason" would force upon us if we accepted its teachings, and since scientism is intolerable, let us make a blind leap, clutching for values. Often the assumption is explicitly made that the values one happens to grab are indistinguishable in value. See for example Charles I. Glicksberg, *Modern Literary Perspectivism* (Dallas, 1970). Glicksberg derives his world view from the prophets of scientism; he takes it as proved that reason can know nothing about value. He then interprets his second-hand philosophy of science as leaving men "free to choose their own values; free to regard themselves as machines or free to control and put to humane uses the nuclear energy they have discovered. . . . *Homo faber* makes God in his own image" (pp. 122–23). The response is, in my view, a hopeless one, since it leaves all cognition under the control of a "reason" that never established its case. For Glicksberg to conclude that irrationality "presides over man's fate," and that the truly perceptive modern author is necessarily a relativist, "forced to realize that art is illusion" (p. 173), is not only radically inconsistent with his own asserted "humane values" (p. 122) but out of harmony with what professionals who think about values have for the most part been saying. Glicksberg cites hardly any serious philosopher, anthropologist, sociologist, or psychologist writing since 1940. The authors he does cite, from any period, he often wrenches from positions that are in fact contrary to his own (for example, Suzanne Langer and Michael Polanyi, p. 5; Koestler, p. 10; Husserl, p. 21; Cassirer, p. 136). Typical of his wrenchings is his use of Whitehead. Whitehead considered his entire philosophical effort as an attack on the unnecessary divorce of science and values; he claimed—I think rightly—to have shown that a full confrontation with the universe reveals that it is value-ridden to the core. For Glicksberg this rich (and demanding) effort at synthesis is reduced to an item in a checklist presumably supporting his own "perspectivism": "the disintegrating flux of the philosophers of the time cult like Alexander, Whitehead, Bergson, and Bertrand Russell" (p. 11).

The journals of literary criticism are full of such irrationalists professing gloom. I do not run into quite so many scientismists, outside the ranks of behaviorists. But see Charles Coulston Gillispie, *The Edge of Objectivity* (Princeton, N.J., 1960): "The noble eighteenth-century faith in natural law involved a fundamental confusion between the declarative and the normative senses of law, between 'is' and 'ought.' . . . For neither in public nor in private life can science establish an ethic. It tells what we can do, never what we should. Its absolute incompetence in the realm of values is a necessary consequence of the objective posture" (p. 154; see also p. 167).

16

versus subjective, matter versus mind, mechanism versus vitalism, scientific reason versus faith or "the heart" or "the wisdom of the body"—and so on. The giveaway in such matters is that the column can be turned into two double columns, all of the terms made useful to either scientismist or irrationalist, just by adding proper adjectives to the opponent's terms.

Often one needs no better adjective than a mere *mere*: my side obtains knowledge of facts, yours asserts mere value. Or: my side respects values, yours deals with mere facts. My side works with reason, yours with mere, or blind, faith. My side does justice to man's highest faiths, yours deals with mere, or sometimes cold, reason. And so on. I have been told that professional writers of pornography use checklists of descriptive terms, both as memory aids and as a way to prevent unintended repetition. For the pornographers of the knowledge-value controversy, I have constructed two double columns, the first to be used by those who want to defend knowledge or science or reason, the second for those who want to defend values. Anyone looking for a chance to add a title to his bibliography and lacking something to say should be able to whip up an impassioned and right-thinking contribution in a week, on either side of the fact-values war. I have not made up the lists; they are culled from my recent reading in the rhetoric of protest and response.

The scientismic columns below give the language of those who seek first the kingdom of knowledge and believe that all will be added

## SCIENTISMIC

| GOOD | BAD |
|---|---|
| known facts | asserted values |
| objectivity | subjectivity |
| reason | faith, prejudice |
| nature as unified material whole | mentalism, "the ghost in the machine," "multiplication of entities" |
| science | opinion, rationalization |
| the proveable, the knowable | the doubtful, the unknowable |
| science as study of the way things are | humanities as study of wishes and desires |
| the scientist | the demagogue |
| proof | assertion, emotion, rhetoric, propaganda |
| the neutral universe | invented values |
| man as physically conditioned | invented notions of "self" and "conscience" |
| empiricism | idealism |

17

## IRRATIONALIST

| BAD | GOOD |
|---|---|
| mere facts | values (the important) |
| things | persons, subjects |
| cold reason | faith, commitment |
| materialism, mechanism | mind, spirit, the soul personhood |
| scientism | wisdom, real knowledge |
| the provable | the significant, knowledge of the heart |
| science as study of cold fact | humanities as assertions of value |
| the destroyer | the prophet or seer |
| proof | sharing of values, Kant's "wooing" |
| the denuded universe | asserted values, needed gods |
| man reduced to machine | the "self," the "soul" |
| reductionism | holism |

unto it; like the angels "bearing the immortal part of Faust into the higher atmosphere," they believe—as all of us truly modern minds have in part believed—that "Whoe'er aspires unweariedly [after knowledge]/ Is not beyond redeeming." Sin though they may along the way, they will be granted final absolution if only they have been true to the quest for knowledge. The irrationalist columns above consist of the same terms as seen by those who pursue values as primary and think of science or reason as somehow the domain of Mephistopheles.

Anyone familiar with particular controversies can fill in the blanks indefinitely. For example, turning to the various campus protests of the past few years, one can construct columns beginning like this:

## SCIENTISMIC

| | |
|---|---|
| neutral university | demagogic university |
| reason and its defense | irrational protest |
| rational senior faculty | mindless students and junior faculty |

## IRRATIONALIST

| | |
|---|---|
| life-denying university | the new, free, open, personal university |
| rationalism as defense of status quo | new truths, beyond reason, of heart, gut, and gonad |
| heartless, dried-up rationalizers of status quo | the new prophets and new Jerusalem |

18

I would not claim, of course, that every warrior in every battle has replaced thought with such sloganizing. But it is astonishing to discover how much of the polemic of our time fails to go beyond the easy dichotomies of these columns; scratch the slick verbal surface of even the most open-minded debate and you will find combatants who have let their positions be defined by a mental chart with two slots only. Or if there is a third, it will be an equally predetermined middle ground: a reluctant concession that reason has its place, a benign smile upon the Lawrentian men of passion, though of course "they go too far." Viewed in this light, our recent open warfare between various intellectual and governmental establishments and the counterculturalists is just one more enactment of a very old mental war—less extreme than the wars and mass tortures of this century, more extreme than the battles you and I had with our moldywarp professors when we were in college. As the quotation from *Faust* reminds us, the battle lines have not changed much since the romantic period, and some would say that they have been drawn clearly—and destructively—since the mid-seventeenth century.

I shall discuss tomorrow how a great, complex philosopher, Bertrand Russell, both suffered from the sharp split between what we can know and what we value and helped to strengthen its hold on the twentieth century, limiting the thought of large numbers of men and women. The split has long since been repudiated by professional philosophers like Dewey, Whitehead, Cassirer, Husserl, and Father Lonergan, to say nothing of the recent surprising development in the heart of linguistic analysis, where everyone is purporting to prove these days that there are value judgments which can be empirically verified and also validated.[8] It has been repudiated—brilliantly I think—by one of the greatest of the philosophers of science, Michael Polanyi,[9] and by many schools of literary criticism.[10] And it has been repudiated by schools

8. My biggest single surprise in reading for these lectures was the discovery of how many "post-modernist" reunions of fact and value there are. I had known about the pragmatist arguments earlier in the century, including Dewey's suggestion that modern dictatorships gain much of their support because "the strain produced by separation of the intellectual and the emotional is so intolerable that human beings are willing to pay almost any price for the semblance of even its temporary annihilation" (*Theory of Valuation* [Chicago, 1939], p. 65). But I had not suspected the rising flood of arguments, especially in the last decade. In Appendix B I give only a selection showing what seems to be a truly astonishing change of intellectual climate.

9. Throughout his works, but especially in *Personal Knowledge* (Chicago, 1958) and *The Tacit Dimension* (Garden City, N.Y., 1966).

10. For example, the Chicago school of literary criticism, in which I was trained more than twenty years ago, pursued the question of how a rationally

of anthropology, where universal values are back in favor, and by many historians, psychologists, sociologists, and theorists of law.[11]

But though what might be called front-line inquirers now often find the split unnecessary, illogical, or harmful, somehow our general intellectual climate—particularly our interdisciplinary and political controversy—continues to rely on it and the pairings that it spawns. Recently in the social sciences, for example, we have had a flood of reactions against a value-free study of man. One might hail these attacks as liberations, did they not so often simply accept the original disjunction and grab blindly for the neglected half. In some of these accounts, Max Weber is the villain, because of his famous championing of a *wertfrei* sociology—for example, in his essay "Science as a Vocation":

> One can only demand of the teacher that he have the intellectual integrity to see that it is one thing to state facts, to determine mathematical or logical relations or the internal structure of cultural values, while it is another thing to answer questions of the *value* of culture and its individual contents and the question of how one should act in the cultural community and in political associations. . . . If he asks further why he should not deal with both types of problems in the lecture room, the answer is: because the prophet and the demagogue do not belong on the academic platform.[12]

Defenders of the value column have enjoyed pointing out, as it is easy to do, that Weber's exclusion of values from the platform is itself the expression of a value, and that by his own terms he has thus become, on *his* platform, a prophet or demagogue. There have been countless similar demonstrations that objective scholarship is not and cannot be objective in the sense of being free of value judgments. These demonstrations are sound enough, in their own terms, but they get us nowhere if they simply embrace the value column, repudiate a rigorous pursuit of genuine knowledge, and leave the assumptions of modernism unchallenged.

Noam Chomsky's famous recent essay "Objectivity and Liberal Scholarship" partially undermines itself with this failure. Chomsky shows easily and conclusively that "liberal scholars," most notably

---

verifiable critical judgment could be established; and Kenneth Burke, in a great series of works, has shamelessly gone on reasoning about values.

11. See Appendix B, sec. 2.

12. As reprinted in *From Max Weber: Essays in Sociology,* ed. and trans. H. H. Gerth and C. Wright Mills (New York, 1946).

Gabriel Jackson in his study on Spain in the 30s, discover what their value commitments allow them to discover, and they overlook what their values lead them to overlook.[13] But Chomsky then writes as if he has earned, with this restoration of values into historical study, the right to impose his own values on history—and without even as much effort to grapple with opposing views as was made by Jackson. That Jackson was not and could not be objective in the sense of recording the Spanish Civil War as it really was, independently of his basic commitments, does not free Chomsky merely to assert a revolutionary history of that war, no longer obliged to meet the highest standards of historical evidence. Chomsky often talks as if all attempts to write honest history are really and always mere disguises for value commitments and that therefore he has a right to push *his* value button—"down with the 'liberal' defense of capitalism"—and see what is churned out.

His obligation, I would have thought, was to give his readers good reasons why his version of the war is in some historical sense better than Jackson's, and not just one more passionate voice to be measured in decibels. To do so he must do more than play with the old double columns, this time labelled "wicked use of 'objectivity' as disguise" vs. "revolutionary commitment to true values." Having plumped for values, he leaves himself sadly vulnerable to any able historian, of any value-commitment other than his own, who asks the simple question: what are *your* standards of validity?

Chomsky can of course reply, and he has done so, that such attacks are simply disguises for the anti-revolutionary values of the attackers. Reading the controversy that his essay has produced[14] is a discouraging business, partly because it illustrates so clearly how many these days still unconsciously accept the split that I am attacking: there may be facts and factual studies somewhere, probably in the physical sciences, and there are values and value studies—but never the twain shall meet. If one recognizes, as we all must, that in the social sciences and humanities values are implicated at every point, even in the assertion of the simplest fact, then of course we are in trouble, because by definition we are caught in whirlpools of Mere Assertion, knowledge being by definition unobtainable about values.

13. Noam Chomsky, *American Power and the New Mandarins: Historical and Political Essays* (New York, 1969), pp. 23–158. There is of course a lively debate among professional historians about whether or how history can be objective and still express the historian's values. See J. H. Hexter, *Doing History* (Bloomington, Ind., 1971), esp. "History and the Social Sciences" and "Garrett Mattingly, Historian."

14. See for example *Encounter* 33 (August 1969): 43–44; ibid. 33 (December 1969): 47–48, 93; ibid. 34 (February 1970): 33, 92–95.

### FIVE KINDS OF MODERN DOGMA

What I am suggesting is that the modernist way of splitting up both the world as it is (value-free nature vs. man's epiphenomenal valuings) and the world as it is inquired into (fact questions vs. value questions) has run so deep in our thought that many have clung to it as other men cling to traditional religious convictions. This point can be seen more clearly if we now turn for a sustained look at the constituent modernist beliefs that are implicit in the four columns, beliefs which permeate our lives, destroy our thought, and defeat our efforts to engage productively in changing each other's minds. They thus corrupt not only our political rhetoric but also our thought about science, about ethics, about art, about love and sex and the media, about child-rearing and about education. Though men and women will be found who accept some of the beliefs while rejecting the rest, it is still not unusual to find modernists who embrace all of them dogmatically—that is, they believe that the doctrines are self-evident and can thus be taken as unargued starting points toward other conclusions.

In practice the dogmas we turn to now tend to travel together, reinforcing each other to constitute the almost overwhelmingly persuasive worldview of modernism. But it will be useful to think of them as falling into five kinds. There are dogmas about (a) the *methods* or means for producing change; (b) the *nature* of the thing changed—the mind or soul or self or person or organism (though I have talked only of "changing minds," I intend the word mind in the broadest possible sense); (c) the *scene* of change—the world in which that thing changed, the "mind," finds itself; (d) the *principles* or basic *assumptions* about truth and its testing—the ground and nature of change; and (e) the *purpose* of change. Every effort to change a mind will appear differently depending on our view of what does the changing, what is changed, how it relates to the whole nature of things, whether or in what sense the change is tested or justified in basic principles, and the purpose of the change.[15]

15. I am aware of help here from both Aristotle's use of four "causes" and Kenneth Burke's "dramatistic pentad": act, scene, agent, agency, and purpose. But I can't effect a precise match with either.

It will be clear that I am tackling only a highly selected list chosen from among many doctrines that might be or have been called modern or modernist; for example: (1) that most troublesome source of doctrines of absurdity—the conviction that though every soul of every person in every culture is of infinite worth, such worth is totally cancelled by death; (2) the belief in the future as somehow more real than the past or present. This belief is closely related to ideas of perfectibility of society or souls (see John Passmore's splendid study, *The Perfectibility of Man* [New York, 1970]). The belief naturally leads to engineer-

## Five Kinds of Modern Dogma

In its scientismist version, the modernist credo that results when the five kinds are held together runs like this: (a) There are no good reasons for changing my mind, especially in questions involving value judgments; there are only motives or drives, and therefore there is no meaning to "should" in the expression "I should change my mind." (b) A mind is nothing but a brain the operations of which are reducible to chemical or physical laws—we don't change minds, we change behavior. (c) The universe is inherently impersonal, indifferent to all human values, and therefore all value judgments are ultimately on an equal footing. (d) Truth is found primarily by critical doubt, by discrediting untrue assertions, by subtracting human preferences or intuitions or values and uncovering the cold hard truth that really underlies our warm inventions. (e) My purpose in trying to change minds about purposes or values or ends can thus only be to make my desires and purposes triumph, since about such matters there is no truth or falsehood; only about means or techniques can men dispute rationally.

The irrationalist version of modernism goes something like this: (a) The heart has its reasons that the reason ignores—and therefore to hell with reason! It is simply what other men use to restrain my freedom or to disguise their true motives. (b) The conscious mind is really a subordinate and potentially limiting element in the total self or soul or spirit of man; the mind may try to think about facts and truth, but the organism drives for superior irrational realizations that the mind with its scientific analysis cannot touch; mind kills spirit. (c) The universe revealed by thought, as instructed by the scientific revolution, is impersonal—God is dead. Therefore I renounce all hope of finding a harmony with it, and I assert my personhood and my values as a rebel against nature. In one alternative version, increasingly pop-

---

ing the present according to the dictates of an imagined future. Such thinking is by no means confined to revolutionary Utopists like Communists or Fascists. It is found in all modern planners and advisers, from the Rand Corporation to Mr. Alvin Toffler, who in *Future Shock* (New York, 1970) imagines a future of accelerated change and then recommends ways to train ourselves to endure; some reviewers rightly questioned his predictions, but none that I saw questioned his unthinkingly modernist way of dealing with them.

To let my picture of the future modify what I do is not necessarily bad; I must do so whenever I control today's actions to prepare for tomorrow's pleasure. Such calculation becomes what I call futurism when it takes the form of imposing miseries on some people today in the name of happiness for some others tomorrow. Futurism is of course especially dangerous when the engineer is not personally required to share in present sacrifice. See Yehoshua Ariely's lecture, *The Future-Directed Character of the American Experience* (Jerusalem: The Magnes Press, 1966).

23

ular in the last decade, I assert that nature and I *are* in harmony, in spite of what science teaches, and I commune with it in deliberate contradiction of what the mind tells me about it. In another, gods or devils as lesser deities live again, battling on my side, more or less ineffectually, against blind or hostile nature or against the older gods. In the world of the irrationalists, each inner voice speaks with absolute authority, and new cults are born daily, some with terrifying consequences. (d) The truth found by reason is trivial or inhuman; scientific reason destroys personal and thus individual truths; the only truth worth having is what I can find for myself in an honest probing of my individuality, that is, in my differences from all other men. (e) Since each man's truth is uniquely valuable for *him,* the purpose of changing minds cannot be to lead us to superior truths *shared* with other men, much less truth shared with all reasonable men. The purpose is to release creative individuality—and this means that one does not marshall reasons for beliefs to produce an enslaving consensus but rather one works on emotions to liberate unique self-expression.

Today in my remaining time I shall look briefly at the first of these five, the motivism that treats the sharing of reasons as mere disguise for the true causes—mechanical for scientismists, suprarational or subrational or prerational for too many of the rest of us.

## "Good Reasons Apply to Means, Not Ends"

About the agency of mental change, the modernist dogma is simple, though its surface manifestations are innumerable: there are no good reasons for changing your mind, except (sometimes) in choosing means or techniques. Choices of ends and of worldviews and of political and religious norms are value choices, and since value judgments are not about matters of fact, there can be no final superiority, in arguing about them, of one line of reasoning over another. What we call reasons can always be seen through as rationalizations or superstructures or disguises or wishful thinking: our minds are really determined, in all of our values, either by nonrational conditioning in the past, or by present motives or drives, many of them lying so deep that we can never find them out.

I call this dogma *motivism,* for want of a better term,[16] and I call

16. I am especially unhappy about the potential confusion with Kenneth Burke's "motives," which include what I am calling motives but which he expands to include all "good reasons," all valid "warrants for assertion or action." Another confusion may occur with the "conscious motives" which one school of psychologists contrasts with drives; their insistence that motives exist, in their sense, resembles my argument for good reasons (see Salvatore R. Maddi, *Per-*

motivism a dogma not because I think that all or most value choices are made on the basis of fully conscious and "scientifically cogent reasoning," but because I find many people assuming, without argument, that *none* of them ever can be. "Look for the secret motive" has at least until recently been a slogan in many disciplines, and the unexamined assumption has been that if you can find it—that is, if you can find a class interest or a sexual drive or a kinship interest or a childhood trauma—you have explained away whatever "surface reasons" anyone offers for his beliefs or actions.

Listen to the sort of thing we take for granted, when applied to other people, as represented by a recent discussion about Norman Mailer in *The Nation:*

> God or the Devil? Mailer is a man interested in first causes. Though he professes a belief in the ultimate unknowability of everything, he is still quite willing to smell out a good guess. He mutters, he ruminates, he suggests problems and possibilities. This might be called psychoanalytic journalism, Mailer going beneath the surface of an event, past the mechanics of it, beyond the social and political realities of it, and into the swamp of its psychology, into the quicksands of the human subconscious that are its real *raison d'être.* Thus, he wonders what the real reason is that makes men want to go to the moon. What is the reason that makes the astronauts want to go? Why did America get to the moon first, and why this special group of Americans, the WASP's?"[17]

---

*sonality Theories: A Comparative Analysis* [Homewood, Ill., 1968], esp. pp. 332–39): "Unconscious motivation is an explanatory construct that should be employed only when it seems relevant, that is, when a person's own account of his goals is unconvincing as an explanation of his behavior. This use of the concept of unconscious motivation is more defensible from the point of view of reason than is that which makes all behavior somehow an expression of unconscious motivation. The latter approach only seems understandable to me if the theorist has some investment in second-guessing people, or in convincing them that he knows them better than they know themselves, or in rendering them pessimistic and distrustful concerning themselves and others" (p. 339).

J. R. Lucas develops the distinction between good reasons and other kinds of causes (though without using my word "motivism") in *The Freedom of the Will* (Oxford, 1970) and in his contribution to *The Nature of Mind* (Edinburgh, 1972). The latter volume—a debate among H. C. Longuet-Higgins, C. H. Waddington, A. J. P. Kenny, and Lucas—is a lively introduction to current issues concerning the "mind"; though the contributors differ sharply among themselves, they would all repudiate the kinds of reductionism I am questioning here.

17. Harry Maurer, "Sacred to Diana," *Nation* 212 (March 22, 1971): 380.

Note the automatic assumption that the real reasons are not the public reasons, that the real reasons have something to do with the subconscious, or with class or racial affiliations that run far beneath the surface. If we were to ask Mailer whether his choosing to study the astronauts was itself defensible with good reasons, he might say— since he tries harder than most authors to apply the same standards to himself that he applies to other men—that his real reasons were also quite other than his conscious reasonings. We have all learned to assume that what determines minds and purposes must be not reasoning but deeper and blinder causes. I would be greatly surprised if a good many of you are not at this moment wondering how I dare call such a belief dogmatic, so obvious does it seem to you.

Bertrand Russell, who will be my chief source of dogmatic quotations in tomorrow's lecture, is a good source here, as he always is when one wants to find a clear clean statement of a representative twentieth century view. Russell everywhere maintains a sharp split between what he calls "the happy realms of exactness where pure thought can disport itself in freedom," and "the doubtful problems in which emotion must have its place." He apologizes for speaking so copiously about the second kind, which have nothing to do with reason or knowledge or even thought. But which kind do we have here, under *R* in his *Dictionary of Mind, Matter and Morals?*

> REASON: I do not mean by 'reason' any faculty of determining the ends of life. The ends which a man will pursue are determined by his desires; but he may pursue them wisely or unwisely. We may assume that the kaiser hoped to increase his power by the war, and the czar hoped to avert revolution; neither of them showed wisdom in the choice of means to these ends. When I speak of 'reason,' I mean merely the endeavor to find out the truth about any matter with which we are concerned, as opposed to the endeavor to prove to ourselves that what we desire is true.

Russell does not say whether his reasoning about reason is of the kind that merely rationalizes a desire or whether it is itself pure. If we asked him whether reason teaches that we *should not* endeavor to find reasons showing that what we desire is true—if we asked in what decalogue this lifelong commandment of his was inscribed—he would, I suppose, laugh at us, so self-evident must seem the rationality of his attack on rationalization.[18]

18. New York, 1952. So far as I know, Russell, the greatest modernist of them all, is the only philosopher of our time so popular and so skillful stylistically

Even though motivism is now on the defensive (as I shall later try to show), men tend to think that statements like the following, which concludes an effort to refute Dewey's "logic of inquiry," establish themselves as they stand, requiring no argument in their defense:

> Ultimately, the controversy between those who base logic upon "truth" and those who base it upon "inquiry" arises from a difference of values, and [therefore] cannot be argued without, at some point, begging the question. I cannot hope, therefore, that anything in the above pages has validity except for those whose bias resembles my own, while those whose bias resembles Dr.

---

that an alphabetical dictionary of his unargued opinions could be of commercial value.

The words *rational* and *reasonable* are equated by some writers, distinguished by others, and they are variously related to words like *knowledge, cognition,* and *thought.* Some recent works on the reasonableness of being moral have distinguished the terms sharply, reserving *rationality* for the capacity to match means to ends, or in some cases both the capacity and the intention to do so (see David A. J. Richards, *A Theory of Reasons for Actions* [London, 1971], pp. 75–79). In this view it naturally follows that some moral demands can be irrational though reasonable; if morality dictates that I go against my "own interests," it becomes reasonable to act in what a utilitarian would call an irrational way.

I see no point in adding to semantic confusion by taking this route, and I have generally used *rational* and *reasonable* as synonyms, reserving terms like *logical* or *calculative* for the special case of "being rational in matching ends and means." The use of the distinction by current philosophers is interesting, however, because it springs from their effort to find firm ground for the point I am making in other ways: that moral arguments can carry intellectual (or reasonable or rational or cognitive) weight, and that it is unreasonable to ignore them or to deny their force. Richards' distinction is used, for example, to buttress his claim that "the principles of morality [are] in an absolute priority relation to the principles of rationality" (p. 227).

This usage is generally followed by those who, working from within religious traditions, reunify reason or rationality and faith (see John E. Smith, *Experience and God* [New York, 1968], and *Reason and God* [New Haven, 1961]). The usage is also followed in another fine book which attempts to grapple with both the scientismist and the irrationalist branches of modernism: Stanley Rosen, *Nihilism* (New Haven, 1969). Rosen works at renovating confidence in "rational speech" wedded with "desire": "I have tried to show the nihilist consequences of the detachment of philosophy from wisdom, or rather of the reinterpretation of wisdom first as mathematical certitude and then as the experience of historicity" (p. 230).

That the reduction of reasons to motives has been seen as a serious threat to all thought about morality can be seen in the immense bibliography that has accumulated about the subject in recent decades. See, for example, the selective thirty-two page "Bibliography of the Philosophy of Action," compiled by Robert McGowan and Myron Gochnauer, in *Agent, Action, and Reason,* ed. Robert Binkley, Richard Bronaugh, and Ausonio Marras (Oxford, 1971).

Dewey's will find in his book just such an exposition as the subject seems to them to require.[19]

About a decade ago, Morton White described the resulting impoverishment of thought among philosophers:

"Ancient Greek philosophy," Kant reminds us, "was divided into three sciences; physics, ethics, and logic," and the logical positivist had neatly ticketed all three. For the positivist physics was cognitively meaning*ful* and a body of synthetic a posteriori propositions; ethics was a body of cognitively meaning*less* statements which had failed to satisfy the verifiability theory of meaning but which could be handled in the emotive meaning section; logic and its sister mathematics were safely analytic. That was the clear-cut picture which had been developed from the dark, mysterious negative of early wittgensteinianism, a picture which still hangs in the studies of many philosophers in England and America.[20]

19. Bertrand Russell, quoted by Peter A. Schouls, "Communication, Argumentation, and Presupposition in Philosophy," *Philosophy and Rhetoric* 2, no. 4 (Fall, 1969): 190.

20. *Toward Reunion in Philosophy,* Atheneum ed. (New York, 1963), p. 13. Since 1963 the picture has been removed by more and more philosophers (see Appendix B). For more extensive accounts of the untenable reductionism implicit when reasons all are reduced to "lower" forces, see Kenneth Burke, *A Grammar of Motives* (New York, 1945), chap. 3, "Scope and Reduction"; Arthur Koestler, *The Ghost in the Machine* (London, 1967), esp. chaps. 1–3; Polanyi, *Personal Knowledge,* esp. pt. 4; and idem, *The Study of Man* (Chicago, 1959): "Backed by a science which sternly professes that ultimately all things in the world—including all achievements of man from the Homeric poems to the *Critique of Pure Reason*—will be somehow explained in terms of physics and chemistry, these theories assume that the path to reality lies invariably in representing higher things in terms of their baser particulars. This is, indeed, almost universally regarded today as the supremely critical method, which resists the flattering illusions cherished by men about their nobler faculties. Our experimental psychology is dominated by a method which aims at representing all mental processes by a mechanical model; depth-psychology represents human behaviour as the outcome of subconscious primitive urges; and the most influential current interpretations of politics and history assume that public affairs are determined either by the force of economic interests or the love of power. Here we have before us that systematic denaturing of human experience by modern empiricism which I denounced in my first lecture—and now is the moment to show, as I had promised, that the true nature of things can be reinstated by accrediting our capacity to establish knowledge by an act of understanding" (p. 64).

See also Harry Prosch, *The Genesis of Twentieth Century Philosophy: The Evolution of Thought from Copernicus to the Present* (Garden City, N.Y., 1964):

"Thus contemporary man can scarcely understand what the older philosophers meant by 'reason' in any way which does not make it look like 'rationalization,'

It is by no means essential to motivism that the denial of good reasons should be in the name of trivial or petty motives. What is essential is that conscious thought, deliberation, open talk about why we should or should not seek this or that value is either ignored or reduced to other deeper or truer causes. But in practice, motivism has often led to a cutting down of man's aspirations and capacities to the "merely animal" or, in a natural further step, to the chemical or physical. As Kenneth Burke has God say to Satan, in a splendid "dialogue in heaven" appended to his *Rhetoric of Religion,*

> "In the name of empirical, scientific observation, the search for motives (men's theorizing on the nature of purpose) will lead to a constant procession of solemn, humorless caricatures that will greatly entrance you in your character as prankster. In the search for academic preferment or for quick sales in the book mart, their teachers and writers will slap together various oversimplified schemes that reduce human motives to a few drives or urges or itches involving food, sex, power, prestige and the like (schemes concocted in keeping with the logic of 'firsts,' but without the proper criticism of such procedures)."[21]

It is astonishing to see how little argument was thought necessary to support motivist assertions, once this century was well under way. As I move now through a full page taken from Russell's *The Analysis of Mind,* I ask you simply to address each assertion with the question, "What evidence would this scientific philosopher be able to offer if I asked him to prove this claim, this connection, this easy inference? And what force, if any, would he claim for the notion that I *ought* to accept his conclusions?" (I have italicized the points at which my own questions become most pressing):

> Our impulses are not patent to a casual observation, but are only to be discovered by a scientific study of our actions, in the course of which we *must regard ourselves as objectively* as we should the motions of the planets or the chemical reactions of a new element.
> The study of animals *reinforces this conclusion,* and is in many ways the best preparation for the analysis of desire. In animals we are not troubled by the disturbing influence of ethical considerations. In dealing with human beings, we are perpetually *distracted* by being told that such-and-such a view is gloomy or cynical or pessimistic; ages of human conceit *have built up* [how

i.e. the 'invention' of reasons which are 'phony,' because they 'rationalize' a behavior which is really irrational" (Anchor Book ed., 1966, p. 334, n. 3).

21. *The Rhetoric of Religion: Studies in Logology* (Boston, 1961), p. 299.

would he prove this causal assertion?] such a vast myth as to our wisdom and virtue that any intrusion of the mere scientific desire to know *the facts* is instantly resented by those who cling to comfortable *illusions*. But no one cares whether animals are virtuous or not, and no one is under the delusion that they are rational. Moreover, we do not expect them to be so 'conscious,' and are prepared to admit that their instincts prompt useful actions without any prevision of the ends which they achieve. For *all these reasons,* there is much in the analysis of *mind* which is more easily discovered by the study of animals than by the observation of human beings.

We all think that, by watching the behaviour of animals, we can discover more or less what they desire. If this is the case—and I fully agree that it is—desire must be capable of being exhibited in actions, for it is only the actions of animals that we can observe. They *may* have minds in which all sorts of things take place, but we can know nothing about their minds except by means of inferences from their actions; and the more such inferences are examined, *the more dubious they appear.* It would seem, *therefore,* that actions alone must be the test of the desires of animals. From this *it is an easy step to the conclusion* that an animal's desire is *nothing but* a characteristic of a certain series of actions, namely, those which would *be commonly regarded* as inspired by the desire in question. And when it has been shown that this view affords a *satisfactory account* of animal desires, it is *not difficult* to see that the same explanation *is applicable* to the desires of human beings.[22]

That a philosopher could leave so many gaping holes, while claiming to believe nothing that could not be proved factually or scientifically, does not prove that his conclusions were wrong. It only shows that he dwelt in a dogmatic climate and could count on his readers' sharing his dogmas. His readers, he always implied, were a small band of courageous folk who had been able to see through the "illusions" of other men. And those of us who happily joined the band—for some years he was to me as to others the spirit of philosophy incarnate—were not expected to pause for questions about evidence.

Motivism is not new. But though many philosophers before the twentieth century developed determinisms, one usually finds, as in Spinoza, that they make a radical distinction between having one's actions "determined" by the truth discovered through active reason and having one's actions determined by brute unthinking preconditions in

22. (London, 1921), pp. 61–62.

the temporal order. From Plato and Aristotle at least until Kant, hardly anyone except a few atomists failed to distinguish some kind of "vertical" lift or pull—a *cause* in the sense of mind meeting truth and feeling drawn to it—from the "horizontal" push given by the chain of past temporal events or material conditions of the body. But in our time, for many men, there is nothing but the temporal order of causes; the world is something like a vast billiard table, with a few of the balls offering rationalizations to explain why they move. In such a world, to explain what anyone believes or does, one looks only to the antecedent bumps and not to the reasons given (the kind of antecedent sought will of course vary from theory to theory).

The reductive motivism that results has never been held as an explicit theory by many outside of the ranks of behavioral psychologists, and even they cannot hold to it consistently. But popularized versions of Marxism and Freudianism and positivism have spread the dogma to the "intellectual masses" who take up ideas in novels, political controversy, middlebrow magazines, and freshman English anthologies. By now it has almost scriptural force: in the beginning was not the word but the causal chain, and his name was sometimes Chemistry and sometimes Drive or Desire, but never Lift or even Pull. And it came to pass that Error was born, and his chosen name was Reason, but his real name was Rationalization. And Rationalization and his wicked prophets did undertake to undermine Push, claiming that reasoning about values, about purposes, could alter Push's unalterable path. But the true prophets were able to unmask the wicked prophets, showing that their vaunted reasonings were themselves clearly dictated by Push. And, lo, there was nothing that anyone could say about anything that could not be unmasked and shown to be truly another manifestation of Push's eternal power. And when men did engage in debate about their deepest concerns, they found that each man could say unto his brother, Racca, thou fool.

## SOME CONSEQUENCES OF MOTIVISM

I shall not try to "prove" that motivism in any of its many versions is false doctrine. If motivism were easily shown to be false, it presumably would not have won so many intelligent adherents in the first place. It is not a simple error—like the notion that the earth is flat or that light has no mass—that can be refuted with a crucial experiment or a logical disproof. It is more like belief in miracles or predictive dreams: anyone who believes that all reasons are disguises for irrational motives of various kinds is sure to find confirming examples wherever he looks, partly because cases of rationalization in this sense are indeed plentiful and partly because belief in the hypothesis leads one to look at other people in a certain way and to find what one looks for.

Motivism is in fact a self-confirming hypothesis with a peculiarly effective twist. Any effort I make to refute it with what I call reasons can be dismissed with the hypothesis itself: "But you try to defend reason only because you are afraid of the truth." Indeed when motivism is buttressed with the dogmas I'll discuss tomorrow, it is, like every other closed intellectual system, well-nigh impregnable.

Consider, for example, how little it will trouble a motivist when I point out that motivism entails fearful consequences with which no one can live for so much as thirty seconds. What I will have done, for the True Believer, is simply illustrate his case. His theory leads him to expect his unhappy critics to be fearful of consequences, and it provides him with a terminology for my efforts: "You have a strong motive—fear of unpleasant consequences—which leads you to reject my account of how minds work. But where are your *reasons*? That fearful consequences follow from a belief is irrelevant to whether it is true or not?"

To which I reply, "Who says? What is the authority for this decision that rules for emotional purification, developed fruitfully in chemistry and physics, ought to be applied in deciding what to believe about human life? Your dictum tells me that I *ought* to behave in one way rather than another. It is thus in competition with the other *oughts* that crowd in upon me. And I want to know why it has superior claim over the dictum that I ought to avoid intellectual convictions that have intolerable consequences."

While waiting for his answer, I feel sufficiently liberated to spend at least a few moments looking at illustrations of the consequences of motivism. And of course I have already given the first one—the motivist faces the consequence of living with a practical doctrine that does not and cannot fit either his own practical life or his mental life, except in a very narrow domain.

A second consequence which for many of us is intolerable is that motivism relieves us, in daily tasks, from responsibility for our actions. A freshman comes to me to explain why his paper is late. "Well, I'd like to say that the problem was too hard for me, but I know that would just be a reason; I don't know what my true motives were, but I guess I was trying to say something to you"—meaning something secret, something deeper than or beyond rational formulation, something much more interesting than any paper he could possibly have written. In some circles it has for some decades been difficult to conduct a genuine discussion: someone is always saying, "Oh, I know why you said *that*! As a tenured member of the English Department, you *had* to." Or, more bluntly, "What would your analyst say to *that*?" Every idea—unless of course it is "scientific"—expresses a need or a secret wish; nothing need be taken seriously as a possible contribution to the truth. The very word *truth* has for many been ruled out of court, and with it the notion that one determinant of what is said *can* be a respect for reasons.[23]

But I am even more interested in how motivism makes hard intellectual and practical problems seem easy. Listen for a moment to part of a paper given me this year by another bright though disorganized freshman—a young man who is coming alive intellectually but who is still likely to read ten prefaces rather than one real book. It was a prideful two-page manifesto entitled "God Exists Because Man Needs Him":

> That there are no atheists in foxholes means that religion is a necessary placebo. The singular quality of all deities is that they are a superhuman authority to whom man can appeal for either pity or help.
>
> Man is afraid of judgment and self-determination. Because man fears accountability he needs the mercy of salvation; because man lacks self-confidence he needs a divine will to intervene against misfortune. Because man is weak he needs to believe there is a father up there looking over him who can both forgive and protect. God exists because man needs him.

When I point out to the author that there is a long history of serious reasoning about whether or not God exists, with some proofs for His existence that highly intelligent thinkers, both believers and atheists, have taken and still take seriously, he says, "But my paper goes on to say that science has shown that all that springs from fear." He clearly cannot believe that I am serious when I suggest that even if he is right, even if such beliefs originate in fear (which is unproved), their truth or falsehood has not by that claim alone been settled.

---

23. The issue of determinism and responsibility is not something that can be dealt with in a paragraph, and it is not reducible to the contrast between a world of hidden motives and a world that includes reasons. Many "determinists"—for example, Spinoza—would have repudiated what I call motivism, since they believed that truth can help determine our actions by entering our minds as reasons. But I suppose that to deny what I am calling reasons is necessarily to deny freedom of choice in any form, and it can lead, as it does in B. F. Skinner, to a program for denying even political and social freedoms. See *Beyond Freedom and Dignity* (New York, 1971).

But protection from having to think about reasons in metaphysics or religion is less to our point than protection from having to think about reasons in political argument. This has been especially clear in dissenters within the academy. Last spring, at the time of Cambodia and the resulting campus protests, a young history professor at my university was asked to do a piece on the planned strike and on faculty members' resistance to the idea of closing the university. As a trained historian, he set himself the task, he said, of trying to deal with "faculty attitudes" during the strike, particularly "the almost religious commitment" of so many of the faculty here to "institutional neutrality" and "the accompanying phobic reaction to 'politicization.' " If we leave aside the bias admitted with words like "religious" and "phobic," we have here a relatively clear historical problem, a problem set in terms of its causes: *why* did so many faculty members believe as they did?

We might think that one fairly obvious kind of answer that ought at least to be considered would consist of the *reasons* they gave for their beliefs. But this analyst made it quite clear from the beginning that for him the overt reasons need not be considered as primary evidence in answering this causal question. "I thought up some swell theories to account for the special characteristics of the faculty culture on the Midway: historical theories, having to do with the Teutonic cum Thomist traditions of UC; psycho-geographical theories, having to do with the seige-mentality associated with living behind Gothic battlements shielding us from the ghetto; institutional theories, having to do with the structures providing for faculty (non)involvement in decision-making."

But he rejected these theories, not because they all ignore what the faculty said, which they do, but because "the more I thought about it, the more it became clear to me that the most important thing about the response of many of my colleagues to student protest, and the accompanying rhetoric about 'institutional neutrality,' is what it reveals about their values, about the extent to which they respond to events in terms of their professed humanistic principles, or, alternatively, in terms of the narrowest, most parochial professional or class interest."

There followed a short argument purporting to show that faculty defend the university because to close the university threatens "their hitherto secure bourgeois existence." Under such subheads as "Escalation and Selfishness" and "Faculty Fastidiousness," the author wrote throughout as if no reader could possibly want to know the reasons faculty gave or what the critic thought of these reasons. The only subject of interest was the *true* class motive *underlying* their surface rationalizations. What they *said* was, of course, mere "rhetoric"—his word—and therefore need not even be reported.

It is possible, admittedly, that the young historian was right; it is possible that not a single one of the arguments given by any of the professors defending university neutrality was worthy of consideration *as a reason.* I don't believe this, of course, but for now my point is not to refute the historian but to provide an instance of how little confidence men have in *reasoning* about such matters. On the one hand, the critic holds a self-evident belief requiring and receiving no argument in its support: to close the university at this point in history is obviously the right thing to do (even though many colleagues whom he says he respects and loves think otherwise). On the other hand, there are these curious people who write long statements saying we shouldn't. How can you account for such a weird thing? Obviously not by looking at their arguments, which cannot be anything other than rationalizations, but rather by probing their underlying emotions and other irrational motives, their class or club or economic interests.

I have time for only one more example of such reductionism, this one from the world of less impassioned inquiry. One whole current school of historians, often called by the ancient name *prosopography,* aims to study how class or family affiliations have served as motives to determine men's actions. In contrast to the search for hidden psychological motives, prosopography looks for hidden kinship loyalties or economic interests, taking for granted the notion that one should look behind the expressed reasons (obviously rationalizations) of any given historical figure to discover his "true motives."

As Lawrence Stone says,[24] "For some scholars, prosopography

24. "Prosopography," *Daedalus,* Winter 1971. Other authors throughout this issue devoted to "Historical Studies Today" inevitably touch on other ways in which historical causes are reduced to this or that version of "blind motives." See especially Frank E. Manuel, "The Use and Abuse of Psychology in History."

Once we are alerted to the ways in which motivism might destroy any discipline that depends on some notion of genuine reasons for belief and action, we discover passionate protests against it wherever men's asserted reasons have been systematically reduced to other causes. See for example Theodore K. Rabb, "The Scenic Tour: A review of *Civilisation* by Kenneth Clark," *Commentary* 51 (June 1971): "While one can agree that Protestants destroyed many lovely images, it is both misleading and untrue to assert that 'the motive wasn't so much religion as an instinct to destroy anything comely' because people were enraged by 'incomprehensible values.' It would be difficult to imagine a more complete misunderstanding—the Protestants knew *exactly* what values the images represented, and they were bent on transforming those values. Their motives, moreover, were *entirely* religious; their overwhelming aim, to simplify religion, was

was not merely a way of ignoring passions and ideas, it was adopted for the specific purpose of neutralizing these disturbing and intractable elements" (p. 56). "There is thus a strong bias toward treating the individual as *homo-economicus,* and to study him primarily in the light of his financial interests and behavior, since this is what the records illuminate" (p. 59). Prosopographers ignore, as he shows, the role of religious conviction in establishing the groupings around Cromwell, seeking instead to find such causes as the dissatisfaction with "downward mobility" that Hugh R. Trevor-Roper finds in the poor gentry, mere gentry, or parish gentry in the Revolution. Such historians are consequently rather "unwilling to build into their perspectives of history a role for ideas, prejudices, passions, ideologies, ideals, or principles. . . . The attention paid by these historians to the tactics rather than the strategy of politics presupposes a society without conviction in which manipulation and wire-pulling are more important than issues of principle or policy" (pp. 63–64).

I don't need to tell you how useful such procedures are when scholars, conservative or liberal, set out to understand (and dismiss) protest groups. When students attack the curriculum, one naturally looks to the way they were brought up—"the Spock generation"—or to their class origins, or to the psychology of fear in which they live; it is a rare thing indeed when someone like Joseph Schwab actually takes seriously the possibility that the curriculum is in many respects intolerably bad, and that at least some of the reasons students offer against it are, like some of the reasons offered in attacks on American society, good reasons.[25]

It is easy to see why, when habits of motivist dismissal are thoroughly established, the quality of our public discourse about common problems should sink so low. If reasoning together cannot ever produce justified changes of mind, what means have we at hand for moving each other? We can only trick each other through superior propaganda—what is often called mere rhetoric. If neither of us has any chance of offering good reasons, I can only trick you, or force you,

---

firmly rooted in a comprehensive set of beliefs. Although they smashed the statues and windows which had perverted Christ's unadorned message, nothing could have been further from their minds than the wish simply to destroy comely things. And it is equally untrue to say that 'religion [was] of course being used as a pretext for political ambitions' in the wars of religion, implying that nobody was really fighting for his faith" (p. 114).

25. Joseph J. Schwab, *College Curriculum and Student Protest* (Chicago, 1969).

or blackmail you, or shoot you—and thus change your mind permanently.[26]

It is true that such a doctrine presents great logical problems to anyone who applies it to his *own* convictions: if *they* have no better support than that they have been implanted in him by conditioning or by uncontrollable and irrational drives, what right does he have to impose them on anyone else? But then, why not? Anything goes that one can make succeed, if the only test of a motive is whether it motivates. Soon we discover that "politics begins at the barrel of a gun," that there is nothing, nothing whatever, to prevent myself and my party from doing anything we can get away with. Universities, those hypocritical places that claim to be the home of reason, are really disguises for the selfish motives of their administrators and professors: they must be, if good reasons do not really exist. And in controversy with their defenders we would be foolish indeed either to listen to their rationalizations or to worry about providing good reasons of our own—except insofar as it is useful to *appear* reasonable.

As I have said, to point to these consequences cannot in itself shake the foundation of motivism, unless one has already begun to question the motivist assumption that repugnant "human" consequences are irrelevant to the truth of a doctrine. Attacks on various forms of motivism have been many and forceful; in my view they have often been convincing. And yet motivism thrives. How can that be?

Without pretending to have any final answers to such a question, I would suggest that any intellectual habit survives *as a habit* only so long as it is useful—which is to say, reversing the position of motivists, only so long as it can point to "consequences," whether intellectual or practical successes, that seem to provide good reason for continuing in the habit, regardless of other consequences that may be unpleasant. A given habit will seem useful provided it seems to answer important questions more successfully than any rival habit. And the fact is that though motivism is both internally inconsistent and destructive of much

26. It should be clear that what I call motivism was not invented in the modern academy. One brand of it is portrayed in *The Republic* when Thrasymachus reduces all reasoning about justice to each man's getting whatever his power enables him to get. A modern version of the reduction of all politics to a juggling of "interests" is attributed to President Nixon by Richard Harris in his study of the debate about Mr. Carswell's nomination to the Supreme Court ("Judge Carswell and the Senate," *The New Yorker,* December 5 and 12, 1970). *Note, May 1973:* Mr. Harris's charges seem mild, in the light of the current Watergate revelations.

that we cannot live without, it is buttressed by an impressive chain of intellectual successes at what might be called the local level. It is inevitable that when psychologists and sociologists and economists probe for hidden motives they will find them—in great abundance. Men do engage in self-destructive rationalizations, hiding their real reasons with verbiage. Men do defend, sometimes, perhaps most of the time, their class interests, and they disguise their defenses with eulogistic terms. Many "rationalists" in the past did in fact blindly accept the reason-emotion split and then grossly exaggerate the role that logical calculation does have or can have in human affairs. The processes we now think of as conditioning and imprinting and genetic determination do play—as all major philosophers have known—a large role in fixing character, or habitual choice.[27] Inevitably any investigator working on the assumptions of motivism will thus always be able to find "mere" motives, because they are always there to be found. And as long as there is no commanding intellectual alternative to motivism and to its buttressing dogmas, so long as many men find that the only knowledge that seems to be obtainable about the world of action and value is knowledge of motives, they will be motivists, even if they suspect that their position is evidently inconsistent or—if made consistent—self-destructive.

We cannot answer motivism, then, with a polemic that simply reverses the attack. Instead, we should seek a way of cutting through the destructive split on which the depredations of motivism are based: instead of trying to prove that men change their minds or should

27. The problem gets handled differently, of course, in different philosophies. The typical modern way was perhaps fixed by Hume: we obviously cannot act without motives, and "reason" itself can never provide motives; only desires and drives of various kinds can do that, and reason comes into its own in adjudicating among conflicting motives. Still, for Hume, in contrast to modern motivists who look so much like him on the surface, reason can operate profitably with the "maybe's" of life, appraising the relative weight of motives that were in themselves neither base nor noble. Thus for this skeptic, a kind of cognitive respectability could be attained in choices about matter of value, because people could easily find good grounds for pursuing *these* values as against *those*. The fear that he had been programmed to prefer the "rational" to the "irrational" did not trouble Hume, but for a modern motivist it is crucial: for him, even our preference for believing truth rather than falsehood is merely the expression of an implanted motive. For a good treatment of this problem, see Warner A. Wick, "Moral Problems, Moral Philosophy, and Metaethics: Some Further Dogmas of Empiricism," *The Philosophical Review* 62 (1953): "That choice does begin in desire conditioned by character or attitude is an old truth which ethical theorists, often given to thin intellectualism, have too seldom remembered. I applaud its rediscovery. But the present issue is whether such attitudes can be criticized by any objective principle" (p. 7).

change their minds only on the basis of abstract ideas and logical proofs —a position easily refuted by even a tenth-rate motivist—we should look for a philosophy of good reasons, a way of discovering how motives become reasons and a way of showing how what we call ideas sometimes can and should affect our choices and sometimes can only fail to do so.

My goal must be, then, not a kind of unanswerable "scientific refutation" but rather an alternative way of slicing the cake. In my next lecture, I shall turn to the remaining four kinds of dogma that have interlaced into what amounted, if I am right, to the almost impermeable religion of modernism. Though this religion has always been proudly "anti-religious," gaining in fact a good deal of its emotional appeal from a sense of courageous rejection of past religious foolishness and wicked deception, it shows many of the characteristics of religious systems—most important for our purposes, the capacity for self-validation by internal reference from one dogma to another.

Its prophets were all proud of their freedom from dogma and of their commitment to doubt; from the perspective of today it is amusing to see just how proud (and how naive) they could sometimes be. Having myself felt the exhilaration of conversion to this religion as I was early disconverted from my inherited Mormonism, I can understand how Arnold Bennett, at 42, could flaunt his chains as proof of his freedom:

> In my opinion [1909] it is absolutely impossible for a young man with a first-class intellectual apparatus to accept any form of dogma, and I am therefore forced to the conclusion that Mr. Chesterton has not got a first-class apparatus. . . . I will go further and say that it is impossible, in one's private thoughts, to think of the accepter of [religious] dogma as an intellectual equal.[28]

Such joyful chants are evoked only by full systems that enable men "with first-class apparatus" to ignore what can be said against this or that part of the system.

None of us in this room really believes that all of his *own* commitments are equally indefensible in the eyes of other men. Everyone, no matter how thoroughly committed to motivism he may claim to be, always exempts at least a part of himself and his values from the dogmas. For the motivist, for example, the commitment to motivism and the command to respect its conclusions as truth are found and supported "rationally," not simply by following blind drives. One "ought"

28. As quoted in Arnold Lunn, *The Flight from Reason: A Study of the Victorian Heresy* (London, 1931), pp. 71–72.

to conduct one's mental life in their light, even though to say so is to assert a value. There seems something fishy about this one exemption, surely. What if the whole edifice were plainly, destructively, and tragically wrong—not wrong in the sense that there are no good reasons for respecting it on some occasions for some purposes, but in the sense that it is totally misleading when applied indiscriminately to the whole of life.

If I say that it is wrong, really, and not just in my own "wishful thinking," I am of course committing the kind of value judgment that is in question. You will, if you are a real motivist, explain why I cling to such values by referring to my upbringing as a fundamentalist Mormon or to my vested interests as a professor or to my sex life or my fears of "the harsh truth." And of course you will ask for proof. We all expect and demand "proof" for our assertions, and surely we are right to do so. A recent convocation speaker at Chicago characterized the university as essentially the place where things are doubted until proved: "If I have a prayer for you," he said, and it was clear that he used the word prayer metaphorically, "it is that you continue to cultivate what we have worked to inculcate—an attitude of benign skepticism about virtually everything—a constant query of 'where is the evidence?' in support of ideas and institutions, new and old." How many times I myself have said the same thing, and felt virtuous as I said it!

But I ask you to think a bit, as I turn now from motivism to the remaining four dogmas, about what would happen to your intellectual and moral life if you reversed that formula, cultivating a benign acceptance—perhaps temporary and tentative, but real—of every belief that can pass two tests: you have no particular, concrete grounds to doubt it (as distinct from the abstract principle to doubt what cannot be proved); and you have *good reason to think all men who understand the problem share your belief.* Reserve your skepticism, during the next twenty-three hours, for the abstract doubts you have been taught. Unless I am seriously wrong about the century in which we live, this exercise will not be easy for you. But if you practice it, you will be ready to look closely at the other beliefs that have surrounded and supported motivism, helping it to survive long after its time was past.

Once he was expounding to Lowes Dickinson his theory that "good" and "bad" had no objective validity. A few minutes afterwards Lowes Dickinson was laughing because the name of somebody Russell disliked had come up in conversation, and Russell had declared in the fiercest tone of conviction: "He is a *scoundrel*!"

Alan Wood

I find it quite intolerable to suppose that when I say "Cruelty is bad" I am merely saying that I dislike cruelty.

Bertrand Russell

As logic improves, less and less can be proved.

Bertrand Russell

Thus rational doubt alone, if it could be generated, would suffice to introduce the Millennium.

Bertrand Russell

Thought is the testing of statements on
the touchstone of the conscience,

. . . . . . . . . . . . . .
Thought is pondering over experience,
and coming to a conclusion.
Thought is not a trick, or an exercise,
or a set of dodges,
Thought is a man in his wholeness
wholly attending.

D. H. Lawrence, "Thought"

When you shoot at a king, don't miss.

Old saying

## TWO | Bertrand Russell's Rhetoric and the Dogmas of Doubt

### RUSSELL AS REPRESENTATIVE MODERN

Motivism survives as one link in a chain of beliefs that was forged slowly and—it now often seems—inexorably by the heirs of Cartesian dualism. I am not going to add one more historical tracing of the three-hundred-year slouching of modern skepticism toward Bedlam to be born.[1] Instead I want to look closely at a representative figure who comes at the end of the line, Bertrand Russell, perhaps the last and greatest modernist to embody to the full both extremes of the creed. As scientismist he became a great prophet of rigorous reason, adding a last chapter to the Book of Degenesis, that record of the dehumanization and defoliation of a Garden from which God and the angels had long since departed. As irrationalist, he became an internationally famous utopian, helping to free action and feeling from thought and thus to establish habits of unargued assertion and intuitive certainty about problems that his scientism taught were beyond the grasp of reason.

I choose Bertrand Russell as my central figure not because he is at the center of present controversies: he is not. But Russell comes

---

1. There have been hundreds, perhaps thousands, of such accounts in this century, some plotted as "the slow and painful triumph of truth," some as "God and man betrayed." The triumphal plot—as found for example in H. G. Wells's *The Outline of History*, Bertrand Russell's *A History of Western Philosophy*, and the even more superficial *Story of Philosophy* of Will Durant—has become rarer and rarer as the century has progressed; but it can still be found, for example, in Charles Coulston Gillispie's *The Edge of Objectivity* (Princeton, N.J., 1960). In recent decades the path of modern thought has been more often seen as a tragic or pathetic or absurd descent into nothingness; in most accounts there is some kind of escape hatch—a religious or existentialist or stoical reaffirmation of values that somehow escape the depredations of skepticism (see, for example, Franklin L. Baumer, *Religion and the Rise of Scepticism* [New York, 1960]). One account that manages to avoid gross myth-making by looking closely at particular thinkers is that of Harry Prosch, *The Genesis of Twentieth Century Philosophy* (Garden City, N.Y., 1964). Prosch's bibliography provides a good beginning on what he considers the four main modes of grappling with the world once it had been secularized: Marxism, existentialism, pragmatism, and the analysts. In Chaim Perelman and L. Olbrechts-Tyteca's *The New Rhetoric: A Treatise on Argumentation* (Notre Dame, 1969) and in other works by M. Perelman one finds a history of modern argument, or rhetoric, in which Descartes, with his method of handling doubt and certainty, started us on the downward path toward a world divided between valueless facts, which can be known, and unreasonable values, which cannot be. See also Vaile Florescu, "Rhetoric and Its Rehabilitation in Contemporary Philosophy," *Philosophy and Rhetoric* 3 (1970): 195.

closer to being representative of the main intellectual achievements and problems of our time than anyone else I can think of. In his role as mathematical logician he early established himself as one of the great innovators, strongly influencing at least two dominant contemporary schools of philosophy. He was often referred to in his lifetime as the greatest philosopher of modern times, and W. V. Quine says that "his philosophical influence, direct and indirect, [since 1901] has been unequalled."[2]

More important to our purposes, as a popularizer of philosophy and propagandist of ideas Russell had a greater role than any figure since—well, if you will not ask for proof, I'll say since Voltaire. In a great flood of popular accounts on subjects ranging from science and logic through ethical and political and educational theory to sex and diet, he presented to our century the image of the wise man thinking, the apostle of reason battling the credulous and quite probably wicked defenders of past dogmas.

Finally, he became sanctified, for many admirers, in the world of action. If I asked which philosopher of all time you would expect to find apotheosized in a dormitory at the University of Chicago, the poster of the benign grey head filling—or so it seems—one whole corridor, your answer would be right: not Aristotle, not Plato, not Hegel, not even Marx, but Bertrand Russell. Ralph Schoenman, editing a book of appreciations late in Russell's life, said that after he had read *Unpopular Essays,* a book that gave him more joy than anything else he had ever read, he came to worship Russell, only half-playfully considering him his candidate for God. He went to England to join Russell and the Committee on Nuclear Disarmament, became a kind of disciple, and

2. "Russell's Ontological Development," *The Journal of Philosophy,* vol. 63 (November 1966), reprinted in Ralph Schoenman, ed., *Bertrand Russell: Philosopher of the Century* (London, 1967), p. 304. See also Quine's "Remarks for a Memorial Symposium," in *Bertrand Russell: A Collection of Critical Essays,* ed. D. F. Pears (New York, 1972). Both volumes testify to Russell's unique importance. The bibliography of Pears' book is especially useful; limiting itself to "writings which are primarily philosophical"—that is, to what I later call "Russell I"—it substantiates his influence in six major areas of philosophy.

For polemical purposes I might have done better to choose a living, romping scientismist rather than the subtle and witty and late Russell—someone like B. F. Skinner whose simple and uncompromising behaviorism illustrates, better than Russell's shifting complex views, what an abstract empiricism can do to obscure what we in fact know. Skinner's polemic for his version of the good society, in *Walden Two* (New York, 1948) and *Beyond Freedom and Dignity* (New York, 1971), shows much more strongly than Russell's the tendency of moral fervor to become totalitarian when freed from the restraints of "good reasons." Another actively threatening target would be Jacques Monod.

finally, when Russell was 95, wrote the gospel according to Schoenman:

> He is 95. All the excitement remains: the energy and the élan,
> the passion for early Church music, the great love of poetry and
> the limitless recollection of cherished lines and passages, the feel-
> ing for drama, the vast knowledge of scriptures and the small
> ironies of old cultures—these things are with him and always
> shared. It is his sensibility, his passion for language, his hatred
> of humbug and pedantry, the great love of irony and paradox
> which excite every moment in his presence. This is the Bertrand
> Russell I cherish and whom this volume honours—the poetry of
> the man, the generosity of which he is unaware, the fullness of
> his life, his rich completion. I celebrate the beauty of Bertie for
> nothing touches this—not the meanness nor the smallness nor
> the hostility of pathetic men ridden with envy and the poison of
> their inadequacy. He needs no metaphor.[3]

Though Russell must have taken some amusement from such
language about himself, I think the tone of sanctification not entirely
misplaced. If a saint is anyone who consciously and voluntarily takes
upon himself, in extreme form, some inescapable and painful state that
other men must suffer, Russell came close to being a saint of modernism. One of the most gifted men who ever lived, he was forced to suffer
acutely its inherent contradictions. The man whom the irrationalist
D. H. Lawrence saw as an apostle of Satan, the man whom T. S. Eliot
could call "permanently precocious" because of his confident bouncy
rationalism, was in fact always torn between what he called his "mysticism" and his "logic." At the time of his work with Whitehead on the
*Principia Mathematica,* for example, a work which by its rigorous demands often drove him to the edge of suicide, he had a mystical experience. Observing Mrs. Whitehead suffering "an unusually severe bout
of pain," and seeing that she "seemed cut off from everyone and everything by walls of agony," he was suddenly overwhelmed by "the sense
of the solitude of each human soul."

> Suddenly the ground seemed to give way beneath me, and I
> found myself in quite another region. Within five minutes I went
> through some such reflections as the following: the loneliness of
> the human soul is unendurable; nothing can penetrate it except
> the highest intensity of the sort of love that religious teachers have
> preached; whatever does not spring from this motive is harmful,
> or at best useless; it follows that war is wrong, that a public school
> education is abominable, that the use of force is to be deprecated,
> and that in human relations one should penetrate to the core of

3. Schoenman, *Bertrand Russell,* pp. 1–2, 12.

45

loneliness in each person and speak to that. . . . At the end of those five minutes, I had become a completely different person. For a time, a sort of mystic illumination possessed me. . . . I did in actual fact find myself in far closer touch than previously with all my friends. . . . Having been an imperialist, I became during those five minutes a pro-Boer and a pacifist. Having for years cared only for exactness and analysis, I found myself filled with semi-mystical feelings about beauty, with an intense interest in children, and with a desire almost as profound as that of the Buddha to find some philosophy which should make human life endurable.[4]

I find the poignant contrasts revealing here—it is as if "exactness and analysis" were, rhetorically speaking, as strongly opposed to "feelings about beauty" and "interest in children" as being an imperialist is opposed to being a pacifist. And the contrast continues, heightened by a deprecatory tone about the "imagined" vision:

The mystic insight which I then *imagined* myself to possess has largely faded, and the *habit of analysis* has reasserted itself. But something of what *I thought I saw* in that moment has remained always with me [my italics].

He was a divided man, then, even by his own account. But I see him as even more seriously torn than he knew. To talk in this way is of course to risk doing violence to a great man, and it is a sure way to prevent giving an accurate reconstruction, whether of any one doctrine, any one work, or any one psychological moment in his life. To slice a man up is a sure way to kill him. But I count on your going back to the books themselves to rediscover his genius, and I reluctantly pay the cost of attempted dismemberment of the man in order to reject the dismembered universe of truth, thought, and action that he helped wish upon us.

I am not thinking of the fact that Russell changed his mind often, and that he can thus be easily quoted against himself if you compare his writings from different decades, or even from different books published within the same year. I find that fact explicable and often even admirable. The division I have in mind is something we have already seen him suggesting about himself: it comes from playing his three seemingly irreconcilable roles to the hilt. Bertrand Russell I, the genius of mathematical logic, sought *certain* knowledge about what he called "matters of fact" or "the world," sought that knowledge so passion-

4. The *Autobiography of Bertrand Russell: 1872–1914* (Boston, 1967), pp. 220–21.

ately that he later wondered whether he had permanently injured his mind in the search. Russell II, the "man of reason," often the man of rational protest, tried to disestablish certain past beliefs and establish the more adequate beliefs taught, so he said, by science and the scientific view of man's motives and possibilities. Russell III, the man of action and passion, the poet and mystic, argued and fought for particular causes in the world, though with a steady nagging awareness that he could not really prove that his cause was just. Thus the split between scientism and irrationalism runs like a thread of torture through most of what he does in all three roles.[5]

## MOTIVISM IN RUSSELL

Let me begin with a bit more about Russell's own motivism. The *Unpopular Essays*[6] that created Schoenman's discipleship contain an especially revealing chapter called "An Outline of Intellectual Rubbish." Russell says that he hopes his account of the "sillinesses" of the past will relieve our gloom about the sillinesses of the present. But what he does is far more than relieve gloom. For the believing reader, his biting ironies about the stupidities of traditional views build a growing sense of modern intellectual triumph, a self-confident glow that helped

5. The notion of talking of more than one Bertrand Russell is by no means original with me; as early as 1918 Philip Jourdain, for example, wrote a fine satire, *The Philosophy of Mr. B\*rtr\*nd R\*ss\*ll* (London, 1918) and quoted *this* Russell (using Russell's own words) against the *other* Russell. James K. Feibleman has traced Russell's positions on philosophical realism through several changes, though arguing that there is a consistently realist base beneath the changes (*Inside the Great Mirror* [The Hague, 1958]). Quine has traced many changes in his "ontological development" (n. 2 above). Russell himself again and again openly repudiated earlier positions. I can think of no philosopher who so often said, "I at one time believed such and such, but now I do not," and I have found him *silently* repudiating earlier positions even more often.

For a detailed consideration of three ethical theories embraced by Russell at different times (belief in nonnatural qualities, "objective" hedonism, and subjectivism) see D. H. Monro, "Russell's Moral Theories," *Philosophy* 35 (1960): 30–50. Monro sees Russell's views as both inconsistent and finally unsatisfactory, but praises Russell, "one of the formative influences on the modern mind," for showing us "what happens when a mind of the calibre of his grapples with the problem" of justifying "moral convictions when all the evidence seems to lead to moral scepticism."

Alan Wood, in *Bertrand Russell: The Passionate Sceptic* (London, 1957), emphasizes the division between Russell's "official moral philosophy" and the real man: "I have always felt certain that Russell, at heart, never believed his official moral philosophy; and the result was an internal contradiction which he himself sometimes recognized but never solved" (p. 98).

6. London, 1950. Except where I indicate otherwise, I have used the London editions.

make these *Unpopular Essays* very popular indeed. Through it all, one sees the wise old ironist, devotee of hard-headed scientific reason, annihilating other men's follies with one hand tied behind his back.

With a glorious insouciance that one cannot help admiring, Russell manages to lump together, as examples of rubbish, Aristotle's notion that man is a rational animal, Ptolemaic astronomy, astrology, all varieties of belief in God, *and* the reported case, source not noted, of a lady in "Northern New York State about the year 1820" who announced to her religious followers that she would walk on water "at 11 o'clock on a certain morning." "At the stated time, the faithful assembled in their thousands beside the lake. She spoke to them saying [note Russell's mock-Biblical language]: 'Are you all entirely persuaded that I can walk on water?' With one voice they replied 'We are.' 'In that case,' she announced, 'there is no need for me to do so.' And they all went home much edified" (p. 145). *There's* rubbish for you—and the implication is that all those other old-fashioned folk—Aristotle and his kind—were just like that.

The whole essay is a joyful, witty, confident dismissal of all past beliefs—he makes no exceptions and he clearly implies that to study the reasons of the past would be absurd. "Perhaps the world would lose some of its interest and variety if such beliefs were wholly replaced by cold science," he concludes. "A wise man [guess who!] will enjoy the goods of which there is a plentiful supply, and of intellectual rubbish he will find an abundant diet in our own age as in every other."

Russell never troubles in this essay to argue against the reasons men have offered in the past for their outlandish beliefs. The sole exception is Aristotle—whom he mercilessly emasculates and then pins to the mat with a bit of clever irony.

> His reason for this view [Man is a rational animal] was one which does not now seem very impressive; it was, that some people can do sums. . . . Now-a-days, however, calculating machines do sums better than even the cleverest people, yet no one contends that these useful instruments are immortal, or work by divine inspiration. As arithmetic has grown easier, it has come to be less respected. The consequence is that, although many philosophers continue to tell us what fine fellows we are [one might mention in this context Russell's own frequent praise of man], it is no longer on account of our arithmetical skill that they praise us (p. 96).

With Aristotle's reasons taken care of, Russell can then go on to look at the *true* motives men had for their totally irrational beliefs.

48

People's beliefs have various causes. One is that there is some evidence for the belief in question. We apply this to matters of fact, such as 'what is so-and-so's telephone number?' or 'who won the World Series?' But as soon as it comes to anything more debatable, the causes of belief become less defensible. We believe, first and foremost, what makes us feel that we are fine fellows. . . . Self-importance, individual or generic, is the source of most of our religious beliefs (pp. 109–10).

Secondly, there is "love of the marvellous." In fact, "every powerful emotion has its own myth-making tendency," for example, our natural impulse to be cruel, or our greed: "The great depression was the direct result of the surviving belief in the magical properties of gold" (p. 121).

Then after more ad hoc pronouncements on foolishness caused by sexual prejudice and by patriotism, he comes to some rules for avoiding "foolish opinions." The rules are marked both by an almost incredible superficiality and an avuncular tone that supports the picture —to those ready to believe—of the wise man able to set us all straight.

The advice he offers that interests us most as we study motivism is to reject all opinions that flatter our self-esteem and those that spring from fear. He here reduces the whole quest for good reasons to a simple negative search for labelled motives or drives. There is of course not a word about what motivates his own quest, except the bit about how much fun it is to see other men make fools of themselves. Somehow the fact that he is shattering idols seems to exempt him—as it did for me as I read him enthusiastically twenty years ago, or as it must have done for Mr. Schoenman more recently—from the charge of believing *his* conclusions because they flatter his self-esteem.

In this and scores of other essays Russell thus reinforced or implanted the dogma described yesterday about the *agency* of mental change; it is all drives, needs, and fears or conditioning by past superstitions, except of course in that narrow range of opinions concerned with the scientific or the "factual," like telephone numbers and World Series scores.

But it is now time to turn to the remaining four kinds of dogma: (2) What is the nature of the thing in which or on which mental change occurs (what is a human being, really, and what do we mean by "mind"?) (3) What is the scene in which this special kind of change, *mental* change, occurs—that is, in what kind of world is the mind placed? (4) What is truth and what are the principles of its establishment—that is, what are the methods that might justify a change of mind? (5) What is the purpose of attempting to change minds? On each of these questions, Russell, like many another prophet of the scientific revolution, has an unquestioned and seemingly unshakeable set of beliefs; though he changed his mind often about some doctrines, his basic assumptions about how the world relates to man remained unchanged.

### DOGMAS TWO AND THREE, THE AGENT AND THE SCENE: MAN AS AN ATOMIC MECHANISM IN A UNIVERSE THAT IS VALUE-FREE

What is man? What is a mind? Throughout Russell's life he was unwavering about what he often called the *scientific view of man:* man is a strictly "natural" product of the same coldly impersonal forces that work in every other part of the impersonal, aimless universe. "For countless ages the hot nebula whirled aimlessly through space. . . ." So begins his famous drama of purposelessness in "A Free Man's Worship" written in 1903.[7] The world of "fact," as discovered by "objective" science, is totally indifferent to man's values.

> Amid such a world ["purposeless," "void of meaning"], if anywhere, our ideals henceforth must find a home. That Man is the product of causes which had no prevision of the end they were achieving; that his origin, his growth, his hopes and fears, his loves and his beliefs, are but the outcome of accidental collocations of atoms; that no fire, no heroism, no intensity of thought and feeling, can preserve an individual life beyond the grave; that all the labours of the ages, all the devotion, all the inspiration, all the noonday brightness of human genius, are destined to extinction in the vast death of the solar system, and that the whole temple of Man's achievement must inevitably be buried beneath the débris of a universe in ruins—all these things, if not quite beyond dispute, are yet so nearly certain, that no philosophy which rejects them can hope to stand (pp. 2–3).

These doctrines were never repudiated, though in less than two decades Russell was shaken by scientific developments into shifting his "neutral monism" slightly in the direction of seeing the indifferent and unified universe as somewhat "more like thought and less like stones" than in this early view. He never doubted that man, with his mind, is not only dependent on the laws of chemistry and physics but

---

7. *Selected Papers of Bertrand Russell* (New York, 1927), pp. 1–15. The essay is still perhaps most frequently encountered in *Mysticism and Logic* (London, 1917), in which Russell himself established the fashion of portraying the mystic and the logician torn asunder.

finally explicable in terms of those laws.[8] His hopes of finding the "laws of human behavior" varied from book to book, and the role assigned to chance was not always the same. But there was never any suggestion that personalist views of the universe and man's place in it might be anything other than wishful longing.

8. See *The Analysis of Mind* (London, 1921), pp. 297–305. After this lecture I was asked how I could question the great achievement of modern thought in seeing man as a harmonious part of nature. The passage does not make sufficiently clear the distinction between being dependent on and indeed unified with nature and being explicable with terms and laws found in the study of physical processes. With Russell's effort in this essay to "reunify" man and nature I am entirely in sympathy; once the scientific revolution had divorced them, all who think about it find themselves struggling to put Humpty Dumpty together again. But my point about Russell and many other modernists is that they have not been sufficiently aware of the ambiguities in words like "nature" and "the world." As some phenomenologists have insisted, if man is really one with nature, then nature is by definition man-like, at least in part; all the phenomena of man's consciousness become part of "the world," and everything Russell has to say about the cold, inert, unknown, and unfeeling universe becomes questionable. From this point of view Russell's neutral monism is really a very unneutral dualism: he has chosen, in his definition of "things as they are," to rule out certain things —including values and feelings—that in fact *are*.

The platitude that "it's all just chemistry" was already pretty tired long before Russell wrote—see for example the satire against Kolya's views in the last section of *The Brothers Karamazov*. And of course it persists—not surprisingly, since there is no direct way to refute it and since if the universe really is a universe, there must be a sense in which the physical and the spiritual or mental are never fully separated. But this is a far cry from assuming that the mental will some day be explicable by laws reducible to the *present* laws of chemistry or physics. For a very late repetition of the dogma from a relatively undogmatic mind, see Thomas Kuhn's claim, in *The Structure of Scientific Revolutions*, 2d ed. (Chicago, 1970), that sooner or later all that happens in the mind will be explicable according to neural laws that can be reduced to the laws of chemistry and physics: ". . . our seeing a situation as like ones we have encountered before must be the result of neural processing, fully governed by physical and chemical laws" (p. 194); ". . . the processes involved must ultimately be neural, and they are therefore governed by the same *physico-chemical* laws that govern perception on the one hand and the beating of our hearts on the other" (p. 195; see also p. 204). These expressions of a faith in "physico-chemical" reductionism seem especially limited when compared with Michael Polanyi's treatment of the reasons for believing that only a hierarchy of explanatory systems, each imposing "boundary conditions" on the one "below," can hope to discover the rules or laws explaining or governing the behavior of higher forms of organization (*Personal Knowledge* [Chicago, 1958], esp. chap. 13, "The Rise of Man"). The immense difficulties facing a physics that intends, sometime in the future, to explain biology can be seen clearly in Erwin Schrödinger's *What is Life: The Physical Aspect of the Living Cell* (Cambridge, 1944). Schrödinger is a true believer, but an honest and subtle one; his complexities contrast strikingly with Russell's simplicities, since they proceed from similar initial assumptions.

51

To scientific common sense (which I accept) it is plain that only an infinitesimal part of the universe is known, that there were countless ages during which there was no knowledge, and that there probably will be countless ages without knowledge in the future. Cosmically and causally, knowledge is an unimportant feature of the universe; a science which omitted to mention its occurrence might, from an impersonal point of view, suffer only from a very trivial imperfection. In describing the world, subjectivity is a vice. Kant spoke of himself as having effected a "Copernican revolution," but he would have been more accurate if he had spoken of a "Ptolemaic counter-revolution," since he put Man back at the center from which Copernicus had dethroned him.[9]

The view of man, the puny, meaningless insect, prevailed, then— except of course whenever Russell felt impelled to defend values to which he was himself deeply committed, values like that of scientific inquiry or of integrity in its pursuit. Then we meet the two other Russells, the vital, idealistic, even Utopian prophet of reason and the passionate mystic and man of action who became famous among nonprofessionals. Russell I still dominated in the sense of setting the definitions, distinctions, and terms in which argument and action take place. But Russell II, the courageous partisan of truth, and Russell III, the savior of the world, never allowed themselves to be silenced by the cold logician for long. They knew that man's life could not be lived without values, and they feared that the scientific world picture which Russell I preached would, when popularized, produce impoverished, dehumanized man.

The conflict between the three Russells comes nicely to a head in a curious essay, "Behaviorism and Values," published in *Sceptical Essays* in 1928. In a critique of Watson's behaviorism, Russell first denies that he is himself a behaviorist, but then apologizes for this critical failure:

> Objective self-criticism, however, compels me to admit that it would be better if I were. In this essay I want to set forth certain difficulties which are felt by persons like myself, who, while accepting what is modern in science, have difficulty in divesting themselves of medievalism as regards what is worth living for. I want to ask, not only what is the logical bearing of behaviourism

9. *Human Knowledge: Its Scope and Limits* (New York, 1948), p. xi.
Needless to say, questioning these dogmas does not establish what they questioned. Though I think that every proposition in Russell's statement can now be said to be debatable, since serious debate is taking place, I would be unhappy to be identified with the opposite of all of Russell's views here.

upon values, but what is likely to be its effect upon ordinary men and women if widely accepted in a necessarily crude form (p. 89).

His answer is a shrewd and accurate prediction of what popular behaviorism will be:

> In old days there was supposed to be a thing called the mind, which was capable of three types of activity, feeling, knowing, and willing. Now it has been ascertained that there is no such thing as the mind, but only the body. All our activities consist of bodily processes. "Feeling" consists of visceral occurrences, particularly such as are connected with the glands. "Knowing" consists of movements of the larynx . . . (pp. 89–90).

He then attacks the conception of human excellence which *seems* to follow—illogically, he claims—from this notion of the world, attacks it in the name of a higher ideal "which has come down to us from Greece and the Middle Ages. . . . I believe this older outlook to be logically reconcilable with behaviourism, but not *psychologically* in the behaviour of the average citizen. In this older outlook, feeling and knowing are considered as important as doing, art and contemplation are thought to be as admirable as altering the positions in space of large quantities of matter" (p. 91).

Then, without so much as a bow toward providing an argument, he asserts: "It may be laid down that every ethical system is based upon a certain *non sequitur*. The philosopher first invents a false theory as to the nature of things, and then deduces that wicked actions are those which show that his theory is false" (pp. 91–92). The trouble with behaviorism is not that it in fact or logic does lead to bad ethical consequences but that, since men are so illogical, they *think*—even the behaviorists think—that behaviorism does have ethical consequences. And as Russell looks at the consequences that behaviorists *think* behaviorism should have, he finds them bad: they would rule out qualities, ideals, subtlety, feeling, all in the name of measurable quantities.

Then this clever, subtle, sensitive but divided man does an amazing thing. Russell I has said he ought to be a behaviorist but can't quite make it. Russell II has worried about the effects of popular behaviorism on mass man. Now Russell III, the man of action, retreats from the whole problem by recommending as his practical solution that ordinary men (whose misreading of the ethical consequences of behaviorism he fears) should be "taught logic": they should be taught logic so that they will learn *not* to reason. "For, if they reason, they will almost certainly reason wrongly" (p. 98)—that is, they will conclude that if man is a machine, certain ethical consequences follow!

Taught real logic—by Russell I—they will learn that nothing ethical follows "logically" from any general beliefs about man's nature.

Quite aside from the witty elitism of this carelessly constructed but prophetic essay, is it not curious that any man of genius could be so casual about the compartments of his mind as he is here? He claims that the values he cares for most are inherited from and supported *solely* by an outmoded worldview that his intellect cannot defend. He then dogmatically asserts that neither that old view nor the new world-view, that of the behaviorists, nor any worldview, can logically entail *any* values. But the "ordinary man" will mistakenly think that the new worldview entails ignoble and corrupting values. So what should we do?

One thing a man *might* do is try to verify in discussion with other men his notions of the noble and the corrupting. As we shall see in a moment, Russell often in fact moves in the direction of attempting this, especially in his middle years. But to end as he does here by lamely recommending the teaching of logic, so that men can see through the mistaken connection between behaviorist principles and bad ethics, is of course to leave all ethics, and indeed all ideals, on a common footing, indefensible with a reason which has been equated with logic. And it leaves Russell with no weapon in defending his ideals except a bit of sophisticated irony about medievalism and about being "out-of-date."

Concerning the nature of the mind and the world it occupies, then—the question of who or what experiences mental change—Russell I has it all his own way. It is he, the objective logician, who pronounces that mind is a peculiar kind of body accidentally tossed up by the cold seas of matter. Russell II is nearly always standing by, of course, to insist that man is after all capable of noble ideals, especially the ideal of being reasonable. And Russell III, from the beginning, insists on radical actions and transformations of society, just as if such things really mattered.

Even when Russell the believer holds the stage, the strings controlling his behavior are held by Russell I behind the scene, as in the stirring conclusion to "A Free Man's Worship":

> Brief and powerless is Man's life; on him and all his race the slow, sure doom falls pitiless and dark. Blind to good and evil, reckless of destruction, omnipotent matter rolls on its relentless way; for Man, condemned to-day to lose his dearest, to-morrow himself to pass through the gate of darkness, it remains only to cherish, ere yet the blow falls, the lofty thoughts that ennoble his little day; disdaining the coward terrors of the slave of Fate, to worship at the shrine that his own hands have built; undis-

mayed by the empire of chance, to preserve a mind free from the wanton tyranny that rules his outward life; proudly defiant of the irresistible forces that tolerate, for a moment, his knowledge and his condemnation, to sustain alone, a weary but unyielding Atlas, the world that his own ideals have fashioned despite the trampling march of unconscious power.

No Christian preacher could affirm his values more passionately than this; Russell the mystic has spoken his truths. But the truths he speaks are spoken by default, imposed upon him by the logician who has told him that knowledge about such important matters is impossible and that in consequence man is, both intellectually and morally, in a desperate plight.

### Dogma Four, the Principles of Knowing

Russell's internal warfare is perhaps even clearer when we turn from the agent and scene of mental change (and the portrait of his seeming rejection of all metaphysics) to the *principles* of mental change and a brief description of his theories of knowledge. As we would expect by now, Russell's epistemology does not remain fixed, either from decade to decade or from book to book in a given period. But there are again certain unchanging assumptions that make his self-divisions significant for us in our quest for a philosophy of good reasons.

The first of these, his beliefs about doubt and certainty, he developed from a tradition willed to him by centuries of western skepticism. Descartes is often praised or blamed for establishing the notion that the way to decide what we know is to look for what we can know *certainly,* and that the way to discover *that* is to find what remains after we have applied the universal solvent of doubt to every belief. It would be more accurate to say that Descartes himself merely brought to a head techniques of systematic doubt that had been adumbrated at least as early as Socrates and explored with greater and greater vigor in later skepticisms.[10] Be that as it may, to Russell it seemed that the history

10. Skepticism is a troublesome word with a confusing history. From our point of view here, what is most interesting is how often it has been adopted as a device for protecting the right to believe in something precious which seems threatened by whatever opposes skepticism. Montaigne was a skeptic in order to protect himself from having to pay serious attention to warring arguments that seemed to tear the church and society apart. The Fellows of the Royal Society in Restoration England were skeptical in order to maintain belief in the kind of scientific inquiry they pursued, and in the kind of universe that made that inquiry possible; they were generally careful to insist that they were not "Pyrrhonists"—complete unbelievers—and they often explicitly exempted this or that religious or philosophical principle from their systematic doubtings (see chap. 1,

of thought revealed triumph after triumph of doubt, with one traditional belief after another overthrown by this or that empirical philosopher or scientist willing to ask honestly, "What can I really prove?"

---

"The Sceptical Critic," in Phillip Harth's *Contexts of Dryden's Thought* [Chicago, 1968]). They all finally, like Russell, believed in Truth and Reason, even while taking as a motto, *Nullius in verba.* "So that the *Philosopher thinks much, and examines* many things, separates the *Certainties* from the *Plausibilities, that which is presumed* from *that* which is *prov'd,* the *Images* of *Sense, Phansie,* and *Education,* from the *Dictates* of *genuine* and *impartial Reason.* This he does before he *Assents* or *Denies* (Joseph Glanvill, as quoted by Harth, p. 9). Note the word "dictates" as contrasted with "education"!

In one definition of the word, it is of course impossible to find any *assertions* of full skepticism; even silent enactments are difficult. A good general rule is: scratch a skeptic and find a dogmatist.

It is hard not to take a wicked pleasure in the paradoxes revealed in the traditionalism of those who preach the achievements of doubt. Russell usually portrays himself as a daring original who followed pure thought in opposition to the benighted believers of previous centuries. But one can scarcely give credit for daring originality to any modernist whose father was a free-thinker and "a disciple and friend of John Stuart Mill," whose parents were both "ardent theorists of reform and prepared to put into practice whatever theory they believed in," whose mother "sometimes got into hot water for her radical opinions," and who as an old man remembers episodes like this from childhood: "I was impressed by the fact that limpets stick to the rock when one tries to pull them off, and I said to my aunt Agatha, 'Aunty, do limpets think?' To which she answered, 'I don't know.' 'Then you must learn,' I rejoined" (*Autobiography,* chap. 1).

It is clear that Russell's own sense of having to overcome the weight of all those benighted bishops came in part from the years he spent under the influence of his devout paternal grandmother. But even during those years he was often in the presence of people like his maternal grandmother, who "had a considerable contempt for everything that she regarded as silly," who ridiculed him for not having read books of "popular science," and who was, in short, like many others surrounding him, "an eighteenth-century type, rationalistic and unimaginative, keen on enlightenment, and contemptuous of Victorian goody-goody priggery." His account of his fear of her ridicule, like his account of the guilt he felt toward his father's mother, cannot—according to *my* antimotivist principles—be used to discredit his ideas; but according to *his* principles, they make a nice ironic commentary on his conviction that religion springs only from fear and desire for self-esteem, while modernist ideas come from independent thought.

A good short introduction to what Russell's immediate forebears believed is given by A. O. J. Cockshut, in *The Unbelievers: English Agnostic Thought, 1840–1890* (London, 1964). Though Cockshut does not mention Russell, he shows that the daring originality and independence and honesty of which Russell was so boastful were platitudes of his boyhood, as was the self-portrait of the coldly rational man of science wedded uneasily to the mystic. See especially the chapter on T. H. Huxley, who boasted that "his mark" on the world would be to free it "from the abominable blur of cant, humbug, and self-seeking which

## Dogma Four

We can distinguish two aspects of this faith. On the one hand, there is a kind of unproved and unprovable conviction that *thought doubts;* that's its job. On the other hand, thought "proves" what can be certainly known. In practice, of course, the word *prove* here takes on a strong connotation of doubting, because the way of proof, as we shall see, is the way of finding what cannot be doubted. But in statement, the paeans to Doubt often sound very different from the cautious words of scientific inquiry:

> Men fear thought as they fear nothing else on earth—more than ruin, more even than death. Thought is subversive and revolutionary, destructive and terrible; thought is merciless to privilege, established institutions, and comfortable habits; thought is anarchic and lawless, indifferent to authority, careless of the well-tried wisdom of the ages. Thought looks into the pit of hell and is not afraid. It sees man, a feeble speck, surrounded by unfathomable depths of silence; yet it bears itself proudly, as unmoved as if it were lord of the universe. Thought is great and swift and free, the light of the world, and the chief glory of man.
>
> But if thought is to become the possession of many, not the privilege of the few, we must have done with fear. It is fear that holds men back—fear lest their cherished beliefs should prove delusions, fear lest they themselves should prove less worthy of respect than they have supposed themselves to be.

Significantly enough these words come from a book affirmatively entitled *The Principles of Social Reconstruction*[11]—telling of

surrounds everything in this present world" (p. 88) and whose summary of his lifelong (conflicting) passions differs from Russell's mainly in being much less anguished: *"Sartor Resartus* led me to know that a deep sense of religion was compatible with an entire absence of theology. Secondly, science and her methods gave me a resting-place independent of authority and tradition. Thirdly, love opened up to me a view of the sanctity of human nature, and impressed me with a deep sense of responsibility" (pp. 95–96). See also Gertrude Himmelfarb, *Victorian Minds* (New York, 1968), esp. "The Victorian Angst." "In fact, the Victorian unbelievers carried unbelief about as far as it could humanly, sanely, go" (p. 302).

11. Bertrand Russell, *Principles of Social Reconstruction* (London, 1916), pp. 165–66. Once he gets beyond his repeated pleas for a "new thought" that will by definition be destructive of past thought and that will make the thinker lonely, his constructive principles turn out to be both admirable and unoriginal: e.g., "The growth and vitality of individuals and communities is to be promoted as far as possible"; "The growth of one individual or one community is to be as little as possible at the expense of another"; "The supreme principle, both in politics and in private life, should be to promote all that is creative, and so to diminish the impulses and desires that centre round possession" (pp. 227, 236).

a shining vision of the society that is to be, of the triumphs that thought will achieve in the time to come, and of the ever-widening horizon of man's survey over the universe. Those who are taught in this spirit will be filled with life and hope and joy, able to bear their part in bringing to mankind a future less sombre than the past, with faith in the glory that human effort can create (p. 167).

How a thought which is essentially "destructive and terrible" will deal with this vision of reconstructed hope and joy is not shown.

If "thought doubts," clearly what it must do if it is to avoid destroying itself is to find what cannot be doubted. In his early philosophical work, he has told us, Russell wanted to discover whether there were any propositions that could be accepted as absolutely certain. Though he often said that nothing is certain, he never gave up the notion that what one should look for, when looking for truth, is the most nearly certain propositions one can find, and certainty was always a function of empirical and logical proving. Such a search means in practice that most of what we consider important will be unknowable because unprovable, and it also means that belief in the universal efficacy of doubt becomes the most certain belief of all.

The scepticism that I advocate amounts only to this: (1) that when the experts are agreed, the opposite opinion cannot be held to be certain; (2) that when they are not agreed, no opinion can be regarded as certain by a non-expert; and (3) that when they all hold that no sufficient grounds for a positive opinion exist, the ordinary man would do well to suspend his judgment.[12]

This sounds innocuous enough until we remember how it relates to motivism, the first dogma: in all judgments about values the experts *do* disagree; in fact there are no experts, since reasons offered are always reducible to motives. Thus in moral and aesthetic judgment there can never be "sufficient grounds for a positive opinion." The philosopher, he says again and again, makes an "unusually obstinate attempt to arrive at real knowledge,"[13] and by real knowledge he always means

12. *Sceptical Essays* (London, 1928), Introduction, pp. 12–13.
13. *Philosophy* (New York, 1927), p. 1. Alan Gewirth has described the inconsistency in our usual way of referring to scientific and ethical experts. Referring to science and scientists, we are tacitly normative: we mean *good* scientists, or *genuine* scientists, not Christian scientists, scientologists, or the many unscientific-minded folk who have somehow wangled appointments in this or that department of physics or chemistry or biology. And of course we find that our chosen experts do in fact turn out to share certain norms of method and definition. But when we argue about ethics we find ourselves saying that there can be

knowledge as nearly certain as possible. Whatever can be doubted is just to the degree of the possible doubt not knowledge.

Values are thus most certainly ruled out of the cognitive domain; I find no evidence that the apostle of doubt ever doubted this central assumption, though he knew that most previous philosophers would have doubted it in his extreme form, and that contemporaries like Whitehead and Dewey thought it untenable. Whenever one finds him speculating about knowledge, whether in the early logical inquiries or in the later investigations of human knowledge and the mind, one can be sure that the questions dealt with will be mostly how we gain knowledge about things like tables and chairs and telephone numbers and historical facts; at the most difficult, we ask how or what we know about our memories or predictions of fact, or about such nonexperienced but factual things as atoms.

Russell II always had trouble with this notion of knowledge. It left him, as a man who wanted to defend the use of "reason" in human affairs, with an embarrassingly limited supply of reasons to give other men for following his various programs of reason and action. In theory, if Russell I were believed, Russell II had available in any practical problem only true knowledge—certain or near-certain conclusions based on empirical observation or rigorous deductions from self-evident scientific or mathematical propositions—or mere emotional appeal and exhortation. Russell I had no place whatever for what traditional philosophers called dialectic, or sometimes rhetoric: the careful weighing of more-or-less good reasons to arrive at more-or-less probable or plausible conclusions—none too secure but better than would be arrived at by chance or unthinking impulse.

But Russell believed, as a first article of faith, that reason should operate in the world of men, and he often tried to discuss how it could do so without violating too blatantly the convictions of Russell I.

In another essay in *Sceptical Essays,* "Can Men Be Rational?" he makes the transition between the two Russells clear; but he does so in such a way as to leave Russell II able to reason only about means; the rest is preaching, useless except on behalf of rationality.

I believe that all solid progress in the world consists of an increase in rationality, both practical and theoretical. To preach an

---

no standards because experts do not agree. Hitler teaches one thing, Gandhi another, and the Godfather something else again. Whether we want to allow for a normative definition of ethics, allowing into the debate only the genuine experts, we must surely recognize the curious asymmetry here (Gewirth, "Positive 'Ethics' and Normative 'Science,'" *Philosophical Review* 69 [1960]: 311–30).

altruistic morality appears to me somewhat useless, because it will appeal only to those who already have altruistic desires. But to preach rationality is somewhat different, since rationality helps us to realize our own desires on the whole, whatever they may be. A man is rational in proportion as his intelligence informs and controls his desires. I believe that the control of our acts by our intelligence is ultimately what is of most importance, and what alone will make social life remain possible as science increases the means at our disposal for injuring each other. Education, the press, politics, religion—in a word, all the great forces in the world—are at present on the side of irrationality; they are in the hands of men who flatter King Demos in order to lead him astray. The remedy does not lie in anything heroically cataclysmic, but in the efforts of individuals towards a more sane and balanced view of our relations to our neighbours and to the world. It is to intelligence, increasingly wide-spread, that we must look for the solution of the ills from which our world is suffering (p. 53).

Twenty years later, in *Human Knowledge*, he made a much more ambitious attack on the same problem. In this book, the sharpness of Russell's earlier separation of knowledge, which is limited to what is "scientific," from all the rest of man's mental life—intuition, feeling, desire—is to some degree blurred. He is clearer about the dependence even of scientific knowledge on data which are on the one hand private but on the other are verified finally in public discourse. And he often shows some awareness both that there are many kinds and degrees of rational credibility and that we have good grounds for "belief" or "credence" about many matters that we cannot, in his terms, be said to know. When he wrestles with the relationship between "subjective certainty," a "psychological concept," and "credibility," which is a "logical concept," he indeed approaches a rhetorical view of how one assesses various more-or-less compelling reasons for more-or-less probable conclusions:

> Short of subjective certainty, a man may be more or less convinced of something. We feel sure that the sun will rise tomorrow, and that Napoleon existed; we are less sure of quantum theory and the existence of Zoroaster; still less sure that Eddington got the number of electrons exactly right. . . . These are matters as to which there is fairly general agreement, but there are other matters as to which disagreement is the rule. Some people feel no doubt that Churchill is good and Stalin bad, others think the opposite; some people were utterly certain that God was on the side of the Allies, others thought that He was on the side of the Ger-

mans. Subjective certainty, therefore, is no guarantee of truth, or even of a high degree of credibility.

Error is not only the absolute error of believing what is false, but also the quantitative error of believing more or less strongly than is warranted by the degree of credibility properly attaching to the proposition believed in relation to the believer's knowledge. . . .

Scientific method, broadly speaking, consists of technique and rules designed to make degrees of belief coincide as nearly as possible with degrees of credibility.[14]

If we did not know from other sources how narrowly Russell defines knowledge, this definition of scientific method could be used, without too much stretching, as a definition of that rhetorical method we are seeking, one that will gauge the relative worth of reasons for assent.[15] Thinking or reasoning or rhetoric in this view would be the

14. *Human Knowledge,* pp. 396–97.

15. "I think, therefore, that everything we feel inclined to believe has a 'degree of doubtfulness,' or, inversely, a 'degree of credibility.' Sometimes this is connected with mathematical probability, sometimes not; it is a wider and vaguer conception. It is not, however, purely subjective. There is a cognate subjective conception—namely, the degree of conviction that a man feels about any of his beliefs—but 'credibility,' as I mean it, is objective in the sense that it is the degree of credence that a *rational* man will give. When I add up my accounts [note that he immediately leaps to a quantitative example] I give some credence to the result the first time, considerably more if I get the same result the second time, and almost full conviction if I get it a third time. This increase of conviction goes with an increase of evidence, and is therefore rational. In relation to any proposition about which there is evidence, however inadequate, there is a corresponding 'degree of credibility,' which is the same as the degree of credence given by a man who is rational. (This latter may perhaps be regarded as a definition of the word 'rational')" (pp. 342–43). He almost gets to "rhetoric" here: the words could be used by any rhetorician to define what he believes the rational rhetorician to be. But there is no hint that the process works on values, on personal judgments, on judgment of persons. See also his summary of his views on scientific knowledge, wisdom, and degrees of credence about questions of value in "Philosophy for Laymen" (*Unpopular Essays*). It is in this essay that he for once toys with a notion of reasonable emotions, under the term "generalized emotions," and he even hints at a doctrine, now widely held by philosophers but surely abhorrent to Russell I, that ethical and logical commands are on the same moral footing: "The interrelation of logical and emotional generality in ethics is an interesting subject. 'Thou shalt love thy neighbor as thyself' inculcates emotional generality; 'ethical statements should not contain proper names' inculcates logical generality. The two precepts *sound* very different, but when they are examined it will be found that they are scarcely distinguishable in practical import." But though even to talk in this way, in 1950, shows a great change from the man who had written *Sceptical Essays,* the essay still reveals a man who divides the world into "science" and "religion,"

art of making our degree of assent (and dissent) coincide as nearly as possible with degrees of credibility—that is, with the best available reasons. The Russell II who emerges here feels the need for such an art, but he can hint at its application only to the narrowest possible range of beliefs. Except for four short pages (396–99) he never treats any question of right conduct or value judgment as a question for possible knowledge at all. And those pages are disappointing indeed. There are two kinds of ethical theory—rule theory and consequence theory: Kant and the Decalogue on the one hand, and on the other the theory that "the virtuous man will act in the way which, as far as his knowledge goes, will *probably* maximize pleasure," according to the "degree of credibility." ("It would have been a good thing if Hitler's mother had killed him in infancy, but she could not know this"—this is the only difficulty he seems to be able to think of about the "consequence" theory, and it is taken care of in his definition with the word *probably*!)

In short, in 1948, even when overtly seeking to deal with "human" knowledge, Bertrand Russell is still pursuing, with only slight modification, his earlier rigorous divorce of mysticism and logic. When he asks about human knowledge, he in effect cannot help concluding that it is all on the side of logic—that is, empirical observation and logical inferences from them—leaving the whole of human conduct to the side of mysticism: instinct, intuition, feeling. "What character in addition to truth must a belief have in order to count as knowledge?" he asks, and the answer is an elaboration of the commonsense belief that there must be "sound evidence": ". . . What is known consists, first, of certain matters of fact and certain principles of inference, neither of which stands in need of extraneous evidence, and secondly, of all that can be ascertained by applying the principles of inference to the matters of fact." And when one asks how to obtain these kinds of proof, the answer is essentially that of traditional empiricism: "matters of fact are those given in perception and memory, while the principles of inference are those of deductive and inductive logic" (p. 155).

He acknowledges the unsatisfactory features in this traditional doctrine, but in the end, after a perfunctory treatment of three theories of knowledge, he ends up with the "traditional [British] view" essentially unmodified. When he returns to Kant's question of the synthetic a priori (can the knowledge we have of "some universal propositions and also of some unexemplified existence propositions . . . be based wholly on experience"?) he is forced to conclude, rather lamely, that our

---

with philosophy useful as a handmaiden to the first and a needed and absolute skeptical restraint about the second.

knowledge of some things cannot be "based on experience," that "empiricism as a theory of knowledge has proved inadequate, though less so than any other previous theory of knowledge," and that in any case the whole inquiry has been inspired by and has exemplified the doctrine that "all human knowledge is uncertain, inexact, and partial. To this doctrine we have not found any limitation whatever" (p. 506).[16]

16. The question of whether all human knowledge is uncertain, including the knowledge that all human knowledge is uncertain, has spawned a great deal of complex debate before and after this dogmatic conclusion by Russell. Norman Malcolm summarizes the issues brilliantly in *Knowledge and Certainty* (Englewood Cliffs, N.J., 1963), especially the first two chapters and "Memory and the Past." Malcolm is particularly useful in his analysis of the notion of "logical impossibility" in Russell's claim that "there is no logical impossibility in the view that the world was created five minutes ago," and of the ambiguities in the notion of possibility, covered by terms like *may* and *might*, in sentences like Russell's "I might have come into existence a few moments ago" (p. 188). Malcolm argues that Russell, like Rudolf Carnap and C. I. Lewis, makes the mistake of identifying "absolute certainty with 'theoretical certainty,'" both being "impossible" because, in all empirical judgments "there remains still," as Carnap puts it, "the theoretical possibility of denying the sentence" (pp. 54–55). Though Malcolm's exposé of the dogmatic circularity of such commitments to theoretical doubt is gentler than I think is justified, he provides the kind of precise, detailed philosophical analysis which my rough-and-ready rhetorical purposes do not require. The important thing for my case is that to doubt on "theoretical grounds" that the world is more than five minutes old is clearly less reasonable, in a most important sense of the word, than to believe that it has lasted a very long time, on the ground that everyone I have ever heard testify on the subject believes that it has. The first test is logical, and I am delighted to learn from Malcolm that it turns out to be logically very weak or perhaps flatly wrong; the second test is rhetorical or social, and it is of course the test that all men naturally use for their beliefs, when they have not been corrupted by general dogmas, religious or antireligious.

Viewed in the perspective of Western philosophical history, the debate between Malcolm and the proponents of Russell's kind of verification is but a local skirmish. It is rhetorically important, at this moment in history, to repudiate the quest for theoretical certainty, because handled as it has been by the logical empiricists it has led to negative conclusions which have rubbed off on all arguments, shaking men's faith in the validity of *any* conclusions. As John Dewey said, in *The Quest for Certainty: A Study of the Relation of Knowledge and Action* (New York, 1929), the logicians have stultified our quest for knowledge pertinent to action by setting up impossible standards for knowledge of any kind.

The effort to reunify the domains of knowing and doing in order to rehabilitate the world of thoughtful action must seem, to anyone who is primarily interested in theoretical, objective certainties, both logically loose and humanly tainted. (I can remember how easily, twenty years ago, I could "refute" Dewey and the whole pragmatic movement by showing that they had "no adequate criterion of truth.") Though I am serious in trying to show the harmfulness of

63

Meanwhile, in arriving at this obviously self-contradictory conclusion, he has conveniently and often explicitly rejected many of the
questions that traditional rhetoricians and philosophers would have

---

the modernist dogmas about fact and value, reason and conditioning, doubt and
certainty, I am aware that other social contexts and other intellectual problems
can still justify arguing for the senses in which reason and faith, fact and value,
are sharply distinct, and for the primacy of doubt. An easy example: In talking
with religious fundamentalists about these ideas, I have often found them too
readily transmuted into simplicities and then embraced: "Yes, yes, there has
been too much doubt in the world; the grammar of assent is what we need, and
the values we assert—however wildly irrational—are just as factual as the scientist's claims." Probably what one should attempt with those good sleepy people is
an old-fashioned skeptical attack. As Richard McKeon says, in the most extensive account of the various dichotomies and fusions that have clustered about
philosophical discussion of "certainty," "facts and values are not simple given
entities but depend on what men think, on what they do, on what they need, and
on what they aspire to achieve" ("The Flight from Certainty and the Quest for
Precision," *Review of Metaphysics* 18, no. 2 [December 1964]: 253).

One of the nicest double ironies in the history of philosophy can be seen in
following the fate of the quest for empirical certainty from about 1900 to the
present. By the time of A. J. Ayer's *Language, Truth and Logic* (1936), the empiricist conviction that "no empirical proposition can ever be anything more than
probable" could produce an absolute pronouncement like the following:

"It is now generally admitted, at any rate by philosophers, that the existence
of a being having the attributes which define the god of any non-animistic religion cannot be demonstratively proved. To see that this is so, we have only to
ask ourselves what are the premises from which the existence of such a god
could be deduced. If the conclusion that a god exists is to be demonstratively
certain, then these premises must be certain; for, as the conclusion of a deductive argument is already contained in the premises, any uncertainty there may
be about the truth of the premises is necessarily shared by it. But we know that
no empirical proposition can ever be anything more than probable. It is only
*a priori* propositions that are logically certain. But we cannot deduce the existence of a god from an *a priori* proposition. For we know that the reason why *a
priori* propositions are certain is that they are tautologies. And from a set of
tautologies nothing but a further tautology can be validly deduced. It follows
that there is no possibility of demonstrating the existence of a god" (A. J. Ayer,
*Language, Truth and Logic*, 2d ed. [New York, 1946], pp. 114–15).

The disastrous fate of such certainties about the quest for certain knowings
through the next twenty-five years, even within what might be called Ayer's
branch of empiricism, should keep us all humble (see John Hick, ed., *The
Existence of God* [New York, 1964]; and Antony Flew and Alasdair MacIntyre, eds., *New Essays in Philosophical Theology* [London, 1955]).

The early Wittgenstein claimed to have found, in his rigorous logic of language, a truth that was "unassailable and definitive"—"the final solution of the
problems" (*Tractatus Logico-Philosophicus*, trans. D. F. Pears and B. F.
McGuinness [London, 1961], Preface). As Russell himself wrote in an intro-

felt obliged to face. When he comes, for example, to the question of how one evaluates probabilities about witnesses, some of them more "probably trustworthy" than others, he gives two short paragraphs and hastily concludes: "But we need not pursue such arguments, which are a matter for lawyers rather than philosophers" (p. 190).[17] He turns immediately to advertising and politics, and claims that only the "unusually sophisticated person" will know how to resist "primitive credulity about testimony." But he feels no need to explain what kinds of knowledge or lack of knowledge justify his using words like *sophisticated* and *primitive*: "I do not want to stray into politics, so I will say no more about this aspect of the belief in testimony" (p. 191). Meanwhile Russell III had always felt free to "stray into politics," though with a more and more desperate tone as the decades of horror and disappointment unfolded.

But it is not only forensic and political questions that are ruled out as beyond the help of knowledge. *Human Knowledge* contains little about how one reconstructs meanings or intentions—Russell simply ignores the whole mysterious art of interpretation of other men's offerings of knowledge. Though he obviously "knew" that men's intentions can be read in literature and in life, that in fact error and hence truth

---

duction to the work: "Mr Wittgenstein is concerned with the conditions for a logically perfect language—not that any language is logically perfect, or that we believe ourselves capable, here and now, of constructing a logically perfect language, but that the whole function of language is to have meaning, and it only fulfils this function in proportion as it approaches to the ideal language which we postulate" (p. x). What a strange assumption this is, looked at today —that language fulfills its whole function only by moving toward the logical perfection of absolute clarity! Russell could say this, even while knowing full well that "in practice, language is always more or less vague," only because he believed that "the essential business of language is to assert or deny facts" (p. x) and that the essential business of philosophy is to discover which facts, if any, are undeniable.

17. I think it is not surprising that one of the most impressive new rhetorics has come from the encounter of a lawyer (and philosopher) with the reasons for confidence in the results of legal reasoning. Do lawyers and judges "know" anything? It is clear that most of what they know is not discovered or demonstrated in processes anything like those that Russell advocates as the only way to know. The result of placing such a question in the context of traditional rhetorical inquiry is *The New Rhetoric* by Perelman and Olbrechts-Tyteca. See also Edward Levi, *An Introduction to Legal Reasoning* (Chicago, 1948); James White, *The Legal Imagination* (Boston, 1973); and Charles Fried, *An Anatomy of Values* (Cambridge, Mass., 1970). But the law is only one of many fields which, as I said in lecture 1, have discovered that much of what they know is theoretically ruled out by the principles of systematic doubt.

are possible in such reading, one would never guess from his writings that degrees of knowledge are obtainable in such matters.[18]

Most flagrant of all, there is no hint of a logic of values, no hope offered to anyone who might want to think about commitments to values and for or against persons and programs. This total exclusion is again perhaps most striking when Russell himself uses value terms and reveals his commitments. We can legitimately ask, surely, what status as knowledge statements like the following can be said to have, if Russell I's conception of knowledge is accepted. If you depersonalize language through education in the use of abstractions, he says, "you can no longer hope to be a poet, and if you try to be a lover you will find your depersonalized language not very successful in generating the desired emotions. You have sacrificed expression to communication, and what you can communicate turns out to be abstract and dry" (p. 5). True, I would say, but neither true nor false according to Russell's own theory. Such bits of wisdom and lore have nothing to do with knowledge.

## THE PREACHER LIBERATED

The notion that we have reason to believe only what has been proved, in the sense of withstanding all possible doubts, cannot be lived with by most of us for even a moment. There is nothing shameful in this, unless logic, mathematics, and physical science, which are also based on "unprovable" assumptions, are shameful.[19] Life would be impossible if it were not so, as Russell well knew.

18. I must add that his own hermeneutical practices were as bad as his neglect of theory would lead one to predict. His *History of Western Philosophy* (New York, 1945) is largely worthless, except as it helps us understand Russell, because almost all philosophers—and especially premodern philosophers—emerge from it looking like absolute idiots. Russell clearly did not believe that any effort to make sense out of all that intellectual rubbish would be justified.

19. As everyone now knows, Gödel "proved" (even in Russell's sense of the word, I gather) that no formal system can prove all of the propositions on which it depends and no system can prove its own freedom from contradiction by its own modes of proof; at least one first step must always be derived or assumed on grounds other than the standards of proof operating in the system. To a mathematical novice, this must seem simply a more rigorous statement of Aristotle's claim that no science can prove its own first principles. Neither claim is equivalent to saying that our choices of first principles need be unreasoned or arbitrary. See, for a careful, brief verbal summary of Gödel's proofs, John von Neumann, "Tribute to Dr. Gödel," *Symposium Papers Commemorating the Sixtieth Birthday of Kurt Gödel,* ed. Jack J. Bulloff et al. (New York, 1969). See also Piaget's *Structuralism,* ed. and trans. Chaninah Maschler (New York, 1970), pp. 32–36.

If this is true, I am not uncovering a shameful fact when I turn to his practical life (in contrast with his philosophy) and find his positions unproved by his own standards. That he takes for granted, in some of his writings, propositions that are doubtful, or at least radically in need of support he does not provide, puts him in no worse case than we all stand in: every passage on any subject, probed as I am now going to probe some words of his, will lead very quickly to a dead end —a point at which the question "And why is *this* true?" finds no further response in the writing itself. But the search for such points of unquestioned certainties can be especially revealing in a man like Russell who prides himself on open-mindedness and frequently claims to believe in no certainty except that nothing is certain.

Consider first a bit of typically oracular prose by Russell III, a passage introducing the book *What I Believe*.[20] To me it is self-sufficient, totally convincing as it stands:

In this little book, I have tried to say what I think of man's place in the universe, and of his possibilities in the way of achieving the good life. In *Icarus* I expressed my fears; in the following pages I have expressed my hopes. The inconsistency is only apparent. Except in astronomy, mankind have not achieved the art of predicting the future; in human affairs, we can see that there are forces making for happiness, and forces making for misery. We do not know which will prevail, but to act wisely we must be aware of both.

I have no trouble accepting the final sentence, with its forceful "must," because the proposition is a truism—and truisms, though often boring, require no proof, especially in prefaces. It would be absurd to say to Russell, the moralist, "Prove at this point that to act wisely I must take into account both the forces making for happiness and the forces making for despair."

What I do have trouble with, however, is reconciling this kind of oracular pronouncement about how to act wisely with anything Russells I or II have to say about knowledge. I have read again and again in his works that truth and knowledge are other kinds of things entirely, and I consequently continue reading *What I Believe* in a somewhat skeptical frame of mind—wondering whether he will ever hint that there is a Russell who doubts every proposition unless it is sustained with logical or mathematical or scientific proofs.

What I come to does not reassure me. Since the conflict in his

20. New York, 1925.

roles cannot be fully appreciated in any short quotation, I should like now to dispute the details of a rather long section from the first chapter of this book.

For brevity, I shall occasionally use a shorthand notation: (1) If I do not comment, Russell has made an assertion which he and I both see as needing support[21] and which he does in fact proceed to support with some kind of argument. (2) If I pause to insert a "Why?" that will mean that I disagree with the proposition or at least that I know it to be sufficiently controversial to need the support *that it does not get.* (3) If I say, "Granted, but . . . ," the "but" will mean "But you, Russell (in contrast with someone who has a place for values in his notions of knowledge and value) have no right to take *this* as proof: according to your own definitions of knowledge and proof, it is merely an assertion of your personal opinion."

R: "Man is a part of Nature, not something contrasted with Nature."

Q: I agree, but this seems to me to be precisely what you deny when you choose to rule out all of man's values as irrelevant to Nature.

R: "His thoughts and his bodily movements follow the same laws that describe the motions of stars and atoms."

Q: Why? What kind of laws? The laws—no doubt extremely general —of Supreme Being? You have rejected those. The law of gravity? Of chemical combination? You have made a huge leap here. [Note that there is no answer; Russell plunges on to other unsupported assertions.]

R: "The physical world is large compared with Man—larger than it was thought to be in Dante's time, but not so large as it seemed a hundred years ago. . . . It is [now] thought—"

Q: By whom? *I* should think what follows still highly controversial (whether in 1925 or 1971).

R: "that the universe is of finite extent in space, and that light could travel round it in a few hundred millions of years. It is thought [again?] that matter consists of electrons and protons, which are of finite size, and of which there are only a finite number in the world."

Q: Perhaps, when put in the tentative form of "It is thought"—implicitly allowing for the fantastic changes that have taken place since you wrote the sentence. But you now use this tentative, unproved, ostensibly scientific assertion as hard evidence for hard conclusions.

R: "The laws of these changes [in electrons and protons] can apparently be summed up in a small number of very general principles,

21. I am assuming that most listeners will share most of my decisions here— an astonishing but justified piece of arrogance, the importance of which will not be clear until the next lecture.

which determine the past and the future of the world when any small section of its history is known."

Q: Why? Here I am in 1971, and I am told by physicists that they cannot agree among themselves about either the number or the nature of the elementary particles. I note that you say "apparently," which again sounds as if you had an open mind, but then you close in on that hard word "determine," which serves as the basis for the curious logic that now follows.

R: "Physical science is *thus* [my italics] approaching the stage when it will be complete, and therefore uninteresting. Given—"

Q: Why?

R: "the laws governing—"

Q: How? You've told me again and again that you don't believe in the laws of causation!

R: "the motions of electrons and protons, the rest is merely geography—a collection of particular facts telling their distribution throughout some portion of the world's history. The total number of facts of geography required to determine the world's history is probably finite."

Q: What does "probably" mean here? You drop it immediately in order to settle dogmatically the immensely controversial questions of whether men's experience of phenomena need be counted among the "world's facts." Thus you prepare for the ten-thousandth repetition of Laplace's hypothesis—in your hands now an established theory—about the determined, computer-like, totally predictable universe.

R: "Theoretically, they [the facts about electrons and protons] could all be written down in a big book to be kept at Somerset House, with a calculating machine attached, which, by turning a handle, would enable the inquirer to find out the facts at other times than those recorded."

Q: Why? Is not this cliché of liberal thought in your time, even when covered by your jokey tone, simply a reassertion of the position to be proved, that man and nature are not only inseparable but reducible to the laws governing atoms?

R: "It is difficult to imagine anything less interesting, or more different from the passionate delights of incomplete discovery."

Q: Granted, but—

R: "It is like climbing a high mountain and finding nothing at the top except a restaurant where they sell ginger-beer, surrounded by fog but equipped with wireless."

Q: Granted, but what is the status of this argument in Russell I's view of how to argue?

R: "Of this physical world, uninteresting in itself, Man is a part."

Q: The original proposition reasserted and still unproved.

R: "His body, like other matter, is composed of electrons and protons, which, so far as we know, obey the same laws as those not forming part of animals or plants."

Q: So far as we *know,* in your sense, we can also say that they *don't.*

R: "There are some who maintain that physiology can never be reduced to physics, but their arguments are not very convincing."

Q: Why? Let's see one. And what about psychology and politics and ethics?

R: "And it seems prudent to suppose that they are mistaken."

Q: Why? What a curious inversion of Pascal we have here! Asserting that the universe is totally reducible to the laws of physics—asserting what Russell I has claimed cannot be proved, just as the existence of God cannot be proved—Russell II falls back on the Pascalian wager inverted: it is *"prudent* to suppose that they are mistaken." Prudent in relation to what ends? Prudence is a value. Why should I be prudent in relation to scientific caution rather than to—say—making life seem meaningful?

R: "What we call our 'thoughts'—"

Q: Why the inverted commas?

R: "seem—"

Q: Why?

R: "to depend upon the organization of tracks in the brain in the same sort of way in which journeys depend upon roads and railways."

Q: What is the argumentative status of this analogy? Many studies, which admittedly you could not have known when you wrote, would question this linear model.

R: "The energy used in thinking seems to have a chemical origin; for instance, a deficiency of iodine will turn a clever man into an idiot."

Q: Granted, but what is the warrant for equating the "energy used in thinking" with *thought itself*? And what is the force of your one example? You have shown that the train can be derailed, but not what makes it go or what built the line or what does the switching.

R: "Mental phenomena seem to be bound up with material structure."

Q: Mere reassertion, made without exploring the ambiguity of "bound up."

R: "If this be so—"

Q: An "if" immediately turned into a conclusion, with no further evidence.

R: "we cannot suppose that a solitary electron or proton can 'think'."

Q: Again the inverted commas.

R: "We might as well expect a solitary individual to play a football match."

Q: Granted, but who ever asserted that individual electrons think, with or without inverted commas?

R: "We also cannot suppose that an individual's thinking survives bodily death, since that destroys the organization of the brain, and dissipates the energy which utilized the brain-tracks."

Q: Well, your thought is present to me now, in 1971, having survived your death. But aside from that, which I assume you will see as only a quibble, what does it prove about your general case, even if I agree that your *particular* mind was dissipated when your brain was?[22]

R: "God and immortality, the central dogmas of the Christian religion, find no support in science. It cannot be said that either doctrine is essential to religion, since neither is found in Buddhism. (With regard to immortality, this statement in an unqualified form might be misleading, but it is correct in the last analysis.) But we in the West have come to think of them—"

Q: Who's we?

R: "as the irreducible minimum of theology. No doubt people will continue to entertain these beliefs, because they are pleasant, just as it is pleasant to think ourselves virtuous and our enemies wicked."

Q: Unabashed motivism here. Would you care to comment on how you would prove the statement? And just how "pleasant" is the notion of a wrathful, jealous God, anyway? Even when you wrote, you could have found many an anthropologist who thought things were a lot more complicated than you say.

R: "But for my part I cannot see any ground for either. I do not pretend to be able to prove that there is no God. I equally cannot prove that Satan is a fiction. The Christian God may exist; so may the Gods of Olympus, or of Ancient Egypt, or of Babylon."

Q: Surely you know that you have here reduced the notion of God's existence to a form unconnected with the proofs offered by philosophers; if the question of God is the question of anthropomorphic "Gods"—Supreme Being reduced to the Jehovah of Christian fundamentalism, or to Apollo and Venus and Osiris and Santa

---

22. Disbelief in immortality is of course an inescapable deduction from the picture of the brain-in-the-mindless-universe that we found above. Any notion of immortality is quite literally inconceivable for anyone who has accepted that worldview. But if for any reason one comes to question that worldview, then every question it settled becomes open again. I do not believe in immortality of the kind that I think Russell is rejecting, but then I do not believe in the existence of the isolated atomic self about which his form of the immortality question arises. The point here is not to argue for or against the belief but to insist on Russell's dogmatism; a question he thought closed is very open indeed and was thought to be still unsettled by many less triumphant speculators even in Russell's own time—for example, William James and Emile Durkheim. I spare the reader (for once) my handy little bibliographical guide to the history of speculation about immortality, beginning with Plato and ending with—shall we say, just to be provocative?—Lévi-Strauss, who I believe never uses the word.

Claus—then you have at best a Pyrrhic victory in a war invented by modernism.

R: "But no one of these hypotheses is more probable than any other: they lie outside the region of even probable knowledge, and therefore *there is no reason* [my italics] to consider any of them. I shall not enlarge upon this question, as I have dealt with it elsewhere."

Q: But even elsewhere you always keep the question in the form: Because I cannot *prove* that there is or is not a God, I choose—prudently—to believe that there is not. Logically the other choice is, in your own terms, equally sound (or unsound), but by ridicule and distortion you make it appear that your side is more reasonable.

And so we go on, through a catalog of flat assertions and superficial arguments that never come within miles of what serious defenders of belief in God or immortality would actually say.

R: "Believers in immortality will object to physiological arguments, such as I have been using, on the ground that soul and body are totally disparate, and that the soul is something quite other than its empirical manifestations through our bodily organs. I believe this to be a metaphysical superstition. Mind and matter alike are for certain purposes convenient terms, but are not ultimate realities."

Q: Why?

R: "Electrons and protons, like the soul, are logical fictions."

Q: How's that again? I was just told that they were the ultimate constituents of reality, no questions asked, and that if I knew their "geography" I could plot the whole history of mankind. Now, to make your point against the soul, you waft them away.

R: "Each is really a history, a series of events, not a single persistent entity."

Q: Why? Is this *knowledge* you give us?

R: "Fear is the basis of religious dogma."

Q: Again!

R: "[I]t is fear of nature that gives rise to religion."

Q: What's your evidence?

R: In dignifying such fear, religion has done mankind a great disservice: "all fear is bad—"

Q: Why? And would you include fear of error, for example?

R: "and ought to be overcome—"

Q: Why? Where does the "ought" come from?

R: "not by fairy tales—"

Q: Why?

R: "but by courage and rational reflection."

Q: Why? Why is courage good in your terms? Why try for rationality if the geography of electrons and protons determines what I think?

R: "Happiness is none the less true happiness because it must come to an end—"

Q: Granted, but—

R: "nor do thought and love lose their value because they are not everlasting."

Q: Why don't they? Only because they have none in the first place?

Now watch the closing paragraphs of the chapter, freed of my carping. Keep in mind Russell's overriding claim that man is a part of nature, not something contrasted with nature.

Many a man has borne himself proudly on the scaffold: surely the same pride should teach us to think truly about man's place in the world. Even if the open windows of science at first make us shiver after the cosy indoor warmth of traditional humanizing myths, in the end the fresh air brings vigour, and the great spaces have a splendour of their own.

The philosophy of nature is one thing, the philosophy of value is quite another. Nothing but harm can come of confusing them. What we think good, what we should like, has no bearing whatever upon what is, which is the question for the philosophy of nature. On the other hand, we cannot be forbidden to value this or that on the ground that the non-human world does not value it, nor can we be compelled to admire anything because it is a 'law of nature.' Undoubtedly we are part of nature, which has produced our desires, our hopes and fears, in accordance with laws which the physicist is beginning to discover. In this sense we are part of nature; in the philosophy of nature, we are subordinated to nature, the outcome of natural laws, and their victims in the long run.

The philosophy of nature must not be unduly terrestrial; for it, the earth is merely one of the smaller planets of one of the smaller stars of the Milky Way. It would be ridiculous to warp the philosophy of nature in order to bring out results that are pleasing to the tiny parasites of this insignificant planet. Vitalism as a philosophy, and evolutionism, show, in this respect, a lack of sense of proportion and logical relevance. They regard the facts of life, which are personally interesting to us, as having a cosmic significance, not a significance confined to the earth's surface. Optimism and pessimism, as cosmic philosophies, show the same naive humanism: the great world, so far as we know it from the philosophy of nature, is neither good nor bad, and is not concerned to make us either happy or unhappy. All such philosophies spring from self-importance, and are best corrected by a little astronomy.

But in the philosophy of value the situation is reversed. Nature is only a part of what we can imagine; everything, real or imagined, can be appraised by us, and there is no outside standard to show that our valuation is wrong. We are ourselves the ultimate and irrefutable arbiters of values, and in the world of value Nature is only a part. Thus in this world we are greater than Nature. In the world of values, Nature in itself is neutral, neither good nor bad, deserving of neither admiration nor censure. It is we who create value, and our desires which confer value. In this realm we are kings, and we debase our kingship if we bow down to Nature. It is for us to determine the good life, not for Nature—not even for Nature personified as God (pp. 14–17).

Thus the idolator of science, having begun with the claim that man is "not something contrasted with Nature," has produced an absolute dualism of cold nature, known by reason, and man's values, asserted but not known. He goes on to "prove," in chapter 2, that *the good life is one inspired by love guided by knowledge,* that though "both love and knowledge are necessary, love is in a sense more fundamental, since it will lead intelligent people to seek knowledge, in order to find out how to benefit those whom they love." The "since" is interesting, especially if one asks whether its use is justified as knowledge. Such concepts of course have nothing to do with terms like "virtue" or "sin" ("for these are conceptions which seem to me to have no scientific justification").

Russell next spends a chapter attacking superstitions, another chapter "proving" that "to build up the good life, we must build up intelligence, self-control, and sympathy," and a final chapter arguing for—or rather, again asserting—the value of a scientifically conditioned benevolence, of justice ("The recognition of the equal claims of all human beings"), courage (to combat that greatest of evils, fear) and, with seemingly equal importance, a rational approach to contraception. The book concludes as follows:

Human nature we should respect, because our impulses and desires are the stuff out of which our happiness is to be made. It is no use to give men something abstractly considered "good"; we must give them something desired or needed if we are to add to their happiness. Science may learn in time to mould our desires so that they shall not conflict with those of other people to the same extent as they do now; then we shall be able to satisfy a larger proportion of our desires than at present. In that sense, but in that sense only, our desires will then have become "better." A single desire is no better and no worse, considered in isolation, than any other; but a group of desires is better than another group if all of the first group can be satisfied simultaneously while in the second group some are inconsistent with others. That is why love is better than hatred.

To respect physical nature is foolish; physical nature should be studied with a view to making it serve human ends as far as possible, but it remains ethically neither good nor bad. And where physical nature and human nature interact, as in the population question, there is no need to fold our hands in passive adoration and accept war, pestilence, and famine as the only possible means of dealing with excessive fertility. The divines say: it is wicked, in this matter, to apply science to the physical side of the problem; we must (they say) apply morals to the human side, and practise abstinence. Apart from the fact that every one, including the divines, knows that their advice will not be taken, why should it be wicked to solve the population question by adopting physical means for preventing conception? No answer is forthcoming except one based upon antiquated dogmas. And clearly the violence to nature advocated by the divines is at least as great as that involved in birth-control. The divines prefer a violence to human nature, which, when successfully practised, involves unhappiness, envy, a tendency to persecution, often madness. I prefer a "violence" to physical nature which is of the same sort as that involved in the steam engine or even in the use of fire. This instance shows how ambiguous and uncertain is the application of the principle that we should follow "nature."

Nature, even human nature, will cease more and more to be an absolute datum; more and more it will become what scientific manipulation has made it. Science can, if it chooses, enable our grandchildren to live the good life, by giving them knowledge, self-control and characters productive of harmony rather than strife. At present it is teaching our children to kill each other, because many men of science are willing to sacrifice the future of mankind to their own momentary prosperity. But this phase will pass when men have acquired the same domination over their own passions that they already have over the physical forces of the external world. Then at last we shall have won our freedom.

I assume that most of you, perhaps all, will gladly and vaguely join me in embracing with Russell the values of love and the good life, knowledge, self-control, harmony, and freedom. And I hope you will share my sense of the poignance of his assertions, made as they had to be against the grain of his skepticism. It is to his great credit that he could not resist fighting for values that he knew he could know nothing about. Knowing that he could doubt the validity of every value assertion, even the ones he cared for most, and equating the known with "what cannot be doubted," he refused to remain silent about values in the world.

The extraordinary consequences for Russell's rhetoric of the divorce between proved truth and asserted values are revealed perhaps most clearly in his brilliant "Reply to Criticism," in *The Philosophy of Bertrand Russell*.[23] He begins with nearly forty pages of carefully reasoned, open-minded, and for the most part charitable and irenic answers to critics of his work on logic, mathematics, scientific theory, and epistemology. Then, with a marked change of tone, he says:

> I come now to what is, for me, an essentially different department of philosophy—I mean the part that depends upon ethical considerations. I should like to exclude all value judgments from philosophy, except that this would be too violent a breach of usage. The only matter concerned with ethics that I can regard as properly belonging to philosophy is the argument that ethical propositions should be expressed in the optative mood, not in the indicative. [Again I want to ask—knowing that he might use his theory of types back against me—whether the argument that leads to this "should" would be couched in the optative, and if so what its cogency would be for him.] Where ethics is concerned, I hold that, so far as fundamentals are concerned, it is impossible to produce conclusive intellectual arguments. [And of course, if arguments are not *conclusive,* the implication is that they have no force whatever.] When two people differ about (say) the nature of matter, it should be possible to prove either that one is right and the other wrong, or that both are wrong, or that there are insufficient grounds to warrant any opinion. In a fundamental question of ethics I do not think a theoretical argument is possible. I do not therefore offer the same *kind* of defence for what I have said about values as I do for what I have said on logical or scientific questions (pp. 719–20).
>
> A judgment of fact—so I hold—is capable of a property called "truth," which it has or does not have quite independently of what any one may think about it. . . . I see no property, analogous to "truth," that belongs or does not belong to an ethical judgment (p. 723).
>
> Persuasion in ethical questions is necessarily different from persuasion in scientific matters. According to me, the person who judges that A is good is wishing others to feel certain desires. He will therefore, if not hindered . . . try to rouse these desires in other people. . . . *This is the purpose of preaching, and it was my*

23. Paul Arthur Schilpp, ed., *The Library of Living Philosophers,* vol. 5 (Evanston, Ill., 1944).

*purpose in the various books in which I have expressed ethical opinions.* The art of presenting one's desires persuasively is totally different from that of logical demonstration, but it is equally legitimate (p. 724; my italics).

Well, it all depends on what one means by "legitimate." Since it is obviously a value term, the final assertion cannot, according to his own views, be validated, only preached. I think that any reader of this transition must conclude that all of the honor goes to the knowledge side and all of the desperation to the preaching side. And if we apply the simple test of whether Russell is careful about his own arguments, we find a shocking degeneration at precisely this point: his replies to his critics, once he has entered the value side, are perfunctory and superficial, without so much as a bow in the direction of trying to reconstruct the critics' arguments. Why bother, since no matter how careful he tried to be, the result would still be only "preaching"?

### Dogma Five, the Purposes of Argument

In observing Russell's importations of purposes into a purposeless universe and his selective applications of doubt, we have seen almost all we need about the fifth aspect of mental change, the purposes for which it is attempted. It is clear that truth or knowledge can operate as goals only when we are engaged with "scientific" questions about "matters of fact." Russell cares deeply about the happiness of mankind and tries to build a world of rational men who will choose a reasonable road to happiness; knowledge, of a limited but useful kind, can be obtained about means and consequences; and man's great hope lies thus, as it did for earlier utilitarians, in a rational and honest calculus of pleasures. But since in support of such ends one has available only a kind of preaching, the prophet and activist who feels strongly that certain values and purposes ought to prevail in the world can have only one rhetorical purpose: to win.

Russell III was passionately concerned to make certain values prevail in the world and to combat values he thought were destructive: "Is it possible to preserve the lover and the poet without preserving the lunatic? . . . Are they so bound up together that when the one is brought under control the others perish? I do not believe it. I believe there is in each of us a certain energy which must find vent in actions [Note the form of this sentence before I complete it: the tone of strong affirmation, surely curious as the conclusion of what is called a *skeptical* essay—I believe, brother, I believe. And here is what I believe: that] there is in each of us a certain energy [a new ghost in the machine?] which *must* find vent in actions *not inspired by reason,* but may find

77

vent in art, in passionate love, or in passionate hate, *according to circumstance"* (my italics).

And suddenly—as happens so often when Russell II seems to be making a rational case for what was after all a very conventional view of man's dual nature—Russell III bursts through and begins to prophesy. What else can he do? If proof about our values is impossible, if rational argument is by definition irrelevant, and if one still believes and cares, the man of action can only woo, exhort, plead, shout, or wheedle. If he has Russell's genius, he will preach well, using all the devices of traditional rhetoric about such matters—except a really careful, respectful treatment of the reasons for or against a given value.

When he grows warm, Russell often sounds as if he were consciously enjoying freedom from rational responsibilities. Don't ask me for reasons—I have already proved to you that reasons cannot be provided. Just palpitate with me, as I run over once again the pious platitudes of the modernist credo:

> Respectability, regularity, and routine—the whole cast-iron discipline of a modern industrial society—have atrophied the artistic impulse, and imprisoned love so that it can no longer be generous and free and creative, but must be either stuffy or furtive. Control has been applied to the very things which should be free, while envy, cruelty, and hate sprawl at large with the blessing of nearly the whole bench of Bishops.[24]

"Respectability, regularity, and routine"; "the whole bench of Bishops"; "generous and free and creative"; "envy, cruelty, and hate" —the triads of virtues and vices roll out; the rhythmical and alliterative reinforcements hammer the doctrines home; but where are the arguments? What are the reasons?

Surprisingly often they are, as here, simply the reasons that one finds in many popular sources today, more than forty years later, from the so-called *Playboy* philosophy to the counter culture as described by Theodore Roszak: on the one hand there is the "cast-iron discipline" of institutions ("modern industrial society") or of inherited norms (those Bishops); on the other there are the asserted "natural" impulses to freedom and joy. Russell, unlike some more recent hedonists, recognizes that man's nature is not unreservedly good—he still sees some need for reason to control the "darker instincts," though he doesn't say how. But the basic rhetoric is that of a simple choice between a good that is intuitively clear—the prophet has enunciated it—and an evil

24. "Can Men Be Rational?" in *Sceptical Essays*, p. 24.

that we inherit from the past or have imposed on us by institutions in the present.

It is interesting to see what happens to the standards of evidence when Russell III has a case to be made.

> Religion, morality, economic self-interest, the mere pursuit of biological survival, all supply to our intelligence unanswerable arguments in favour of world-wide co-operation, but the old instincts that have come down to us from our tribal ancestors rise up in indignation, feeling that life would lose its savour if there were no one to hate, that anyone who could love such a scoundrel as so-and-so would be a worm, that struggle is the law of life, and that in a world where we all loved one another there would be nothing to live for.[25]

Unanswerable arguments? Bertrand Russell talking of unanswerable arguments? Unanswerable arguments provided by religion and morality? But of course the purpose here is to sway men, and we can forget all about what we know about knowledge of values.

It is not surprising that this apostle of reason, who had preached the impossibility of reasonable argument about what matters most, should have moved, along with many others in this tortured century, further and further away from argument toward mere assertion, and finally toward laying his body on the line, the last resort of those who feel that reason has failed. Whereas his protest against World War I had included published arguments about justice and war, arguments presented with a good deal of care, his protests as the years went by became more and more oracular, often with a final appeal to physical resistance and even—in the first hysteria after Russia developed the atomic bomb—to threats of violence.

Even when his protests remained verbal, they inclined toward statements urging others to lay *their* bodies on the line—*demonstrating* in this modern sense and throwing to the winds all concern about earning the right to say *quod erat demonstrandum*. In 1954, when the present generation of demonstrators were infants, he said in a radio address about the hydrogen bomb,

> Remember your humanity and forget the rest. If you do so, the way lies open to a new paradise. If you cannot, nothing lies before you but universal death.[26]

Michael Scott comments on that marvelous historical moment when two members of Russell's group, the Committee for Nuclear

25. *Authority and the Individual* (London, 1949), p. 20.
26. As quoted in *The Times* (London) obituary, 1970.

Disarmament, staged a sit-in on Russell's drawing room floor. When they "refused to move or let him get on with his work," Russell, who had recently staged a sit-in at Parliament Square, called the police and had them removed "in the name of the law." They claimed he had violated his own principles. Scott sees these people as merely silly, and explains Russell's action with what I take to be a good version of popular Russellism:

> While not suffering such foolishness kindly, Russell is one of the most kindly and tolerant of men. But his tolerance is not an easy going indulgence or acquiescence in things which he believes to be wrong. His belief is his point of view and it may be wrong. His tolerance is rather a positive delight in variety and in the conflict which this inevitably implies in the whole order of things. The art of civilization is the pursuit of these conflicts (remember—they are built into the "whole order of things") in a rational and civilized manner, not either by deceit and trickery or the mere use of *force majeur*. Hence his opposition to all forms of bigotry or dogmatism.[27]

In other words, Russell was tolerant of all except those of whom he was not tolerant. His beliefs were his "point of view." He was often compared to a Christian preacher, and the comparison is apt. But there is this crucial difference: a preacher and his audience have certain shared standards of conviction that make of them a rhetorical community: even when a fundamentalist preacher relies on proofs from the Scripture that would make non-fundamentalists scoff, he is not cheating, because *he* believes that such proofs make sense, and he wants his audience to believe with him. If pressed, he would be able to say that his arguments are defensible in the highest courts of reason as he conceives reason. And this means that everyone, whether inside the rhetorical community or outside, must admit that he has a *kind* of answer to anyone who persists in asking "why."

But preacher Russell believed that he could not defend his own preachments with any kind of knowledge. He could not finally believe in his own arguments, except as a way of winning. At best he could only lapse into sincerity, as it were, forgetting that every rhetorical effort was equally noncognitive and thus equally powerless in affecting a critical mind.

No wonder he became more shrill, through the mounting catastrophies of his century: the horrors of World War I, of Nazism and Stalinism, of World War II and the atomic bomb, and the various ab-

27. "Civil Disobedience and Morals," in Schoenman, *Bertrand Russell.*

surdities and cruelties of the Cold War. As the world seemed to him to get worse, his beliefs about how it should work gained wider acceptance and his personal following increased—partly because of his deserved reputation as a courageous warrior. Doctrines which at one time had got him jailed were becoming widespread; disciples were gathering about the master. Personal and circumstantial temptations to be merely oracular became harder and harder to resist. Though the desire to be a philosopher survived through the forties, we find more and more of the improviser, the man who knows what he knows because of how it feels. Though Russell had always been known as a man who would win at all costs, he had generally claimed to be bound by standards of social utility. As he said in *Education and the Social Order,*

> The fundamental defect of Christian ethics consists in the fact that it labels certain classes of acts "sins" and others "virtues" on grounds that have nothing to do with their social consequences. An ethic not derived from superstition must decide first upon the kind of social effects which it desires to achieve and the kind which it desires to avoid. It must then decide, as far as our knowledge permits, what acts will promote the desired consequences; these acts it will praise, while those having a contrary tendency it will condemn. Primitive ethics do not proceed in this way.[28]

But seventeen years later the prophet is no longer bound even by social utility. In *Authority and the Individual* he begins to explore those moments—so important in his later public life—when the individual must pit his feelings even against the useful. Listen to him as he imports unanalyzed and unproved conceptions of the good and the best into his discussion of the "Individual and Social Ethics":

> Prophets, mystics, poets, scientific discoverers, are men whose lives are dominated by a vision; they are essentially solitary men. When their dominant impulse is strong, they feel that they cannot obey authority if it runs counter to what they profoundly believe to be good. Although, on this account, they are often persecuted in their own day, they are apt to be, of all men, those to whom posterity pays the highest honour. It is such men who put into the world the things that we most value, not only in religion, in art, and in science, but also in our way of feeling towards our neighbour, for improvements in the sense of social obligation, as in everything else, have been largely due to solitary men whose thoughts and emotions were not subject to the dominion of the herd.[29]

28. (London, 1932), p. 68.
29. (London, 1949), p. 113.

It is, so far, a revealing passage. We see Russell's own sense of lonely opposition to authority and the herd, buttressed by the typical modernist assumption that human values are invented in solitary opposition to what other men say. But the values seem no longer bound to "social utility"; somehow those lonely prophets have begun to look like goods-in-themselves, a hunch that is confirmed in the next paragraph:

> If human life is not to become dull and uninteresting, it is important to realize that there are things that have a value which is quite independent of utility. What is useful is useful because it is a means to something else, and the something else, if it is not in turn merely a means, must be valued for its own sake, for otherwise the usefulness is illusory.

Yes, yes, go on, one wants to shout: show us how it is done. You're on the right track at last—the track that you might have discovered earlier if you had not been so sure that none of the traditional philosophers had anything to teach you. Now show us *how* you will determine what goods are worthy of being considered ends in themselves.

But the passage shows where such a search for final causes will end: with whatever is not dull or uninteresting. A curious turn indeed, one that no doubt includes, among the ultimately interesting values, the value of the lonely prophet, his sprightly prophesying an end in itself!

Such a prophet will find an almost unlimited rhetorical repertory waiting for him when he descends from his mountain. If he is to win (that is, become one of "those to whom posterity pays the highest honor"), he can use every device of persuasion save one: solid argument about the values he has discovered. What will replace such argument is "mere rhetoric," and it will tend to be the rhetoric of personal demonstration. Russell has told us again and again that we can have no knowledge about values, ends, purposes; we can commune about them, perhaps, and even give our lives for them, but we cannot know anything about them or demonstrate them in any sense other than personal testimony, laying our reputations or our bodies on the line.

## THE TRIUMPH OF RUSSELL'S MODERNISM

In the Prologue to his *Autobiography*, probably written when he was well into his nineties, Russell said, "Three passions, simple but overwhelmingly strong, have governed my life: the longing for love, the search for knowledge, and unbearable pity for the suffering of mankind. These passions, like great winds, have blown me hither and thither, in a wayward course, over a deep ocean of anguish, reaching to the very verge of despair." Rereading him for this lecture I have again and again wondered how this brilliant, sensitive, torn man kept only on *this* side of the "very verge of despair." Pursuing a "true method of Ethics," as for everything else, in "inference from empirically ascertained facts,"[30] he was passionately committed to moral, aesthetic, and cosmological beliefs that his readers—according to his own teachings—had every right to ignore. What ground for hope could he have, if, as he said, his disapproval of Hitler could not be defended in the courts of reason, and his arguments against evil and cruelty had no more validity than Hitler's propaganda?

In the early letter from which I have just quoted, we find a sudden astonishing affirmation of moral imperatives—astonishing, that is, coming from this empiricist: "What first turned me away from utilitarianism," the young man says, "was the persuasion that I myself ought to pursue philosophy, although I had (and have still) no doubt that by doing economics and the theory of politics I could add more to human happiness." We have by now learned to expect no defense of his right to use the word "ought" in that sentence, even though it is so obviously not drawn from any empiricist's lexicon. "It appeared to me," he goes on, "that the dignity of which human existence is capable is not attainable by devotion to the mechanism of life, and that unless the contemplation of eternal things is preserved, mankind will become no better than well-fed pigs." This is, clearly, one of many threats posed by the triumph of the modernist dogmas—but without giving up the dogmas, where is one to go for evidence that there is meaning in the word "dignity," that "contemplation of eternal things" should be preserved, that to be a contented pig is worse than to be a discontented philosopher?

Russell goes on in that letter to argue that to be philosophical does not on the whole tend "to happiness. It gives moments of delight, but these are outweighed by years of effort and depression." "*How* outweighed?" one wants to ask. On what scale? But of course he has, within a few sentences, forgotten his empiricist creed—and has grown warm with a prophetic fire. And once warmed, the young man could leave the world of factual support, or even everyday rhetorical argument, far behind:

> It seems to me now that mathematics is capable of an *artistic excellence* as *great* as that of any music, perhaps *greater*; not because the pleasure it gives (although very *pure*) is comparable,

30. Letter to Gilbert Murray, April 3, 1902, in *The Autobiography of Bertrand Russell, 1872–1914* (London, 1967), appended to chap. 6.

either in intensity or in the number of people who feel it, to that of music, but because it gives in *absolute perfection* that combination, *characteristic of great art,* of *god-like freedom,* with the *sense* of inevitable destiny; because, in *fact,* it constructs an *ideal* world where everything is *perfect* and yet *true* (my italics).

Pulling himself back down to earth, he carries on with more "unearned" value terms:

Again, in regard to actual human existence, I have found myself giving honour to those who feel its tragedy, who think truly about Death, who are oppressed by ignoble things even when they are inevitable. . . . I hold all knowledge that is concerned with things that actually exist—all that is commonly called Science—to be of very slight value compared to the knowledge which, like philosophy and mathematics, is concerned with ideal and eternal objects, and is freed from this miserable world which God has made.

And he concludes with an attack on "this ghastly world of ignoble degradation, in which only virtue is punished and vice lives and dies happy and respected."

We have seen that Russell at one time lamented the likely effect of behaviorism, if Watson's doctrines ever became popular. One can play exactly the same game with Russell's views, regrettably without having to resort to speculation. Partly because of his own prolific and skilful polemics, Russell's beliefs spread rapidly throughout the century, in more or less corrupted form, until they are by now part of the intellectual equipment, if it can be called that, of a very large number of our contemporaries. When they talk about knowledge, they say that nothing is certainly known and that nothing is even probably known about values. When they talk about values, they talk like the freshman I quoted yesterday—about the value-free universe and the relativity of all opinions and the resulting legitimacy of any sincerely asserted commitment. And when they act they act passionately and with a sense of righteous certainty: they "remember their humanity" and "forget all the rest," and they are extremely impatient when the new paradise Russell helped teach them to expect does not come *now*.[31]

31. The best account I know of how the combination of moral absolutism and passionate skepticism has worked in our time is Michael Polanyi's. See esp. *The Tacit Dimension* (Garden City, N.Y., 1966), chap. 3: "A similar fusion of unprecedented critical lucidity and intensified moral passions pervades our whole civilization, inflaming or paralyzing both reason and morality" (p. 56). "We have, then, moral passions filled with contempt for their own ideals. And once they shun their own ideals, moral passions can express themselves only in anti-

I cannot sort out with any confidence the causes of this triumph of modernist views against the kinds of refutation I shall touch on tomorrow. To what degree did Russell merely reflect, and to what degree did he implant and strengthen the disastrous divorce I have used him to represent? However it happened, the world has been taught that when push comes to shove, reason has nothing to say: generations of doubters and passionate protestors have lost all faith in the possibility of effective protest *with the mind.* And if you cannot really protest with your mind, then finally all you can do is lay your body on the line. You may have to do so anyway, when authoritarian irrationalists have determined to kill you rather than talk with you. But my point is that all three Russells in their different ways had told men that if they found it seeming right to do so, if their consciences told them that other men were flatly wrong and they themselves flatly right, if their visions of truth and justice were in conflict with those of other men, arbitrary decisions about right and wrong could "rightly" be imposed upon those others. Thus the worldview of modernism has given support both to self-righteous authoritarians of the right and to their spiritual brothers who use violence to attack the "rational establishment" from the left. A thoroughly articulated, seemingly impregnable system of dogmas has sliced the world into two unequal parts, the tiny domain of the provable, about which nobody cares very much, and the great domain of "all the rest," in which anyone can believe or do what he pleases.

The road through such a slicing—of objective from subjective, of fact from value, of self from nature, of knowledge from action and feeling—is in fact many roads. It would be foolish to seek a simple, unified organon, hoping that at last we could eliminate differences among men and establish a great single new truth. That isn't how things work. But it is time to recognize that there are a good many reasons to question the modernist dogmas, and there are many alternative ways to *remember our humanity* without forgetting *all the rest.*

---

moralism" (p. 58). "The unprecedented critical lucidity of modern man is fused here with his equally unprecedented moral demands and produces an angry absolute individualism. But adjacent to this, the same fusion produces political teachings which sanction the total suppression of the individual" (p. 59).

An assertion which outstrips the evidence is not only a blunder but a crime.

T. H. Huxley

Because collaboration is a fact, because it is inevitable, because it spreads into a highly differentiated network of interdependent specialities, the mentality of any individual becomes a composite product in which it is impossible to separate immanently generated knowledge and belief.

Bernard Lonergan

I do not believe in the creed professed by the Jewish church, by the Roman church, by the Greek church, by the Turkish church, by the Protestant church, nor by any church that I know of. My own mind is my own church.

Tom Paine

The reason of man, like man himself, is timid and cautious when left alone, and acquires firmness and confidence in proportion to the number with which it is associated.

Madison

In an intellectual age there can be no active interest which puts aside all hope of a vision of the harmony of truth. To acquiesce in discrepancy is destructive of candour, and of moral cleanliness.

Whitehead

A man is necessarily talking error unless his words can claim membership in a collective body of thought.

Kenneth Burke

# THREE | The Dogmas Questioned

In my first lecture I promised to grapple with the highly general question of when we should change our minds, not just about what people call matters of fact or about what is "scientifically proved" but about value questions—about what we should admire, what we should do, what political protests we should support, and what institutions reject. I then described a great world religion, modernism, the dogmas of which, if accepted uncritically, make my promise absurd. If man is essentially and adequately defined as an accidental collocation of atoms in a value-free universe, if he can in no sense be said to choose among more or less good reasons but rather is always simply driven or motivated or conditioned, and if the only method for discovering knowledge about such matters is to apply the universal solvent of doubt in order to prove what cannot be doubted, then the purpose of offering reasons, in all nonscientific domains, cannot be to change men's minds in the sense of showing that one view is genuinely superior to another. It can only be to trick or sway or condition or force or woo men to believe or do what the persuader desires.

Men will in fact continue, in this view, to "change each others' minds" in another sense, even in that part of life in which scientific proofs are not available: they will produce changes in what men do and in what they say they believe. But the difference between good and bad persuasion will become simply a difference in skill, not knowledge or wisdom. Except in scientific matters, education and mutual inquiry will become indistinguishable from propaganda or "mere rhetoric."

The test of any mode of influence now becomes whether it works; the whole range of ways to influence men becomes a single indiscriminate conglomeration of devices, to be chosen simply on the basis of likely effectiveness in gaining agreement or compliance. Brainwashing, subliminal advertising, operant conditioning will be only technically different from each other and from psychoanalysis; reasoning with an opponent will be always seen as disguised trickery or, at best, "control."

In this view the how and the what of mental change can still be studied rationally, meaning scientifically: sciences of information theory, group dynamics, propaganda analysis, behavioral therapy, and semantics will be devised to explain how men in fact are conditioned to change. All of these will have ethical commands built into them, some of them openly, more of them in disguised form: "men *ought* to be logical"; "men *ought not* to be swayed by anything but scientific proof";

"thinking straight is a kind of defensive study, a way of keeping your dukes up at all times"; "men ought to be trained to recognize irrelevant emotional appeals"; and so on. B. F. Skinner, the best known scientismist of our time, often tells us how we *ought* to think about so-called values: "We do not say that simple biological reinforcers are effective because of self-love, and we *should not* attribute behaving for the good of others to a love of others"[1] (my italics).

Many freshman English texts—those new mass media studied by hundreds of thousands of Americans—have in the past several decades been defensive rhetorics in this sense. Accepting without question the dogmas of scientism, they have taught—as I accuse myself of having taught, during my first losing battles with freshman composition— that the goal of all thought and argument is to emulate the purity and objectivity and rigor of science, in order to protect oneself from the errors that passion and desire and metaphor and authority and all those logical fallacies lead us into.

As a teacher of literature I naturally lived an entirely different and more romantic life, asserting values aggressively and cheerfully, though often becoming cross with my students if they denied—using principles derived from my scientism—the literary values I tried to educate them to embrace. It should have been clear to me that the very word *educate* was suspect, if modernism were right: whenever I touched on values, all I could do was indoctrinate, unless in some sense the pursuit of literary values is reasonable.

1. *Beyond Freedom and Dignity* (New York, 1971), p. 110. Skinner protects himself from the charge of inconsistency in his use of value terms in two ways: "The text will often seem inconsistent. English, like all languages, is full of prescientific terms which usually suffice for purposes of casual discourse. . . . The book could have been written for a technical reader without expressions of that sort [even without the implicit *oughts*?], but the issues are important to the nonspecialist" (pp. 23–24). More important, he would say that his moral imperatives are all conditionals: *If* you think that people ought to behave as I say, *then* you ought to follow my program (see chap. 6, "Values," esp. p. 112).
Needless to say, such protective coloration will not work for anyone reading him from nonbehaviorist points of view: the scholarly surface cannot conceal the presence of hundreds of unargued preachments. For example: (1) "These reactions to a scientific conception of man are certainly unfortunate. They immobilize *men of good will,* and anyone concerned with the future of his culture will do what he can to correct them" (pp. 212–13; my italics). (2) Mentalist explanations are bad, he tells us, because they bring "curiosity to an end" (p. 12). Leaving aside the obvious objection that *curiosity,* like *good will,* is certainly a mentalist term, why should I, in his terms, care? His formal answer, not provided when the term is used, would be that without curiosity my culture cannot survive. But it is clear that Skinner would, like the rest of us, value curiosity even if it had no survival value, and for reasons he does not mention.

Taken at face value, modernism thus sharply divorces all genuine thought or knowledge from those faiths we find in all nonscientific discourse. What had once been a domain with many grades of dubiety and credibility now becomes simply the dubious (for scientism) or the arena of conflicting faiths (for irrationalism). Where classical philosophers and rhetoricians saw gradations from ignorance to wisdom, we are given only a vast domain of ignorance or glorious personal preference. Where they saw a need for eloquence in the service of wisdom, so that moral and political and even metaphysical truth might be given its best chance for success in the world, we are given only a contest of skills and devices in the service of warring preferences and impulses and desires. Rhetorical probability, based on what is "commonly sensed," becomes propagandistic plausibility.

Such disastrous consequences of modernist dogmas could not be considered, for modernists, as genuine reasons for rejecting those dogmas. Irrationalists will gladly accept the license to reject any doctrines that are inconvenient or unpleasant, seeking rather truths of the "heart" or "body." And of course scientismists expected from the beginning that the objectivity[2] they sought would disregard human results and follow

2. Though many now argue that such objectivity is impossible, since even the physical sciences and mathematics depend—and not just logically—on assumptions and values that cannot be objectively demonstrated, it is still often expressed as the ideal of human inquiry. C. C. Gillispie, for example, includes, along with a serious and sound account of how human desires have often delayed particular discoveries in the physical sciences, a completely nonscientific and unargued running polemic for objectivity and impersonality in all things— except perhaps art. "The Latin genius speaks out in Galileo. His is the passionate objectivity of Machiavelli, which says that wishes do not signify—this *is* how the world works. He stripped from the skeleton of the cosmos the obscuring layers of sentience and pious moral and edifying lesson, and left as object of the search the hard, straight bones of Euclidean dimension" *The Edge of Objectivity* [Princeton, N.J., 1960], p. 40; see also pp. 197–201).

For social scientists, the questions are usually more complex—not only whether this or that kind of objectivity is desirable or possible in any science but also whether studying human beings requires a different method from that used in natural science. The issues are far trickier than I have been able to suggest here (see, for example, Dorothy Emmet and Alasdair MacIntyre, eds., *Sociological Theory and Philosophical Analysis* [London, 1970], esp. articles by Alfred Schutz, Sidney Morgenbesser, and Jürgen Habermas). The whole phenomenological movement could be described as an effort to show that man can make an end run around the forces of scientific objectivity and come out on the other side whole. A good introduction to the issues now being debated in this immensely diverse movement can be found in two books edited by James M. Edie, *Phenomenology in America* (Chicago 1967) and *New Essays in Phenomenology* (Chicago 1969). It is significant, I think, that in the second volume, one whole section is devoted to repudiating the irrationalism that threatens on

only where the evidence leads. I could therefore go on till doomsday showing that, as "everyone already knows," modernism is intellectually and morally and politically intolerable; I would not, according to the dogmas themselves, have said anything against them, only against our failure to face unpleasant truths.

But consider once again just how strange a thing it is that we should feel no *argumentative* force in disastrous consequences. To show that a given truth destroys the possibility of life, and indeed, if taken with full seriousness, turns on itself and denies the possibility of truth itself, surely should constitute some reason for reconsidering such a "truth." But I know better than to rest with this argument today: as modernists all, we know that such thinking is not thinking but "wishful thinking," "rationalization." Indeed we often act as if the painfulness of a conclusion should reinforce our conviction: if it hurts it must be true.

### Changes of Scene and Dramatis Personae

I am not attempting in these lectures a direct and full disproof of any of the dogmas; the effort would be futile, because according to the dogmas themselves such matters are not amenable to proof. My hope is only to cast some doubt on doubt and to suggest grounds for confidence in exploring some forms of assent that have been suspect. But I think it is important to remind ourselves, as we begin, of how many major figures over the past three hundred years have attempted a systematic disproof of one or more of the dogmas.

To describe the full range of their attacks would require a lengthy history of thought from Descartes to the present. Perhaps I should say several histories, because the results would look very different depending on the historian's assumptions about the history of ideas. The history would differ, for example, depending on whether the historian thought it possible to deal with individual dogmas, or subdogmas, in isolation (Arthur Lovejoy, for example) or believed on the contrary that no idea can be caught alive except in its original context (for example, Harry Prosch). But what is a proper context for an idea? Very different histories will result, depending on whether we seek to relate a given refutation of a given dogma to the complete philosophic statement in which it is found (in which case, for example, we would give a full account of Kant's philosophy in order to show how Kant refutes the notion of a cold, hostile, and indifferent universe); or seek rather to re-

---

the left flank whenever scientism is repudiated on the right (pt. 2, "Nihilism and the Absurd").

late each idea to the social and artistic currents and political forces surrounding it (for example, Marxists or Hegelians); or to the whole symbolic life of man (for example, Kenneth Burke, *A Grammar of Motives,* pt. 2). Further differences would depend upon whether the historian was more interested in metaphysical questions of substance or in epistemology or in questions about language or action.

Even if one narrows the field, as I am now going to do, to questions of how the mind is defined and how its works are divided, complexities still abound. The divorce between the logical or calculating or experimenting mind, the sole producer of *knowledge,* and the valuing organism that irresponsibly commits itself to *all the rest* will be attacked in different ways, depending on convictions about what *the rest* amounts to. To choose terms for what is left over after the certainly provable has been deducted is already to commit oneself to some possibilities and to rule out others. It makes a great difference, for example, whether one's description of "the rest" distinguishes or lumps together terms like *intuition, will, action, choice, value, feeling, motive, drive, emotion, experience, wisdom, eloquence, the heart,* and so on. And as polemicists on all sides too frequently forget, the same word can cover contradictory concepts in two different systems; *reason,* for example, sometimes appears on the scientifically proved side and sometimes in opposition to it, and *knowledge* is sometimes contracted to mean only what is empirically known, sometimes expanded to include the statistically probable, or even the intuitively probable.

Aware of such complex differences among both philosophers and historians of thought, I offer the following "reminder of authorities on my side" with fingers crossed. As history it is surely useless. As classification of philosophers it is dangerously misleading. But as serious rhetoric, offering the good reasons of expert testimony, it can be taken as a preliminary effort at shaking confidence: look at all these major figures who have chosen *not* to divide up the mind, and hence the world, as modernists tell me I must if I am to qualify as thoroughly modern. (I do not really get around to establishing testimony as a valid kind of reasoning until the next lecture, yet I need it here; that's how life is in the domains of rhetoric. I ask the reader to add to the experts I now call to the stand, those I cite in Appendix B).

I have accused modernism of dividing man's responses to the world into two unequal parts, one of hard knowing and the other of soft faith or commitment. As we turn to refutations, it will be useful to divide the second part once again, into commitments or purposes on the one hand and feelings or passions on the other. We now have a tripartite picture of the human organism that is presumed to experience

91

a change of mind, and the word *mind* has been immeasurably extended beyond the narrow calculator praised by scientismists or damned by irrationalists. Every human being believes certain things to be true, acts for certain ends, and feels in certain ways, but we attach feelings to thoughts and actions in diverse ways. Belief or thought or knowledge, action or will or choice, feeling or emotion or passion occur in every theory of thinking, acting, or feeling; and though the terms shift, each of the three domains always appears somewhere, even if only for long enough to be dismissed as illusory or irrelevant. In this view, the challenge presented by the successive real triumphs of science, and by the related depredations of scientism and the defensive wails of irrationalism, was that of an arbitrary and destructive divorce of man's powers of thought from his necessity to act and his inescapable emotive life.

For scientismists, there has always been the promise of an ultimate reunion off somewhere in the future, when science will have been able to re-ingest all those other matters and then finally explain them. Behaviorism has only made explicit what all scientismists have hoped for: a way of reuniting science and values and feelings and actions under a scientific aegis. Both the enthusiasm and the hostility aroused by behaviorism result from its power as a representative extreme. We saw that Bertrand Russell at one time felt that he ought to be a behaviorist but couldn't quite make the grade. Russell was able to live with the resulting cognitive discord, though he struggled against it. Less protean minds have tried harder for harmony, either going all the way—behaviorism is perhaps now more widely espoused than ever before—or seeking for some other harmony between nature and value.[3]

## Nature and Knowledge Revivified

One obvious possibility is to develop a religious or metaphysical counterpart to behaviorism—that is, to try to build new pictures of man-in-nature that will see men's values as inseparable from God's or nature's values. To the claim, "All values and emotions and preferences are simply the result of environmental controls that can be described in the language of scientific fact," many have replied, "The universe is made of, or permeated by, values; all (or many) facts can and should

3. I must repeat that what follows is, like almost everything in my absurdly brief encyclopaedia of all thought since God died, a terrible oversimplification. My truncated catalog of harmonies lumps together philosophers with many different languages and methods, and it thus distorts each of them. I take little comfort in knowing that everybody else's classification seems to me unfair to most or all of the views classified.

be described in the language of value or purpose." All of man's ethical and political and aesthetic and emotive life is thus taken back into the natural, and new ways are sought for talking about the old scholastic notion of an analogy of being between God and man.[4]

Thus the reduction to the physical is countered by an elevation to the metaphysical. To see nature or "the way things are" or—in Wittgenstein's words—what "the case is" as essentially including human processes and values leads to new speculations, now to be found in great numbers, about how values are embedded in reality. This was, as I understand it, the major effort of Whitehead: "It should be the task of the philosophical schools of this century," he said, "to bring together the two streams (the one from Descartes and the other from Leibnitz) into an expression of the world-picture derived from science, and thereby end the divorce of science from the affirmations of our aesthetic and ethical experiences."[5] By changing one's picture of the natural world from the mechanical, value-indifferent thing that Russell clung to, despite his many reservations, to a picture of the world as a collection of self-fulfilling (and hence valuable) processes or "procedures of organization," one can import values back into the domain of knowledge. In this view it is naturally good for all natural processes to be fulfilled; if the universe is, in its ultimate constitution, a pattern of purposes—directed processes and relations—value is inextricably bound in its workings, and man's valuing can be as rational as his most scientific endeavors.

4. For a popular but effective effort to restore religion by "expanding the natural," see Peter L. Berger, *A Rumor of Angels: Modern Society and the Rediscovery of the Supernatural* (Garden City, N.Y., 1969), chapter 3, "Theological Possibilities: Starting with Man." The word *supernatural* in Berger's title is perhaps misleading, because for most readers it will suggest "what goes against reason." Berger is on the contrary trying to discover a reason that will first "relativize the relativizers" and then establish the reasons for considering what is true about man-in-the-world. His "reaffirmation *adversus modernos*" often moves towards a "rhetoric of assent."

5. "Science and Philosophy," in *Science and the Modern World* (New York, 1925), pp. 184–85. His major effort at reunion was of course *Process and Reality* (New York, 1929): "Philosophy finds religion, and modifies it; and conversely religion is among the data of experience which philosophy must weave into its own scheme. Religion is an ultimate craving to infuse into the insistent particularity of emotion that non-temporal generality which primarily belongs to conceptual thought alone. In the higher organisms the differences of tempo between the mere emotions and the conceptual experiences produce a life-tedium, unless this supreme fusion has been effected. The two sides of the organism require a reconciliation in which emotional experiences illustrate a conceptual justification, and conceptual experiences find an emotional illustration" (p. 23).

Whitehead's process philosophy is only one of many efforts in this direction, though perhaps the most impressive. One could even describe Marx's scientific materialism as a redefinition of reality that makes possible a science of ethics and politics without reducing them to physics; and the Hegelian idealism that Russell first embraced and then rejected could equally be described as a grand effort to reunify, under scientific laws of how the world really acts, parts of the world and of man's nature that had been alienated from each other.[6]

Recent decades have seen many further attempts to reconstitute a universe in which values inhere in the nature of the facts. Revivals of Thomistic metaphysical inquiries in the work of Etienne Gilson, Jacques Maritain, and Bernard Lonergan;[7] phenomenological inquir-

6. It is absurd even to provide a note documenting a statement so general, so ambiguous, and hence so controversial that substantiation could come only in long discussion. At the time I wrote the sentence, I had been reading some Marx, a great deal of Russell, and most immediately the following recent works of Alasdair MacIntyre: *A Short History of Ethics* (London, 1967), esp. chap. 15, "Hegel and Marx"; *Marxism and Christianity* (New York, 1968); and *Marcuse* (New York, 1970), esp. chap. 3, "Marcuse's Interpretation of Hegel and Marx." The whole controversy around the works of Marcuse illustrates again and again how desperate many men are to find some definition of the self and of the world that does not leave an absolute divorce between the alienated autonomous self and the world of inert and valueless nature. It also shows how distressed the modern mind feels when any assertion is made, from any point of view, that values are found in facts, not necessarily imposed upon them.

There were of course many earlier attempts to counter the march of science by rediscovering values in nature, perhaps the best known being various organicist efforts in the Romantic period. Goethe's effort to rehabilitate color as *in nature,* not simply a secondary quality that can be ignored by science and hence by philosophy, was part of a grand vision of a Nature that at every level of organization embodied values according to that level; Gillispie writes as if Goethe's claim that Newton's theory of color was false could be refuted with some sort of objective and crucial experiment—see Gillispie, *The Edge of Objectivity,* pp. 192–98: "Romanticism began as a moral revolt against physics, expressed in moving, sad, and sometimes angry attempts to defend a qualitative science, in which nature can be congruent with man, against a measuring, numbering science which alienates the creator of science from his own creation by total objectification of nature. . . . Indeed, the renewals of this subjective approach to nature make a pathetic theme. Its ruins lie strewn like good intentions all along the ground traversed by science" (p. 199). As if the ruins of theories advanced by objective scientists did not lie strewn fully as thick!

7. Bernard Lonergan's *Insight: A Study of Human Understanding* (London, 1957; New York, 1970) strikes me, on a superficial reading, as another major challenge to secular world views. The rhetorical trouble, however, with all such works springing from an explicit religious commitment is that they are so easily dismissed as mere rationalizations: Lonergan is *Father* Lonergan, and that takes care of *him.* For hundreds of years now religious synthesizers have cropped up

ies into our modes of knowing facts in feeling and value, and feeling and values in the factual; and logical inquiries into "good reasons" by recent inheritors of the "ordinary language" tradition; these and many others have been challenging the divorce of fact from value, of the subjective from the objective, of the world of inert and value-free nature from the world of man's desires.[8]

## Nature as Will or Act

A second possibility is to expand the domain of action or will to repudiate or encompass the scientific picture of a value-free world. We find innumerable modern existentialisms claiming that though the universe, scientifically considered, may be absurd or unknowable, we can honestly

---

regularly, some of them, like Etienne Gilson and Lonergan, first class. Occasionally one will hit the popular imagination—that part of it that longs for an intellectually respectable way to be religious. Bergson earlier in this century managed to fuse popular evolutionary science with popular religious needs (while also doing serious philosophical work that the public ignored), and his *élan vital* was as much the rage in "intellectual circles" as the more recent effort of Teilhard de Chardin to build hope in the inevitable upward spiral of evolution toward a grand future fusion of religion and science. To me such optimistic accounts of *future* marvels of intellectual integration are misleading; the essential problems of harmonizing the parts of our minds and contrasting aspects of the world are unlikely to change, and they must be met in the world as it is now.

A good brief bibliography of religious efforts to confront "a world that asserts the death of God" can be found in Michael Novak's *Belief and Unbelief* (New York, 1965). Novak himself wrestles well with the subjective-objective split, exploring knowledge of persons and of Personhood under the concept of "intelligent subjectivity."

8. For further interesting expansions of nature to include man's experience, see W. T. Jones, *The Sciences and the Humanities: Conflict and Reconciliation* (Berkeley, 1965), and Paul F. Schmidt, *Rebelling, Loving, and Liberation: A Metaphysics of the Concrete* (Albuquerque, N.M., 1971). The latter includes a good brief bibliography, especially of works of "metaphysical rebellion."

Valuable phenomenological "expansions" can be found in Eugene T. Gendlin's *Experiencing and the Creation of Meaning: A Philosophical and Psychological Approach to the Subjective* (New York, 1962); Maurice Mandelbaum's *The Phenomenology of Moral Experience* (Baltimore, 1955), esp. chap. 1; and John J. Compton's "Natural Science and the Experience of Nature," in *Phenomenology in America*, ed. James M. Edie (Chicago, 1967). All of these works in a sense resist my categories; Gendlin's, for example, which I have found especially helpful, could just as well be cited in the section below called "Reality as Feeling," as an expansion of "feeling" or "experience" to encompass the world. Since Gendlin attempts a postmodernist comprehensive view, one that will do justice both to science and to our modes of experiencing, he resists my categories more effectively than some programmatic rebels who cheerfully reduce the world either to idea, will, or taste.

affirm our purposes, and thus escape the trap of meaninglessness. What we *know* is our own existence, and we can *will* that existence to be whatever we want it to be, in opposition to the absurdity of the universe that created us. We need not worry over rational doubts about free will or the objectivity of values: we can simply affirm ourselves and thus in a sense come to know our freedom.[9]

It has seemed clear to many philosophers, though perhaps not to many lay intellectuals grasping at straws, that this existentialist affirmation leaves us in a sense right back where we started, with our minds divided. Though our human dignity and freedom are in one sense restored, an essential part of the mind has been violated. Popular existentialism has always been full of shrill attacks on reason and the mind, and the shrillness springs, I think, from a sense that something is wrong somewhere still: Bertrand Russell I and B. F. Skinner are laughing at us up their sleeves. What fools these affirmers of absurdity be, not to recognize as we do that these affirmings are logically—and thus rationally, and thus finally—indefensible.

To me a much more satisfactory effort at reunification under "will" was that of the pragmatists, especially Peirce, Dewey, and James. Our *purposes* and their fulfillment are here taken as something we really know, and scientific knowledge becomes a special case of fulfillment of human purpose—the purpose to know. Logic is no longer here an abstract propositional logic seeking truths that are certain, objective, divorced from man's needs and desires: it becomes instead the logic of inquiry, and inquiry is a process informed by purpose and hence by human values. That I desire certain qualities, know and pursue certain relations, and "live my purposes" can here no longer be relegated to

9. Again here the footnote could be longer than the book, ranging from Schopenhauer through Dostoevski's deliberately irrational heroes who choose error in order to maintain freedom, down through Camus' "affirming rebel" to some recent existentialists and "left-phenomenologists." The footnote, if written, would be a complicated one, because one of its points would have to be that the very authors who claimed to embrace irrationalism were in fact rationalists: if someone tells me that I should act irrationally because it is right to do so in order to combat rationalism, he is easily shown to be, from another perspective, a higher kind of rationalist. Recent irrationalists like Jung and R. D. Laing and Norman O. Brown are all passionate believers in their own kind of reasons; as they reduce the world to will and to willed feelings, they go on assuming that there is an "ought" to these matters, somewhere, and that their writings can help men to see reasons for the oughtness. For a sensitive account of a reason beyond reason—of the effort, in Wallace Stevens' words, "to reason with a later reason"—see Harold Bloom, *The Ringers in the Tower: Studies in the Romantic Tradition* (Chicago, 1971), esp. chap. 20.

epiphenomena—purposes are as real and known as anything can be, and the world and nature are thus transformed.[10]

## Reality as Feeling: The Wisdom of the Body

A third possibility is to expand the domain of feeling to absorb all of what is called thinking and all other grounds for action. Sometimes the new center is an undefined feeling, as in Hemingway's repeated formula

---

10. The history of modern pop thought contains a great deal that I am baffled by, but nothing is more puzzling than the neglect of the classics of pragmatism. Here is a major literature that if read seriously would undermine popular talk about "the void," "the meaninglessness of life," and "the inherent loneliness and alienation of every man and woman." I name only four major works out of many: William James, *The Principles of Psychology* (New York, 1890), and *The Varieties of Religious Experience* (New York, 1902); John Dewey, *Art as Experience* (New York, 1934), and *Logic, the Theory of Inquiry* (New York, 1938). There's no use in moralizing about such matters, but it is amusing, when not distressing, to see so much now being written about the self-evident condition of man, the nation, and the universe without taking account of the arguments of James or Dewey, Peirce or Mead.

If one index to our culture can be said to be the kinds of chrestomathies fed to college freshmen, we are in a period of mindless exaltation of the will, in contrast to the pragmatists' effort to *think* about it and with it. See, for example, for one of the more serious efforts in the genre, *The Discontinuous Universe: Selected Writings in Contemporary Consciousness,* ed. Sallie Sears and Georgianna W. Lord (New York, 1972). Note how the modernist dogmas roll out as the editors, in their introduction, count on what all true moderns know: "In the absence of a god, 'unsponsored' like the rest of their generation, [the authors collected here] have spent their lives in the midst of the most terrible human possibilities without any real conviction that man can or even wishes to check himself before he destroys or maims the remaining life on his lone, already befouled, planetary home. In the face of such bleakness, their continuing will to create is itself an affirmation. . . . This art, however, is not easy. The writers here agree that man must impose some kind of order upon reality [which of course has none of its own] if he is to survive without being overwhelmed by confusion and inner disintegration. Yet the structures he has evolved . . . seem to them more a series of metaphors than anything else, . . . arbitrary, interchangeable, with their ideal aim of corresponding to structures that 'really' exist in the universe forever unverifiable." "The need for coherence, moreover, gains its urgency from the persistent, at times excruciating sense of chaos that has been central to modern experience and that carries to an extreme conclusion the fascination of the nineteenth century with nothingness, disintegration, and death." "The relation between the consciousness of chaos, which at its extreme finds something alien and terrible both within ourselves and in reality—and an indestructible if 'occasionless' commitment to objects of beauty marks perhaps the broadest outlines of contemporary sensibility" (pp. v–vii). Some of the authors called to march behind such a banner will, I think, be surprised (for example, Kenneth Burke, Lévi-Strauss, Hannah Arendt, Bruno Bettelheim).

that what is good is what feels good, or Lawrence's attacks on the murderous intellect in the name of the darker gods. Sometimes it is art or a metaphysic of art, as in Wallace Stevens' notion of a supreme fiction, or Nietzsche's early claim "that art, rather than ethics, constituted the essential metaphysical activity of man, . . . [and] that existence could be justified only in esthetic terms. . . . God as the supreme artist, amoral, recklessly creating and destroying, realizing himself indifferently in whatever he does or undoes."[11] Or it becomes some physiological center of wisdom, as in Wilhelm Reich's offering of salvation through orgasm, or Norman O. Brown's celebration of the "polymorphous perverse." And sometimes it has been a carefully articulated philosophy in which Platonic identities of truth and goodness with beauty (or art) are explored, as in the work of George Santayana.

In all these views, taste or sensibility or—as in Henry James— "quality of consciousness" becomes the supreme arbiter; art can become the last, best schoolmaster or legislator of the world. What we call wrong is simply what is ugly; the final test of truth, even in the sciences, becomes elegance or harmonious simplicity. The arbiter is not what we cannot doubt, as in scientism, nor what we can know of totality, as in metaphysical renovations, nor what we find has instrumental value, as in pragmatism, but what we find gratifies our most delicate sensing apparatus.

11. "A Critical Backward Glance" (1886), commenting on *The Birth of Tragedy from the Spirit of Music* (1871), as translated by Francis Golffing in *The Birth of Tragedy and The Genealogy of Morals* (New York, 1956), p. 9.

The history of answering scientism with aesthetics would be as long as the others, perhaps beginning in the eighteenth century with philosophies of "taste," but certainly stressing the development of various aestheticisms in the later nineteenth. For a good recent account of one strand in the increasing substitution of beauty as the one last and supreme standard, see David DeLaura, *Hebrew and Hellene in Victorian England: Newman, Arnold, and Pater* (Austin, Tex., 1969). See also such classic passages as the conclusion to Walter Pater's *The Renaissance,* and Wallace Stevens' marvelous poem, "Sunday Morning."

It is misleading, of course, to "place" any philosopher who works analogically. Kenneth Burke, for example, can be quoted to prove that he reduces the world to artistic categories: In *Permanence and Change* (New York, 1935) he says he is trying to provide a "corrective of the scientific rationalization" with a "*rationale of art*—not however, a performer's art, not a specialist's art for some to produce and many to observe, but an art in its widest aspects, an *art of living*" (conclusion of part 1). But his views are so comprehensive and his tactics so diverse that one might just as well argue that he is capturing art for a philosophy of practice, or conflating both to build an adequate "science" of man's universe. Which is another way of warning against taking my placements here as anything more than an assembling of witnesses—hints about how many thinkers have provided "correctives of the scientific rationalization."

There is no theoretical reason why such views must lead to extreme expressions of irrationalism; it can be as reasonable (as I shall suggest later on) to follow the reasons of art as the reasons of scientific inquiry. But in practice the hyperrationality of scientism, of reducing the world to nature, has been countered by the two branches of the countermovement of the late '60s: the political activists, reducing the world to blind will; and the counterculturalists, reducing it to blind feeling. A leader of the Weathermen group cries, "principles-schminciples," in the name of action without thought or feeling, and Leary cries, "Tune in, turn on, drop out," in the name of feeling as against either thought or action.

## Divers Orders, Divers "Logics"

All three of these directions have thus yielded, I think, both philosophically cogent refutations of the modernist slicings and popular reductions that restore the slicings and fight for the superiority of this or that slice. The philosophers would be decisive for anyone who took the trouble (sometimes immense, as in the case of Whitehead, and always great for anyone who begins with different presuppositions) to understand them. If my goal were to find a single systematic philosophy that could be embraced once and for all, I clearly ought to choose one of the three and develop—from a conflation of "the genuinely known" or the "validly willed" or the "truly felt"—my alternative to modernism. But it is immediately clear, when I say that all three have yielded decisive alternatives, that I am exploring a different, pluralistic direction. My goal is (once again) not to establish a philosophy: my concern is with a befouled rhetorical climate which prevents our meeting to discover and pursue common interests. What we must find, I think, are grounds for confidence in a multiplicity of ways of knowing. Such grounds need not be what was sought by philosophers who based themselves in science: a theory providing fixed and proved principles from which all genuine reasoning could proceed. It need only be a revitalization of what we naturally assume as we go about our intellectual and practical business in the world: namely, that there are many logics, and that each of the domains of the mind (or person) has its own kind of knowing.

There have been comprehensive philosophies built on just this assumption. For Aristotle (and Aquinas and Maritain), there is first the domain of theoretical truth, which can be sought in every subject matter but which can yield "positive" knowledge only in natural, mathematical, and logical inquiry; in other subjects we can have probable or useful knowledge but not certainty. There is, secondly, the domain of practical deliberation, which must take into account whatever scientific knowledge is available but which in itself must at best be imprecise and chancy; still, as everyone knows, there really is a difference between a wise man and a fool, or between a good senator and a bad; and part of the difference is in what they know. Finally, there is productive activity and thought about it, yielding a knowledge of how to make and enjoy the graces of life that life's other natural processes fail to provide; the arts are created and enjoyed not in a meaningless, relativized bedlam of "what each person happens to like" but in communities that share, through direct experience and through talk about it, the knowledge of good makings.

What I am attempting here is, however, a considerably looser assemblage of good reasons than such systematic philosophers construct. There may be, though I doubt it, a grand new philosophical synthesis hiding in the wings somewhere, or looming over the horizon —some smooth beast ready to stride proudly toward the twenty-first century to be born. But even if there is, we will not be in a condition to attend to it until we can once more believe in the ultimate value of attending. If finding such a belief depends on establishing a single philosophy, the history of ideas would seem to teach that we are doomed. But if there are good reasons for confidence in the values of discoursing together, then we can get about our business, whatever that may be: philosophers disputing the merits of rival philosophies, the rest of us finding other rhetorical communities that will differ from problem to problem, discipline to discipline, political and social need to political and social need. If we can find some way to rely on our common sense —what we "sense" and know in common—we can once again trust whatever standards of validation our reasonings together lead us to.

We do not begin, then, with theories about the mind or knowledge or the universe or semantics. Instead we remind ourselves of our experience—good empiricists all—and of the fact that when we make mistakes, whether in political and ethical choices or in aesthetic judgment, we find that they always include bad thinking as well as "feeling." When we look at either the fanatics or the hyperrationalists who seem to us most threatening in what they do to their fellow men, we find as many signs of bad thinking and corrupted emotion in one group as the other. Fanatics are always "reasonable" in the sense of seeing rational connections between their abstract principles and their conclusions; their irrationality often consists in choosing the wrong principles validated by an inadequately considered group of "significant others." They have lost their "common sense"—they do not test their commitments by seeking a genuinely common ground shared with the relevant fellow creatures. And the value-free scientismist is from this point of view equally irrational, because he too has chosen, on abstract principles, a validating group that ignores what the common sense he shares with his fellows would teach.

Let us forget, then, for a while, the strangely compelling, seemingly self-evident notion that we know with one part of our minds or souls or selves or bodies, and will or feel with some other part. We can then search for what we agree on, what we meet in, where we *are* together.

## DOUBT AND ASSENT

The full meaning of the choice I am making, with its deliberate embrace of circularity, will be clearer as I go along. For now it is enough if you will entertain the possibility of a kind of social test for truth: "It is reasonable to grant (one *ought* to grant) some degree of credence to whatever qualified men and women agree on, *unless* one has specific and stronger reasons to disbelieve." Abstract commands to "doubt pending proof" are now to be replaced with the ancient and natural command to "assent pending disproof." We will weigh many kinds of evidence, including testimony and authority; we will work as hard at discovering good witnesses as Russell would work at spotting logical fallacies. We will thus appraise more or less dubious reasons, assenting to the degree that *in the particular case* seems warranted.

You will remember that the dogma I am here proposing to replace teaches that we have no justification for asserting what can be doubted, and we are commanded by it to doubt whatever cannot be proved. In that view one never is advised (except by those who have an axe to grind—disreputable pushers of values, religious or political fanatics, mere rhetoricians) to see the capacity to believe as itself an intellectual virtue. Though few have ever put it quite so bluntly as the young Russell in his more prophetic moments, to doubt is taken as the supreme achievement of thought. The burden of proof is thus always placed on assent: to say, "I will believe unless I am given a *reason* to doubt" is self-evidently absurd.

## THE CRITERION OF FALSIFIABILITY

In its most sophisticated form, the principle of doubt becomes, in Karl Popper's widely influential development, the "criterion of falsifiability." We do not know anything, Popper says, unless we know the operations that might disprove it if it were untrue, and unless we know that those operations do not in fact falsify it. Popper's criterion, already implicit in much intellectual activity, rapidly became a commonplace; it seemed to provide the most precise formulation of the only good way to rid the world of its intellectual rubbish. Notice how Edmund Leach assumes that an appeal to it will buttress his unsympathetic account of Freud and his questions about Lévi-Strauss's theories:

> Lévi-Strauss on Myth has much the same fascination as Freud on the Interpretation of Dreams, and the same kind of weaknesses too. A first encounter with Freud is usually persuasive; it is all so neat, it simply must be right. But then you begin to wonder. Supposing the whole Freudian argument about symbolic associations and layers of conscious, unconscious and pre-conscious were entirely false, would it ever be possible to *prove* that it is false? And if the answer to that question is 'No,' you then have to ask yourself whether psycho-analytic arguments about symbol formation and free association can ever be anything better than clever talk.[12]

12. Frank Kermode, ed., *Lévi-Strauss* (London, 1970), chap. 4, p. 54. Popper's basic formulation, modified in later works, is in *Logik der Forschung,* trans. as *The Logic of Scientific Discovery* (London, 1959; 2d ed., 1968).
Popper is simply the best-known source of what one finds everywhere expressed. Antony Flew, for example, suggests that religious expressions like "God exists" or "God loves us" must be declared meaningless unless we can say precisely how they would be falsified: "And to know the meaning of the negation, is as near as makes no matter, to know the meaning of that assertion. And if there is nothing which a putative assertion denies then there is nothing which it asserts either: and so it is not really an assertion" ("Theology and Falsification," in *New Essays in Philosophical Theology* [London, 1955], p. 98). But of course there is an ambiguity in the word *nothing;* Flew means by it "nothing empirically falsifiable," but it is obvious that people who say "God lives" mean to deny many things—only some of them empirically testable. Their expression denies *something,* but Flew's own closed system has already defined that something as nothing, because whatever it is, it cannot be found empirically.
Popper himself often comes close to recognizing how limited in usefulness his criterion really is, and he can skirt very close to the kind of rhetorical principles of knowing that I here advocate. He begins his inquiry with an attack on positivists because their principles required them to throw out scientific generalization along with metaphysics, and he then admits that the criterion of demarcation "will . . . have to be regarded as a *proposal for an agreement or convention.* As to the suitability of any such convention opinions may differ; and a reasonable discussion of these questions is only possible between parties having some purpose in common. The choice of that purpose must, of course, be ultimately a matter of decision, going beyond rational [that is, scientific or logical] argument" (*The Logic of Scientific Discovery,* 2d ed., p. 37; my italics). But see n. 5, in which the "of course" is qualified. ". . . Looking at the matter from the psychological angle, I am inclined to think that scientific discovery is impossible without faith in ideas which are of a purely speculative kind, and sometimes even quite hazy; a faith which *is completely unwarranted from the point of view of science,* and which, to that extent, is 'metaphysical' " (p. 38; my italics). But

Here there are only two choices: either a doctrine passes this test, or it is nothing but "clever talk."

The test is a powerful one, in dealing with certain problems; I use it myself in trying to test my own guesses about how literary works are put together.[13] But stated as a universal dogma it is highly questionable, as Popper himself sometimes seems to acknowledge. How, we may ask, does one know that *it* is true or valid? Can the criterion itself be put in falsifiable terms according to its own dictum? I would say that it cannot—that it claims status as knowledge without satisfying its own demands. (It is also, by the way, a value judgment on human intellectual operations, put in the form of a factual claim, and as a value judgment it is not, according to the dogmas, falsifiable.)

Aside from presenting this logical difficulty, the test is obviously crippling when applied to our practical lives. If we know only what survives after we have done our best to doubt, we are driven to conclude that most of our action has no cognitive base, since we must almost

---

he moves immediately to "knowledge," and his view of what is corroborated knowledge is unwavering (see p. 267). Note the phrase "completely unwarranted"—*its* warrant is surely feeble if the whole scientific enterprise is impossible without "unwarranted faith." If making a whole edifice of inquiry possible does not give some kind of warrant to these "purely speculative," "hazy," "metaphysical" notions, it is clear that *no* practical argument about any matter whatever could possibly have force as knowledge.

That the test cannot be applied rigorously even in mathematics is, I gather, shown by the strange cases of the *principle of choice* and the *continuum hypothesis* in set theory. "Gödel proved that neither of the two can be disproved with mathematical means. For one of them we know that it cannot be proved either." And yet we cannot get along without them—or at least we could not in 1969. See John von Neumann, "Tribute to Dr. Gödel," in *Symposium Papers Commemorating the Sixtieth Birthday of Kurt Gödel,* ed. Jack J. Bulloff et al. (New York, 1969).

The most thoroughgoing answer to the assumption that all knowledge is found by applying systematic doubt or the criterion of falsifiability is Michael Polanyi's in *Personal Knowledge: Towards a Post-critical Philosophy* (Chicago, 1958); see esp. pt. 3, chaps. titled "The Logic of Affirmation," "The Critique of Doubt," and "Commitment." See also Thomas A. Langford and William H. Poteat, eds., *Intellect and Hope: Essays in the Thought of Michael Polanyi* (Durham, N.C., 1968).

13. For a shrewd application of Popper-like methods to literary criticism, see Ronald S. Crane, "On Hypotheses in 'Historical Criticism': Apropos of Certain Contemporary Medievalists," in *The Idea of the Humanities* (Chicago, 1967). For a clever popular account of the absurd results of the criterion in dealing with the question of whether pornography is harmful, see Peregrine Worsthorne, "Thoughts after Longford: Porn and the Liberals," *Encounter,* May 1973, pp. 90–91.

always act on propositions that have not been proved in this sense. "How can you argue that men should be reasonable," a colleague asks, "when you know that we never have enough information to be *sure* about anything. I take a stand, on this or that war, on this or that act of injustice, and my choices cannot be rational because I simply cannot know enough." He is right, if "to know" must mean to be certain, to have scientific proof, to have propositions that have been tested by the criterion of falsifiability. But this is not in fact the choice we make.

Being reasonable in practical affairs is more like a process of systematic assent than systematic doubt. If my wife says, "I have a sudden terrible pain. Call a doctor quick!" I must and will act at once. Only if I have specific reasons to doubt her—if I know, let us say, that she is a notorious and sadistic practical joker—do I have warrant to intrude doubt into the process of assent. I do not and should not pause for skeptical probings, for proof; and I certainly should not take time to rephrase my hypothesis, "she is suffering," in falsifiable form.

Nor do I take time to bring to conscious testing the moral principle, "When my wife suffers, I ought to try to help." If I know anything, if *anything* about my life and the world makes sense, I know that this principle holds. Yet if I did pause to see whether it could survive the tests of systematic doubt, I would have great difficulty even in phrasing it in a form that could be falsified by any standard empirical test.

How could one do so, even if one had time for prolonged testing? "*If* it is true that one ought to help a loved one or friend in pain, *then* I should call the doctor." No empirical tests seem to follow from any version I can devise. "*If* it is not true that I ought to help a loved one in pain, *then* I have no moral command to help my wife now." The conclusion is absurd, but only because its absurdity follows from my knowledge that the premise is absurd, and *that* knowledge comes from principles of assent that cannot be stated in falsifiable form. Even if, as I believe, they are principles that will finally withstand the most aggressive philosophical probing—like that, for example, of Plato, Kant, or the recent analytical philosophers I have mentioned—they will not withstand the scientific test of falsifiability. As Popper says of various faiths held by science, there are no strictly empirical observations (as even Bertrand Russell finally admitted) that could falsify either the proposition "Thou shalt help thy neighbor" or its opposite, "Thou shalt ignore thy neighbor's pain."

But let us push a bit further. "*If* it is true that one ought to help a friend in pain, *then* it must be true that if I do not help him, I will suffer, in my conscience." Here at last is a proposition in testable form: if it is false, my conscience won't hurt, and I know that my conscience usually, perhaps always, hurts when I act against the proposition. But I have really made no progress in satisfying empirical demands, because I will be told that the evidence is subjective and that therefore it does not hold. Besides, my conscience is simply the product of conditioning. Factual statements cannot, the dogma runs, validate normative statements—the question remains whether my conscience *ought* to hurt. Thus the proposition is not really falsifiable. "If . . . , then it must be true that she will not help me when I am in need," or "if . . . , then it must be true that society will fall apart, because it depends on people helping each other." Both of these might conceivably be tested, but not *until it is too late*. Besides, I know (on other grounds) that these consequences are not my main reasons but secondary arguments I fall back on only because men working with systematic doubt have put me on the defensive.

Finally, "if . . . , then it must be true that I would find life intolerable in a world in which husbands ignored their wives' needs." Again the experiment cannot be performed, and even if it were performed, it would yield only subjective "nonreplicable" results. ("What does *intolerable* mean, scientifically speaking?") If the principle turned out to be true and the experiment replicable—in the sense that what I found subjectively intolerable everyone else found subjectively intolerable—the result would still come too late: society would already have become intolerable for everyone.

Meanwhile, of course, the doctor has not been called, because I have pretended not to know something I know very well: that I ought to try to help when I encounter pain in a loved one.[14] I know this through the way I know the world in the first place, that is, through a willing assent to the process of making an intelligible world with my fellow creatures. Together we have constructed and named a world, and just as I know what doubt means only through assent to other men's namings, so I know what at least some of my responsibilities are.

We have learned, we moderns, to chant the qualifications: "there are many borderline cases"; "the circle of my duties is not clearly defined in advance"; "I cannot possibly respond adequately to all the pain of all my friends, let alone my neighbors"; "men seem more often than not to deny my knowledge by hurting each other, and the proposition thus seems to be 'falsified' daily, hourly." But how strange it is that such qualifications, real and troublesome as they can be, should have

14. The principle of course applies to all fellow creatures, not just to those we love; in some ways the argument is cleaner, as Kant taught the world, when affection is not involved and duty counters other inclinations. My more sentimental example is chosen to represent a kind of knowledge that even the least altruistic reader will share.

been allowed to obscure the essential ground that is being qualified. None of the qualifications makes any sense unless the original process of knowing-through-assent makes sense, because each of them depends on assent to communal definitions and norms which if tested by systematic doubt can be quickly destroyed.

### SYSTEMATIC ASSENT

In view of these troubles with systematic doubt, it scarcely seems unreasonable to try out other ways of looking at what we know. Instead of making doubt primary, let us see what happens if we know whatever we can agree together that we have no good reason to doubt, whether or not we can apply other more formal tests of doubt. In this view, assent becomes the prior act of knowing: what we believe together with sureness is given "the benefit of the doubt"; the doubts I entertain must offer reasons for themselves at least as good as I have for the initial belief.

The differences between the two formulations may not at first seem great, but their consequences differ tremendously, as would be shown if I paused here to listen to the chorus of objections that have occurred to some of you. Am I not now forced to accept any piece of silliness that any fanatic wants to advance, provided only that he can get somebody to assent to it and that it cannot be clearly refuted with particular disproofs? Charles Manson will be confirmed by the assent of his witches, Hitler by his SS troops, every Christian sect by its hundreds or millions of adherents, and indeed every political and religious program by its ability to present witnesses.

There is a kind of plausibility conferred on this objection by the widespread conviction that you can't "prove" a general negative. "You can't *prove* that there are no ghosts." "You can't prove that alchemy is a false system, or that astrology doesn't work." "You can't even disprove the existence of God."[15] We would be left floundering in conflicting nonsensical schemes if we accepted all the views that we can't really disprove.

15. J. N. Findlay, asking "Can God's Existence Be Disproved?" concludes that it can be, but his disproof is surely one of the weirdest maneuvers in the history of thought; as G. E. Hughes suggests in one of several replies the disproof has generated, it can best be described as "The Ontological Disproof," "an argument from the analysis of a concept to [its necessary] non-existence." See "Can God's Existence Be Disproved?" a discussion by J. N. Findlay, B. E. Hughes, and A. C. A. Rainer, in *New Essays in Philosophical Theology*, ed. Antony Flew and Alasdair MacIntyre (London 1955). Findlay's argument and reply to critics are found on pp. 47–56, 71–75; Hughes' criticism on pp. 56–67.

If giving up the principle that doubt is the essential, primary tool of thought meant embracing everything not refutable in this scientismist sense, I would thus be forced to accept abstract doubt in self-defense. But it is clear that we are again here victimized by a needlessly narrow definition of proof and disproof. As William James said in "The Will to Believe," when we decide to believe pending disproof we are not suddenly flooded with every belief that anyone offers. We begin only with those beliefs that really recommend themselves to us, whoever we are and wherever we find ourselves. We are all moderns or postmoderns here, and most of us have as part of our structures of perception a belief in natural law as firm as Hume's or Bertrand Russell's. Though we may not be as sure of what the laws of the universe are as Hume the skeptic seemed to be, we needn't give ready credence to any report—of ghosts or astral projection or flying saucers—that does not in some degree fit our own experience. Since I have never seen a ghost and do not even know anyone personally who has claimed to see a ghost, and since most people I know who have thought about it do not believe in ghosts, I give my tentative assent to our collective experience. I need no disproof, though at the same time I see quite clearly that all of us could easily turn out to be wrong on this one; there are so many countervailing "experts" claiming to be heard. When I meet, as I did last year, a young Forest Service employee who believes that men on earth can project themselves instantaneously to Venus and back again, I do not grant assent pending disproof; I have no impulse to assent at all, since the claim runs counter to all of my experience. Similarly, I have very good specific reasons to doubt many of the claims of alchemy and astrology and phrenology, and I can therefore doubt them, for those reasons; on the other hand, if I find, as I do with the alchemical "humours," a certain kind of poetic truth overlooked in simpler modern psychologies, I needn't embrace all the chemical guesses simply because I have demoted the criteria I use in rejecting them. I have no need for a supreme, abstract command to doubt whatever has not been proved, as long as I am ready to reject whatever *has* been disproved. The geology of the Old Testament and the physiology of (say) Descartes have been disproved; I reject them. But I do not as a result leap, like Bertrand Russell cataloging the "intellectual rubbish" of the past, on every Biblical or Cartesian claim to truth that I cannot specifically prove.

Thus nonsense is no more threatening in this view than in any other, so long as I do not require scientific *dis*proof of what is nonsensical. If "we" know that a belief is nonsense, we will not believe it, even if we cannot disprove it in any scientismist sense: in this respect, my new formulation simply accepts what is in fact our practice when faced with absurd doctrines that we cannot disprove.[16]

What is thus demanded by the principle of systematic assent is more rigorous thought than is customary about who "we" are, the group of relevant judges, the axiological experts whose shared experience confirms what we know together. Nobody ever gives equal weight to every voice. What satisfies us in practice, though the practice always can and should be refined, is the discovery that a given belief that fits our own structures of perception and belief is supported by those qualified to know. It is true that we often make the mistake of reversing the process, conferring the status of qualified expert on someone because he agrees with us. But this elementary human error, found in all groups, does not invalidate the conviction that a belief is confirmed *in some degree* whenever "someone who knows" shares it.

This is in formal structure—as Michael Polanyi among others has shown—the process of validation used even by scientists for a great share of their scientific beliefs. No scientist has ever performed experiments or calculations providing more than a tiny fraction of all the

16. The process is nicely illustrated whenever anyone advances an irrefutable but implausible hypothesis. When P. H. Gosse, Edmund's father, tried to refute evolutionary theory with his *Omphalos* (London, 1857), he argued that the world had indeed been created all at once, about 4004 B.C., but that of course it had been created with all of the geological strata and fossil records that it would have had if it had evolved through endless time. At the moment of creation everything had to be in order for a going universe, right down to faecal matter in Adam's colon. Now there is simply nothing in logic or in empirical science that could ever refute that position. It cannot be falsified, but neither can the scientific belief that it was designed to combat. Those who believe in a single natural order would of course say that Gosse violates the law of parsimony, that to invent the hypothesis of such a whimsical God is to complicate the world rather than explain it. But every man prefers his own way of applying Ockham's razor, and it is clear that no theory of evolution has ever been as simple and efficient and parsimonious as Gosse's, judged from his own point of view. With it he can account for any future scientific discovery about the world, while his opponents must go on debating about spontaneous mutation and natural selection and percentages and missing links. If scientists really believed only what they can state in falsifiable form, they would have struggled—hopelessly—to devise crucial experiments that would test Gosse's views as against their own anti-catastrophism. Or they would have felt driven to show that Gosse's theory was in fact untestable and therefore meaningless.

But nothing so absurd happened. Though there were some negative reviews, Gosse was mainly refuted by the old-fashioned method of silence and indifference. Nobody felt the least bit threatened, and since he could get nobody else to take his views seriously, they were by that fact alone "refuted" and properly ignored.

scientific beliefs he holds; the whole edifice of science depends on faith in witnesses, past and present—on testimony and tradition. There is nothing wrong in this, Polanyi argues; indeed, science would grind to a halt were it not so. Though scientific traditions of faith often support errors, making it difficult for new and sounder ideas to be embraced, no one could begin or carry through any experiment, to say nothing of writing a paper or attending a scientific conference, without relying (blindly?) on the traditions that make such errors inevitable.

Thus science is, in its larger structures, validated by the same social processes that I am arguing for in "all the rest." Even when we look in detail at how an individual scientist thinks when he is testing his ideas, we find, Polanyi suggests, that the appeal is more to an ideal "universal scientist" than to any particular person or group.[17] The scien-

17. See, for example, *The Tacit Dimension* (Garden City, N.Y., 1966), esp. pp. 63–64: "The popular conception of science teaches that science is a collection of observable facts, which anybody can verify for himself. . . . But it is not true. . . . In the first place, you cannot possibly get hold of the equipment for testing, for example, a statement of astronomy or of chemistry. And supposing you could somehow get the use of an observatory or a chemical laboratory, you would probably damage their instruments beyond repair before you ever made an observation. . . . Scientists must rely heavily for their facts on the authority of fellow scientists." See also ibid., pp. 67, 80.

For a perceptive account of some of the problems encountered when scientists attempt "persuasion" and "conversion" in matters not amenable to what they think of as proof, see Thomas S. Kuhn, *The Structure of Scientific Revolutions*, 2d ed. (Chicago, 1970), esp. chap. 12 and "Postscript," secs. 5–7. For Kuhn there can be no proof except empirical, logical, or mathematical proof. Nevertheless, in matters not amenable to such proof there can be "good reasons for being persuaded," and we need, if we are to understand this kind of reason, "a sort of study that has not previously been undertaken" (p. 152). A new rhetoric?

In my judgment, Kuhn fumbles the question of "good reasons," because he is unwilling to question his assumptions that in choices of values and paradigms, neither party to a dispute can be "convicted of a mistake. . . . There is no neutral algorithm for theory-choice, no systematic decision procedure which, properly applied, *must* lead each individual in the group to the same decision" (pp. 199–200; my italics). In other words, unless absolute proof, decisive for all inquirers, is available, one cannot speak of mistakes or of correctness of choice. One is either totally, demonstrably mistaken, in a scientific sense, or no correction is possible. And yet "good reasons" are somehow possible, and in the truncated rhetoric that Kuhn offers, it is clear that he is moving toward a notion of a reasonable persuasion that would be as respectable, in its way, as scientific proof (see pp. 153–59). But despite his awareness that the fact-value and objective-subjective distinction have become mere tags and can sometimes be destructive of thought, he allows himself to imply, again and again, that most of the reasons scientists might offer in debate about theories and values are necessarily more

tist is most convinced that he is right when he is most nearly convinced that *any* thoroughly informed and rational—that is, any thoroughly qualified—human being would agree with him.

We will follow the same rule. Needless to say, the various fanatical defenders of nonsense or viciousness, even if backed by millions of SS troops, cannot claim that kind of support. The Nazis, for example, could never claim that all reasonable and informed men would be forced by reason to agree to the extermination of all Jews: self-evidently, the Jews must be included in any reasonable decision about their fate, and self-evidently, without even the need for consultation, they will be known to disagree with any attempt at a consensus about their extermination.

But we need not go so far from this room to illustrate the procedures I am playing with. Suppose we say that we here "know"—that is, have good warrant to assent to—whatever *everyone in this hall* really believes, regardless of whether we can think of abstract arguments about why his belief is not proved by other tests. Instantaneously our domain of knowledge is immeasurably increased, just as it was immeasurably decreased by the slow triumph of scientism from Descartes to Russell. Our knowledge is of "whatever we have good reason to believe," in the sense of "having no good reason to doubt." There will of course be gradations of such knowledge—truth will no longer be made up of what is certain, in contrast to "all the rest." When any belief seems self-evident and we find empirically that we can think of nobody who in fact doubts it, we will be sure about it; when we find, as we usually will, that some men deny what we all agree to, we will be less sure but still able to act on our knowledge with confidence, so long as we think we could persuade any reasonable person. But when we find ourselves or the postulated experts disagreeing, we will become more tentative in proportion to their qualifications and our own sense of where the good reasons lead us. And finally, we will be aware that there can be a genuine conflict of this kind of knowledge, in those areas where genuine values in fact clash: we have no reason to assume that the world is rational in the sense of harmonizing all of our "local" values; in fact we know that at every moment it presents—as in the conflict of values exhibited by every slaughterhouse and every feeding time in the wilderness—sharp clashes among good reasons. The sparrow and the sparrow hawk each has its reasons which reason, with a little effort, can ferret out, but we need not expect to find, at this local level, a Reason that

---

subjective and hence somehow less respectable than their scientific endeavors (see esp. p. 156).

will persuade the hawk to starve itself or the sparrow to sacrifice itself joyously to the hawk's noonday meal.[18]

In short, there is no assumption here like the one found in that growing cult of so-called reason, the Ayn Rand objectivists, that all truly reasonable men will always finally agree. On the contrary, it is assumed that reasonable men of differing interests, experience, and vocabulary will disagree about some questions to which reason, nevertheless, must apply. Consequently they not only can but must, by virtue of their common problems, search for meeting places where they can stand together and explore their differences about the choices life presents.

## What Do We Know about Ourselves and Our "World"?

What do we know about the *arena of change,* the mind or self, if we know whatever no one in this hall seriously doubts? Remember: we must not cheat and fall back into modernism. It will not do to say, "Of course I can doubt that, if I put my mind to it." In this game you are allowed to doubt only what you cannot *not* doubt, only what you have persuasive reason *to* doubt. If I seem to repeat myself, it is partly because I know from my own experience how hard it will be for some of us not to claim doubt except when we *really* doubt.

18. See Alan Gewirth, "Categorial Consistency in Ethics," *Philosophical Quarterly* 17 (October 1967): 289–99; idem, "Positive 'Ethics' and Normative 'Science,'" *Philosophical Review* 69 (July 1960): 311–30. Those who know classical rhetoric will be aware that I am experimenting with the old notion of the *topoi,* those places, *loci,* or shared "standpoints" where good arguments could be found because in them men did in fact discover warrantable beliefs. The *topoi* have often been treated as simple devices of trickery: you probe around in a "place" until you find some assumption, however ridiculous in your own view, that your opponent will accept, and then you argue from it to conclusions you want him to adopt. But what would happen if you probed and found what assumptions your own intellectual convictions *really rest on,* then tested them against other people's assumptions, and finally concluded with more or less confidence, depending on who agrees with you and for what proffered reasons. You would thus be developing as you went along a collection—or perhaps to be fashionable I should say a "structure"—of more or less probable (*probe*-able, *prov*able) assumptions, assumptions that become principles usable not only in argument but in your own inquiry.

The collection of topoi from which such principles come would have become an organon, always to some degree shifting and uncertain, but reliable in discovering not only what you yourself believe but what you *should* believe: you should accept whatever you discover in testing discourse with others who are reasonable and in any sense qualified.

Instead of making an a priori list of topics at a high level of generality, as those who revive classical rhetoric sometimes do, I shall pursue the consequences of this notion inductively, as we inquire here together into our shared beliefs.

1. You and I and Bertrand Russell know, as surely as we know anything, that men are characteristically users of language.[19] Though we don't know much about the language of other animals, we do know, more surely than we know anything about the stars or the nucleus, and immeasurably more surely than we know about the chemistry of man's brain, that men in all ages and cultures have employed symbols—not just the grunt language of immediate signs or pointing, but modes of referring both to particulars not present to the senses and to concepts that generalize intelligibly about particulars. We know this not simply by a tautological use of definition: "What I mean by man is a symbol-using animal." We know it from innumerable observations and reports of all known human cultures: all have language. In other words, we know that what we are doing at this moment—discoursing together, trying to understand each other—is done in some form by every man and woman in all cultures in all ages. Even the deaf and dumb "become human," as Helen Keller and others have argued, the moment when language in this sense enters their lives. I am hungry; let's go hunting. I think it will rain; let's build a shelter. I love you; let us mate. I have

19. I would expect many readers to be troubled by my use of words like *know* and *knowledge*. Why raise unnecessary objections with such terms? Why not use a less offensive term like *warrantable belief* or *defensible opinion*? But I think the offense may be fruitful. In the matter of what to call knowledge which fails to pass the scientist's tests, see Kuhn's "Postscript": "Perhaps 'knowledge' is the wrong word, but there are reasons for employing it. What is built into the neural process that transforms stimuli to sensations has the following character-istics: it has been transmitted through education; it has, by trial, been found more effective than its historical competitors in a group's current environment; and, finally, it is subject to change both through further education and through the discovery of misfits with the environment. . . . But it is strange usage, for one other characteristic is missing. We have no direct access to what it is we know, no rules or generalizations with which to express this knowledge. . . . The knowl-edge . . . remains tacit" (*The Structure of Scientific Revolutions*, p. 196). But the knowledge I am discussing is often not tacit but tested in symbolic exchange.

Perhaps the fullest development of our present route—exploring consensus as a source of reliable knowledge—is the rhetorical philosophy of Cicero, with its appeal *ex consensu gentium*. Since the insecurities in any such method are ob-vious, it has always been easily refuted by those who are seeking either harder facts or less transitory and more transcendent ideas. For a concise discussion of Cicero's "operational" method see Michael J. Buckley, S.J., *Motion and Mo-tion's God* (Princeton, 1971), esp. pp. 95–96 and pt. 2. Much of what I am say-ing is influenced strongly by Richard McKeon: see for example "The Uses of Rhetoric in a Technological Age: Architectonic Productive Arts," in *The Prospect of Rhetoric*, ed. Lloyd F. Bitzer and Edwin Black (Englewood Cliffs, N.J., 1971); "The Methods of Rhetoric and Philosophy: Invention and Judg-ment," in *The Classical Tradition: Literary and Historical Studies in Honor of Harry Caplan*, ed. Luitpold Wallach (Ithaca, N.Y., 1966).

just discovered that the sum of the angles of a triangle will always be 180 degrees; let me show you.[20]

2. Not only do we talk and write and create art and mathematical systems and act as if we shared them: we really do share them, sometimes. Sometimes we *understand* each other. That is, we are often successful in exchanging ideas, emotions, and purposes, using not only words but a fantastically rich set of symbolic devices, ranging from facial expressions that seem much more resourceful than those available to other animals, bodily stances, dancing, music, mathematics, painting, sculpture, stories, rituals, and manipulation of social groups in war and politics. Except for occasional monstrous births, each man born of woman infers grief, anger, love, through symbolic interchange. Even madmen go on, for the most part, talking and painting and singing; those who recover usually report that even in the depths of madness the process of inferring other people's conditions through symbolic clues goes on at a great pace. Some investigators would even argue that human madness consists precisely in this process running to riot; though animals can be conditioned to various forms of breakdown, only human beings can suffer from a wild excess of symbolic activity, with too little exchange and too much private inference. What we ordinarily mean when we say that a deformed birth is a "mere puppy" or "only a vegetable" is at the other end of the scale of normality: symbolic interchange as we know it is impossible, and the condition of being fully human has not been attained.[21]

20. The literature on signs and symbolic languages is immense, but the relatively popular account by Susanne Langer, based in part on Cassirer, is still perhaps the best introduction (*Philosophy in a New Key* [Cambridge, Mass., 1941]). I have not read thoroughly her recent effort to develop a "science of mind" as approached through "feeling"—to find a common ground between science and art in a study of symbols (*Mind: An Essay on Human Feeling,* vol. 1 [Baltimore, 1967]), but it looks like one more voice in the rising chorus of attempts to transcend the destructive dichotomies of modernism. See for example her attack on the objective-subjective distinction and on efforts to reduce all proof to "the quickest possible mathematization" (pp. 37–38). Her effort to describe the "idols of the laboratory," chap. 2, clearly springs from the same heretical impulse as my decision to describe modernism as a dogmatic religion.

Along with extensive and informed argument, she provides an important bibliography.

The recent explosion of interest in "semiotics" as the theory and analysis of signs (what I am calling symbols) is documented in two special issues of *TLS* (October 5 and 12, 1973). It is nice to see that at least one "pragmatist," C. S. Peirce, is at last coming into his own.

21. Efforts "to produce psychopathological syndromes in nonhuman subjects by means of experimental techniques" (Harry F. Harlow and Stephen J. Suomi, "Production of Depressive Behaviors in Young Monkeys," *Journal of*

In short, we know other minds, sometimes, to some degree. That we often do not, and that the knowledge is never complete, is at this point irrelevant, though it has been sometimes talked about as if it proved that we are all hopelessly alone.[22]

3. Not only do human beings successfully infer other human beings' states of mind from symbolic clues; we know that they characteristically, in all societies, *build* each other's minds. This is obvious knowledge—all the more genuine for being obvious. What an adult man or woman is, in all societies, is in large degree what other men and women have created through symbolic exchange. Each of us "takes in" other selves to build a self.

---

*Autism and Childhood Schizophrenia* 1 [1971]: 246) are to me in themselves depressing, when they are not infuriating. Harry Harlow and his colleagues go on torturing their nonhuman primates decade after decade, invariably proving what we all knew in advance—that social creatures can be destroyed by destroying their social ties. His most recent outrage consists of placing monkeys in "solitary" for twenty days—what he calls a "vertical chamber apparatus . . . designed on an intuitive basis" to produce "a state of 'helplessness and hopelessness, sunken in a well of despair' " (p. 247). Among criticisms Harlow cites, the one by L. S. Kubie most clearly dramatizes the symbolic knowledge I am emphasizing. Kubie argues that "the behavior seen in disturbed humans is only a symptom of a basic underlying disorder which involves a dysfunction of symbolic processes" (Harry F. Harlow and William T. McKinney, Jr., "Nonhuman Primates and Psychoses," *Journal of Autism and Childhood Schizophrenia* 1 [1971]: 373, citing Kubie's "The Concept of Normality and Neurosis," in M. Heiman, ed., *Psychoanalysis and Social Work* [New York, 1953]. Harlow mentions no criticism of the morality of his work.

22. There is of course an enormous literature about how or whether we know other selves. Different problems emerge in different formulations. If I begin by assuming that I know "my own case," and ask how I could prove the existence and similarity of other minds, I land in a problem of deciding what proofs are valid, and whether this or that analogy of my person with others can validate my inference that they have minds like mine (see Norman Malcolm's "Knowledge of Other Minds," *Journal of Philosophy* 55 [1958]: 969–78, a reply to A. J. Ayer's analogical proof in "One's Knowledge of Other Minds," in *Philosophical Essays* [London, 1954]. Both essays are conveniently juxtaposed in Donald A. Gustafson, ed., *Essays in Philosophical Psychology* [London, 1967]; the bibliography of this volume, which includes discussions of subjects like "intending," "excusing," "heeding," and "dreaming," is a useful guide to work in the analytical mode). But if I begin by admitting that I do not know myself in isolation from others, that the very language in which I ask the question of how to prove the existence of other minds is inescapably social, I see that I know that other minds exist as well as I know that mine does. To some behaviorists this will get us nowhere, since I do not even know that *I* have a mind. But to us here, at this stage of these lectures, knowing what none of us here has ever doubted for a moment, the behaviorists' claim is a clear example of abstract dogma run riot.

114

Other animals, too, are to some degree formed by their fellows,[23] but the difference between the power of symbolic influence in man and in all other creatures is—as all students of society and culture have noted—tremendous. It is true that we all have some sort of common genetic base, and that base *may* include, as some recent theories would suggest, a kind of universal determination of the basic patterns of human speech, in all languages.[24] But the existence of language and hence of a greatly enriched power for symbolic influence has meant that men are fantastically malleable by their fellows.

4. What is more, we know that we characteristically *intend* to change our fellows by symbolic devices, to "make them" or at least make them different. Though it is true that much of the cultural molding of minds that goes on, especially in childhood, is quite habitual or unconscious, people universally intend meanings, and hence intend changes of mind in other people (perhaps I should remind you once again that I am using the word *mind* much more broadly than is often the case: it includes those operations of the brain that are often attributed to the "gut" and "heart"; intentions in this sense need not be conscious).

5. Further, we are endowed with the capacity to infer intentions, not just in the linguistic sense of meanings but in the sense of purpose. One of the most curious impoverishments in the long retreat I have described is the exclusion of intentions from knowledge. At first, in the seventeenth century, intentions were excluded from the heavens, but as in all the other progressions of scientism, what was first denied to God was later denied to man: purposes became unknown and unknowable. And they are unknowable, if one accepts from the beginning that one knows only what one can prove by observation. I can observe only actions and physical processes: nobody has ever observed a purpose direct, except in himself, "subjectively." But we all know (in our new sense of the word) that everyone can sometimes "read" intentions successfully.

This point is sufficiently important to justify spending a bit of time on it. There has been a good deal of work on intentions and how we know them, but for the most part it has been ignored, until very recently,

23. See, for example, Stuart A. Altmann, ed., *Social Communication among Primates* (Chicago, 1967).

24. Noam Chomsky's fame is in part a grateful outcry from a starved public: perhaps there is, after all, a scientific basis for believing that all men are brothers-in-the-logos! See his *Cartesian Linguistics* (New York, 1966) and *Aspects of the Theory of Syntax* (Cambridge, Mass., 1965). His theories about universal grammar are still undergoing hot debate.

by modernists attempting to be rigorous about what we really know.[25] We really know only facts, and intentions are not facts but states of mind. We do not *know* them, even in ourselves: they are intuitive states of consciousness. We certainly do not know them in others; rather, we infer them and our inferences have at best a very low level of probability. Or so one tradition says.

I would like to suggest, in contrast, that of all things I know, some intentions, both of myself and of other persons, are what I know most surely. We should not allow ourselves to be confused because we often are mistaken about intentions; they are of course easily faked, as con men teach us daily. But to admit that we make mistakes about some intentions no more rules intentions from the realms of knowledge than to say that we make mistakes about the physical world forbids knowledge about the physical world. The question is whether in knowing intentions we ever know something that is real, whether they are, as William James and other pragmatists insisted, matters of fact, even though clearly they are also in one sense subjective. If we do, then I think we not only have good reason to repudiate the hard distinction between objective and subjective worlds, but we also have a major step in the discovery of how facts and values are combined.

Of all the kinds of intention, the most revealing to us here are those found in works of art. When someone paints a picture or tells me a joke, when someone writes or performs a tragedy, when someone recounts the Passion according to St. Matthew in a Gospel or in an oratorio, I can sometimes come to understand and share his intentions and the shared intentions of others participating with me; and I sometimes know them with a sureness that has often been overlooked. That the resulting knowledge is a kind of indwelling (as Polanyi calls it), that it includes subjective states not provable or demonstrable by ordinary hard tests should not trouble us by now in the least.

Suppose I were to violate decorum by telling a joke at this solemn moment, and suppose further—oh, fond fantasy!—that it is as uproariously successful as the best joke you've heard in the last year. And then suppose a critic were to tell you that you do not know whether I was

25. See, for example, G. E. M. Anscombe, *Intention* (Ithaca, N.Y., 1957); and E. D. Hirsch, Jr., *Validity in Interpretation* (New Haven, Conn., 1967). The first is in the tradition of linguistic analysis; the second is strongly influenced by the phenomenologists, especially Husserl and Gadamer. Both would agree (though in different languages) with my elementary claim that we know intentions. For a careful account of current debate about intentions as causes, see Georg Henrik von Wright, *Explanation and Understanding* (Ithaca, N.Y., 1971), esp. ch. iii. I deal with intentions more fully in *A Rhetoric of Irony* (Chicago, 1974).

joking or not, that for all you really can prove, I was intending to communicate my tragic sense of life. What we know, in his view, is what we can prove, in his notion of proof. I submit that we would have every right to call him unreasonable, dogmatic, and in fact a bit foolish, because our communally shared knowledge of joke telling, its purposes, its conventions, its effects, is very secure stuff indeed. My joke would of course reveal other intentions than merely to make you laugh: you would know, at this stage of my third lecture, that I intended the joke and the laughter as illustrative. If the critic tried to convince you that I intended anything else by it than to make you laugh in order to illustrate our communal understanding, you would have every right to call him unreasonable, or even—if you wanted to be playfully contentious— unscientific.

But let us rise to more formal literary jesting, choosing as a second illustration a piece of the kind of stuff that some modernists like to say demonstrates how ambiguous everything is and how impossibly isolated we all are: of course I mean irony. You will look for a long time in scientific treatises on communication without finding any analysis of even the simplest ironies. Indeed, even in the philosophers who specialize in "ordinary language" one finds almost nothing about a symbolic practice that is so ordinary that you and I experience dozens of instances of it daily; I have searched with reasonable diligence through the works of Wittgenstein, for example, and with all his talk about language games, I find almost nothing that even approaches an account of the intricate game you and I securely play when we open, let us say, that marvelous novel, *Pride and Prejudice*: "It is a truth universally acknowledged, that a single man in possession of a good fortune, must be in want of a wife."

We experience this sentence—that is, we take it in as a complex ironic meaning, a very special kind of indirect and intricate kind of unspoken point. We reconstruct an elaborate set of meanings quite different from the surface meaning of the words, and we conclude that we have understood Jane Austen's special brand of irony. She does not think that all wealthy bachelors are seeking wives; she knows that it is *not* a truth *universally* acknowledged but a belief held only by a very special kind of social group. In fact, her point includes the notion that some people, especially needy and greedy mothers with unmarried daughters, are eager to find wealthy sons-in-law; it also includes the extraordinarily complex notion—one that you and I have not the slightest difficulty with—that such people are proper objects of ridicule. What is more, it includes Jane Austen's inference about *us*, a flattering but justified conception of our powers to reconstruct unstated subtleties!

Our performance together is, like mental meetings through other kinds of figurative language, too intricate to allow for brief explanation. But even without the full account that I have recently attempted in *A Rhetoric of Irony,* we can see that to claim to reconstruct such an intention is to claim an important and neglected kind of knowing.

I say that I know Jane Austen's intentions with the sentence, at least in its main lines. But can I really call what I know in this sense knowledge? It is clearly subjective, it cannot be proved by any deductive chain of reasoning or by any ordinary laboratory experiment, and it is obviously doubtable both in the sense that many readers will not see it and can doubt it honestly and in the sense that anyone who is determined to doubt what cannot be demonstrated can *say* he doubts it.

Yet if I remember that the dogmas of scientism are themselves unproved by observation and then ask whether I have good and adequate reasons for my conclusions, I see at once that I *know* what Jane Austen intended with the sentence far more solidly than I know many conclusions dignified with the name of knowledge—for example, that the universe is ten or twelve billion years old, or that Shakespeare wrote *Romeo and Juliet,* or that energy equals mass times the speed of light squared. All of my reasons are what some objectivists would call subjective, but they provide, when added together, a very solid platform indeed. Here are the main ones that occur to me, but there are undoubtedly others:

a. First, I have my own strength of conviction. As everyone knows, and as Russell never tired of saying, "subjective certainty" is no criterion of truth. But of course "everyone" has been wrong: it is *one* criterion, though one that is, like all the others, unreliable. My conviction is in itself worth something, though not a great deal until it is challenged and I have a chance to see how strongly it can stand up under probing. Convictions vary in intensity, and thought about them reveals that some which feel certain are in fact only hopes and wishes (though the *only* should not be used to mean *necessarily* false) while others, like my conviction that Jane Austen's intent is ironic, look stronger and stronger the more I push at them with further tests of their strength.

b. Agreement with other "subjects." If I have read a sentence as ironic and I find that all about me readers are taking it literally and defending their view with confidence, my degree of conviction should diminish—though only to the degree that I have good reason to trust their judgment; it can never be a matter of simple democratic vote.[26] About

26. My statement ignores the complicating fact that all of us can apparently be shaken out of our firmest convictions, including those we think of as scientific, by mere social pressure, if it is heavy and prolonged. Experiments

this sentence I have in fact never met anyone except totally inex-
perienced readers who saw no ironic joke, and even they were easily persuaded that they had missed the point.

---

proving such malleability, which have been often used as shocking evidence for
the relativity of values, can be read as showing that we are indeed made in symbolic exchange and that our moral and aesthetic worlds are constructed by the
same processes of validation as our scientific worlds. See Peter L. Berger and
Thomas Luckmann, *The Social Construction of Reality: A Treatise in the Sociology of Knowledge* (Garden City, N.Y., 1966), esp. part 1, "The Foundations of Knowledge in Everyday Life."

The fact that one or a million voters have been persuaded is never in itself
adequate reason for concluding that they are right. In rhetorical inquiry we
must always take into account both the reasons and the voters' qualifications.
Aristotle makes this point partly by his way of defining rhetoric. It is not the
art of persuading, or of winning in an argument. It is the "faculty of observing
in any given case the available means of persuasion" (*Rhetoric*, 1355b–25; Rhys
translation). The best rhetorician who ever lived might easily fail in a given
"impossible" situation, as Burke failed to persuade the British parliament to
change their policies toward the American colonies. My definition, of course, goes
further in the direction of evaluation even than Aristotle's; if rhetoric is the art
of discovering warrants for assent, the notion of finding good reasons, not just
what look like reasons, is built in from the beginning.

Confusion about this point is as widespread as the sharp and simple distinction between "factual" and "evaluative" statements. Consider for example what
a student will learn from the following exercise, given by Young, Becker, and
Pike (*Rhetoric: Discovery and Change* [New York, 1970], p. 211): "Classify the
following statements as either descriptive or evaluative. Descriptive statements
usually can be verified empirically; evaluations usually cannot. As a guide, ask
yourself whether it would make sense to vote on each statement. An evaluation,
being a matter of opinion, can be voted on; to vote on a descriptive statement,
however, would be absurd, since it can be verified empirically.

1. John lives at 25 Avon Street.
2. The food was poor.
3. I am a freshman.
4. I am only a freshman.
5. He's a beatnik."

Quite aside from the point that both (1) and (3) *could* be highly charged with
value in certain contexts, what is the validity of saying that (2), (4), and (5)
might be voted on? Their validity or falsehood is of course established communally, in some kind of intersubjective agreement. But does it make sense to
say that they are in no way descriptive? If I am served spoiled meat, or concentration-camp soup, and I say, "The food is poor," my statement is as factual, as descriptive, as (1) or (3). Moving to less extreme examples the same
claim can hold: "The soufflé is poor" will be descriptive of a fallen soufflé, among
those who know what a good soufflé is. Soufflé experts and concentration-camp
inmates, both served the same poor soufflé, will probably vote differently; the
latter might say, "The food today was marvelous," meaning "by comparison."
Both groups would be right, but again their conflicting descriptions are both
factual and evaluative; the rightness is not found in a vote but in a discussion that

Let us take a vote, by show of hands, of those who have read *Pride and Prejudice:* How many of you think you know that an ironic jest was not intended? (Pause.) Well, the level of intersubjective agreement shown by your unanimity about the sentence is, I would say, at least as high as about any current scientific proposition except the almost universally accepted (though unprovable) assumption that nature will somehow always and everywhere be the same. I read in the morning paper, under the headline "Laws of Universe Put into Question," that "rarely in history have theorists [in the physical sciences] questioned so fundamentally the percepts of their time"—this in a report from an international conference. I am not surprised. But you could shock me into catatonia with the headline, "Majority of Experts at Annual MLA Convention Deny Irony in Austen's Works."

I am not making the foolish claim that the level of agreement will be similarly high about all other literary interpretations; naturally I have chosen what I take to be a clear and simple case, since if I can earn the right to call even one act of subjective literary interpretation *knowledge,* I have broken, irremediably, the hard division between the subjective, personal world of feeling and value and the objective, impersonal world of knowledge and truth or reality.

c. Coherence with other kinds of knowledge. The circularity of all proof about anything becomes highly evident here—but with no resulting scandal. My conviction that the sentence is ironic was arrived at in a "flash of intuition," as I found its literal meaning incompatible with many things that I know and then discovered a new ironic meaning compatible with everything I know. Now, testing the truth in the hard light of good reasons, moving around the circle in the opposite direction, I find that the intuition was indeed coherent with every relevant piece of knowledge I can think of, whether I look at the work itself or at so-called external evidence.

Looking at the rest of the novel, we find that it fits the sentence only if I read the sentence as ironic. Within a few lines, for example, I find Mr. Bennet refusing to acknowledge the "truth *universally* acknowledged"; unless Jane Austen is a slovenly novelist—and every-

---

shares understandings. (A group of experts might of course properly vote on two excellent soufflés.) Finally, it is not hard to think of contexts in which a jury might find itself voting on (1), or a panel of deans voting on the truth of (3).

The authors go on to suggest that the student make comparable lists and explain "the basis of your classification. Are any of your statements difficult to classify? If so, why?" One hopes that many students will finally see that the reason for difficulty lies in the original disjunction.

thing in my field of awareness tells me that she is not—the incongruity between literal statement and literal fact must be intended. Therefore: irony. Secondly—and here feeling becomes an inescapable part of hard knowledge—the sentence and many others like it ("Wickham is my favorite son-in-law") give delight in themselves and as a growing pattern of human vision *if* they are read as I have read them, ironically. They yield nothing but insipidity if read otherwise. These are value judgments, of course, and we all have been told that value judgments are one thing, and knowledge and fact quite another. But again we see the claims as flatly wrong. My knowledge is inextricably bound with my conviction that this kind of pleasure is valued by myself and other readers, and that our valuing was intended by Jane Austen. (That she shared it is perhaps less sure but still highly probable; what *she* felt and valued is harder to know than what she intended *me* to feel and value).

It would be tedious to run over all of the good external reasons I have for thinking that the sentence is ironic: what Jane Austen said about her work; what every critic says about Jane Austen or about this novel or about this sentence; what expectations are built by her other works; and so forth. If I find—as I do when I come to other sentences in Austen—that some experienced critics see them as ironic and some do not, my confidence about them should diminish, but only to the degree that is required by the reasons given. I will call my convictions knowledge only when I have good reasons shared—or at least share-able—with weighty witnesses. And I will expect, as in even the "hardest" of the scientific fields, that there will be borderline cases in which the intersubjective sharing of reasons yields no resolution.

d. A final criterion is teachability or corrigibility. If we know what we can teach other men to know, by showing how we correct mistakes about it, my knowledge of Jane Austen's irony is knowledge. Every English teacher has had the experience of difficulty in teaching ironic works. But no teacher has ever had more difficulty teaching students to see this kind of irony than every science teacher has had in teaching the elementary concepts in his field. There are perhaps some readers who are irony blind, just as there are many students who cannot seem to grasp simple mathematics or simple physical processes. But their errors are corrigible, if they will attend to arguments of correction. I'll warrant that a larger percentage of your students will share your knowledge of Jane Austen's intention in that opening sentence—and without unfair bludgeoning—than all but the best science teachers can get to understand the second law of thermodynamics.

6. A sixth kind of knowledge we share is inseparable from what has gone before: in knowing intentions we often know them under the

aspect of values. (Perhaps we always do, but that step is not essential to us here.) My knowledge that Austen is teasing is apprehended as a set of shared values—both the values that are being played with and the value of the act of play. To ask whether my propositions are propositions of fact or propositions of value is meaningless, because they are inextricably both.

If a skeptic says that though I can infer Austen's intentions, I know nothing about their value, since other men might value them differently, particularly if they were from another culture, I can reply that such disagreements, though real, have nothing to do with the claim. The question is whether anyone whose opinion the skeptic respects *on this subject* would quarrel with the claim. If there is anyone here today, at this hour, who thinks that the world would not lose an important value if it lost Jane Austen's kind of irony, let him speak up now.

To clarify this point about our inference of value *as we infer intention to create value,* here are two more examples:

a. It is Easter time, 1971, and I am sitting in Orchestra Hall in Chicago, listening to Bach's *St. Matthew Passion.* After the final grand chorus, climaxing more than three hours of listening, I sit in the silence —we have been asked not to applaud—with tears in my eyes. As I recover what we call my "self" slightly, I become aware that my wife on one side and my sixteen-year-old daughter on the other are weeping too, and that in fact handkerchiefs are visibly and audibly at work all over the hall. As we get up to leave, I meet a friend who is ordinarily loquacious; he lowers his reddened eyes and does not speak. Later in the corridor, another friend, ordinarily fluent, says, "That was really . . ." and bogs down, unable to say what it was, really.[27]

Now I ask you, what do I *know* about the various persons and acts implicated in this "sentimental" experience? I am not asking you only what I feel (though it is true that part of what I know is what I feel) but what I know, using standards as rigorous as you care to devise. I submit that I know a good deal about Bach's artistic intentions across the gap of nearly two hundred and fifty years—not of course his motives, in the sense of my first lecture, but his artistic reasons, what his art was designed to do or be. If someone says to me, "Bach really intended to make you laugh, not weep, with that final chorus," or, "The whole thing was in fact an elaborate parody or put-on—in fact a satire composed to attack the foolish pretensions of believing Christians as well

---

27. A curious light on where we are, as we move toward the end of this century, is given by my guess that some of you are embarrassed by my literal account of our emotional responses, while others are silently applauding my courage here in risking sentimentality!

as the conventions of baroque choral music," I know that he is wrong. I may still be wrong in many details of my "reading," but if so it will not be because he is right—the issue cannot be resolved by saying that his opinion is right for him and mine is right for me.

(My sense of sureness is partly a product of my intense feeling, and I must consequently be cautious. A questioner after this lecture said that all of this was mistaken because he sees the *St. Matthew Passion* as a grotesque piece of sentimentality, a work that could never move *him* to a deep emotional or spiritual experience, though it tries hard enough. But it seemed to me that the objection itself confirmed my point: he did not and could not doubt that the work intended an effect in that general range of effects. Even the skeptic thus knew something about the music that we sentimental weepers also knew. What is more, I'm sure that he would concede if pressed that Bach's attempt, though for him a relative failure, was not worthless. If I gave him a choice between attending to it for three hours and attending to my own soulful rendition of "Red Sails in the Sunset" repeated steadily for the same period, we know that he and every music lover in the history of man would choose Bach. Here's consensus enough for my purposes.)

My confidence about shared intentions and values is thus a product of my final feeling multiplied by the conviction that all other listeners who have ever qualified themselves by really listening to that music would agree with me, regardless of whether they shared the feelings on a particular hearing: nobody has in fact ever suggested the interpretation of Bach as satirist of Christianity or of musical conventions and we can say with great confidence that no informed listener ever will.

What is more, I can say roughly the same about the meanings of the tears in my wife's and daughter's eyes, as also of what they report about the concert afterwards. They have shared with me Bach's intentions and my valuing of those intentions, and we thus know a great deal about each other through the sharing. If a skeptic suggested to me that my daughter was faking the tears in order to gain credit with Daddy, I would safely bet far more on my reply than on the conclusion of most arguments in the latest copy of *Science*. It is by no means certain, and I cannot prove it to you. But I would be mad indeed if I refused to credit it as knowledge, just because it is not subject to standard empirical tests.

There will of course be loose edges about this knowledge—the total content of her response will be much different from mine, and mine will have elements in it that Bach could not have intended. What is more, different conductors will read the score somewhat differently. But such peripheral vaguenesses affect this conclusion in no degree whatsoever. There are simply vast numbers of moments, most of them less complex than this, about which I can be sure that the central intentions of other minds are what I in fact receive.

    b. I shall now create an art work, a neatly turned couplet:

> The Beatles are greater than Bach
> And Einstein is smarter than Mach.

Is there anyone here who would like to argue that my artistic achievement and the intentions you infer behind it are superior or equal in value to any famous poem I might now quote—say Blake's "London"? (Long pregnant pause!) But if we all agree, as we seem to, surely we have again found a value judgment that is factual—subjective, yes, but not in the old sense; artistic values can be known, at least some of them can be, and judgments about them *can* be factual, in precisely the sense that a judgment that Arnold Palmer is a better golfer than I am is a value judgment and a factual judgment simultaneously: we know the criteria and the achievement, and though the act of relating the two can be more difficult and hence more often controversial in artistic and moral matters than in sports or mouse-trap making, the process of mutual validation by qualified judges can be as valid in one case as the other. The whole problem is reduced, as Hume said, to determining who are the qualified judges.

    Many of us here have qualified ourselves in some degree in the judgment of poetry. It is easy to imagine a challenger who will say that he knows as much about poetry as we do and that we are wrong: Booth's simplicity and clarity are better than Blake's metaphoric fuzziness. Is the question of our comparative expertise subjective or is it "a matter of fact"? Clearly the dichotomy has become meaningless. Nobody here, we know, will accept the skeptic's preference for Booth's poem. We have known many instances of consummate skill in poetry, and the question of whether our skeptic's experience qualifies him as a challenger is a question of fact—regardless of how difficult it is to determine. If he is to persuade us to reconsider, he must, in practice (and in our rhetorical theory), win adherents who seem to us qualified as experts in the question. And this is just another way of saying that he must convince us that he knows the facts about what words like *better, skill, couplet,* and *art* mean.

    It is important to be clear that we are not agreeing merely to the fact that we all agree, or that we all prefer Blake to Booth. You and I know that the difference in quality is not merely a matter of preference or a matter to be settled by vote; except when we are being doctrinaire skeptics, we know that the one is a better work of art, according to every criterion except usefulness as an example in this lecture. In other words, some preferences are merely subjective, in the old sense, and some are also objective—intersubjectively validated, as some sociologists put it. They can, like judgments of other factual matters, be right or wrong; they are corrigible in responsible discourse.

7. Finally, we know that despite these many agreements, men's firmly held values, known and tested in these ways, often conflict; we produce a great flood of value-ridden rhetoric directed, as it were, against one another. We talk ceaselessly to each other—and quite evidently have done so from the beginning—trying to show that *this* value is genuinely superior to *that*. And we all do so as if persuasion really mattered, and as if choices among values could be judged as really right or wrong. Rhetoric in this sense is not something that was invented at an advanced stage of civilization when men began to make highly formalized speeches in law courts and public assemblies. It was practiced when the inventor of the wheel said, "Hey, fellows, here's something interesting I want to show you—it's more important than your dice game." It was practiced when the first mother or father went beyond simply caressing or physical restraint and managed to convey, in sound or picture or sign language, "No, *because* . . ." or "Good *because* . . . ," completing the primitive sentence with a reason not present to the senses at the moment.

This speculative point about the origins of language in opinion exchange is usually made about material objects and the words that stand for them symbolically; we all know about Helen Keller and her leap into the human community when she learned that the letters traced on her hand meant *water*. But it is impossible, I think, to separate the first real symbolic usage—the first time even a seemingly neutral word like *water* or *fire* was used to stand for water or fire not present—from intentions to assert value (and thus, potentially, to change other minds about value). That's precisely what such usage is—an intention to "call to mind" and thus place some sort of value on what is not sensibly present. When anything is called to mind, in this sense, mind is changed. There is always an implicit "ought," if only "You ought to attend to *my* way of perceiving and naming."[28]

28. I will grant, cheerfully, that rhetoric in this sense must be said to be present long before what we usually call language comes in: value-loaded intentions and knowledge of intentions are clearly present in the higher animals. The speechless dog that calls its master's attention to danger is engaging in simple rhetoric; those still speechless ancestors of ours, the day before language was invented, were no doubt using rhetoric, expressing their intentions as we do, with pointing, poking, and grunting. There is a sense in which even the lowest animals can be said to intend meanings or to influence the rest of the world rhetorically; I would not even resist defining the universe as essentially rhetorical: it is created,

## THE SELF AS A FIELD OF SELVES

Now then: What is a "mind" and what is a "self" in this rhetorical view? It is *essentially* rhetorical, symbol exchanging, a social product in process of changing through interaction, sharing values with other selves. Even when thinking privately, "I" can never escape the other selves which I have taken in to make "myself," and my thought will thus always be a dialogue.

Quite obviously, this is not an unprecedented view of man's rhetorical situation. When men thought of themselves as children of God, made in God's image, created to enact a sacred drama of choice between salvation and damnation, their selves were in no sense self-subsistent; they could in no way be considered "alone," because they were not essentially unique. Soul spoke to soul through shared channels. If "I" chose to believe what "you" argued, I would not do so in total isolation or total freedom: there was God's truth and our common natures between us, mediating our exchange. Our selves were contingent upon a higher order of reality that determined, finally, the purpose of our arguing at all, the grounds of our proof, and the validity of our conclusions. Thus underlying many discussions of "the soul" and of "common sense" in medieval and early Renaissance and Enlightenment philosophy is a steady awareness that total autonomy is inconceivable, just as total difference of purposes would be. At heart men were not only all equal in the eyes of the Lord, they were fundamentally made of and thus subject to the same Reason.

This Judeo-Christian view of man as God's creature is only one of innumerable traditional and "primitive" ways of grounding a valid rhetoric in notions of the self as essentially defined in its relations. Every Platonic philosophy, for example, sees the self as "participating" in suprapersonal forms that are somehow more real than the undeniable differences found between particular selves. Similarly, modern pragmatisms and social psychologies see the self as found only in a social matrix that is in some sense more genuinely real than any of its units viewed in isolation.[29]

---

as Whitehead says, in processes of interchange among its parts. Each least particle—whatever that turns out to be—just like each gross beast and "dead" star, could be defined as a steadily changing "field of influences," receiving, processing, and transmitting "information." Such a heady flight, however, takes us nowhere; we have only turned "rhetorical influence," originally a literal concept, into a foggy metaphor.

29. See for example George Herbert Mead, *Mind, Self, and Society: From the Standpoint of a Social Behaviorist,* ed. Charles W. Morris (Chicago, 1934);

Modernists, as we have seen, rejected all such views, replacing them with two grand myths of the self.

---

and John Dewey, *Human Nature and Conduct: An Introduction to Social Psychology* (New York, 1922), esp. pp. 85–87 and pt. 4, sec. 4.

There are many problems in relating this view of the self as essentially social (in Aristotle's terms, "political"; in Dewey's, "part of a public"; in Skinner's "a product of social contingencies"; in traditional terminology, "one child of God among many") to the value, which in some sense we all share, of the unique and irreplaceable individual. One problem lies in discussing what picture of the self the individual can or should live with, when he knows that most if not all of his self is not strictly his. Given too little sense of self, and various forms of mental sickness threaten. But the complementary sickness-unto-death has been recognized for millennia: the egoism that requires the not-self to surrender or die. Western, and particularly Christian, thinkers like Pascal have been most troubled by the unbridled ego and untamed id, and we now see the end of this road in the behaviorist claim that we must give up the autonomous self entirely—everything about every self is explicable as "conditioning" (but note how, in traditional theology, everything in the world as lived was called "the conditioned" in contrast to the unconditional).

Another form of the problem arises when we ask how a society that has given up religious sanctions can protect itself from the ravages of individualism without falling into Maoist-style or Skinnerian suppressions and controls. I see no reason to be confident that this problem can be solved. But I feel sure that neither a return to traditional dogmas, a reassertion of the value of the individual person, nor the various modern totalitarian socialisms can solve it as a problem; they would eliminate the problem by cutting off one source or another, either the valued person or the truth about our dependent social being. If there is a solution other than these surgical eliminations, only an open, rhetorical form of inquiry is likely to find it: if there are no supra-individual values, there are no values; values can only be found by "individuals" who acknowledge, in responsible discourse, their *essential* dependence on each other.

A remarkable and much neglected early effort to redefine the self was that of Lord Shaftesbury (Anthony Ashley Cooper, 1671–1713). More fully than anyone else I know until Kant, Shaftesbury realized the threat of scientism to all notions of a reasonable pursuit of virtue or of defensible political action. He is particularly good on the definition of a person or self as not an isolated thing but a mode of existence or way of being—an essentially "public" process—and on the purpose of rhetoric, which, like the purpose of government and of life itself, is to achieve a certain quality of "being together with other men." Good rhetoric, open communication, in his view is not merely a means to the ends of efficiency or justice or progress but an end in itself. Michael Denneny, to whose as yet unpublished work I am indebted for sending me back to Shaftesbury for the first time in nearly twenty-five years, sees him as looking to a public that can share (and test) its values by discovering its common sense of things. See *Characteristics of Men, Manners, Opinions, Times, Etc.*, ed. John M. Robertson (London, 1900).

For an exploration of notions of the self in modern times see Richard McKeon's "Love, Self, and Contemporary Culture," in *The Problem of the Self*, ed. P. T. Raju and Alburey Castell (The Hague, 1968).

The myth offered by scientism, based originally on genuine achievements of science, goes something like this:

In the beginning, nature, which consists of countless jiggling bits controlled by statistics and the gloomy law of entropy, accidentally spawned life, which then accidentally evolved, according to the statistical laws of chance, into what we call men and women, or human beings, or—when we are feeling in need of flattery—persons, selves, or even rational animals. These enormously complicated mechanisms have special needs because of their complexity, but essentially they are meaningless atomic units in a universal order (or disorder), behaving according to the rules that govern the bits of nature from which they sprang.

In a fairly recent version of this myth, each of these innately isolated creatures is innately competitive and aggressive, following an instinctive territorial imperative. But this is really only a natural development from the essential view of the person as isolated unit. In that view, "I" have a mind or brain and body, "mine." Other men and women have minds and bodies, "theirs." The brains bump into each other, just like the bodies, and exchange forces in doing so; the brain itself works essentially as a collection of bodies, on a Newtonian model. The bodies that bump the hardest produce the strongest effect. In some naive versions of this interaction it is possible for "my" mind to work on "yours" without in itself being affected; rhetoric is manipulation. More sophisticated versions take into account a principle something like the physical law that every action produces an equal and opposite reaction, so that minds affect each other according to their relative mass. In recent theories of human communication one gets a definition of society in terms of atomic minds exchanging bits of information, and there are many theories which claim to discover a scientific basis for value judgments in a new categorical imperative: thou shalt maximize the quantity of information exchange.[30]

30. For example, Aaron Katz, who sees man as essentially an "organism programmed by nature to fill [a natural, inherent] information gap and thereby achieve maximum adaptation for his species" (quoting Allen Newell). "The concept of 'information' (knowledge) is no longer restricted to physical and biological science," Katz tells us, "but is coextensive with all human experience" ("Prospectus," a mimeographed comment on his "Toward High Information-Level Culture," *Cybernetica* 7, no. 3 [1964]: 203–45). And of course he would say that information exchange is coextensive with all experience, because the whole "theory of man as information processor" is an effort to see man as part of a nature that is essentially an information-processing mechanism. The study of man in this view becomes "the study of man performing maximally in the direction of fulfilling his species' goal of maximizing information." Value thus

The "personal" problem for each isolated self is to discover enough knowledge about nature (including other selves) to control it. The goal of life is to increase human happiness (that is, maximize pleasure for each atomic unit) by increasing human mastery of nature, the total environment, through increased knowledge. Individuals are of course not free in any real sense, but they can find self-satisfaction in contributing to the inevitable march of science: freedom consists in bursting the bonds of ignorance and learning to control nature through mastery of its own laws. If you are troubled about your "self" and its role in all this, that is because you've been hanging around muddle-headed humanists too long; forget about unanswerable questions and get back to your rewarding work as a functionary in the legions of progress—or, in recent pessimistic accounts, in the tiny bands of rational men struggling to postpone ultimate catastrophe.

The irrationalist myth of the self looks of course very different, but it is really based on the same assumptions about the helplessness of reason employed by the isolated self. The scientismists are right about how it was "in the beginning," and the problem for each of us social atoms is to create some sort of freedom for himself, some escape from the depersonalized self that the scientific myth grants us. My salvation can be found only by salvaging something in me that is not subject to the scientist's laws. I probe and probe, I peel off this layer and that layer, but everything I look at has, in fact, been analyzed by some scientist or other and explained as subject to law or control—that is, it has

---

comes back into the universe, and man realizes one of the values of the universe; information processing is by definition good, and the more of it the better. Man, as the supreme processor, has now discovered a rational way of talking about values! "The third law states that the amount of information is proportional to the 'quality' of the culture, the quality being its capacity for information processing. This involves such measures as 'creativity,' 'objectivity,' and 'ego-strength.' "

It is not my purpose to reject this self-validating position, though the mechanical style would make a tempting mark. Nothing you and I do could escape Mr. Katz's net: the method is inherently all-encompassing. Given the world-view that has, for many men, become self-evident—the view of the universe as a vast and immensely complex machine—it might be said to be an inevitable development. In a mechanistic universe we find man's values, hard, inescapable facts of man's nature. How do we study them? Clearly the only way is to translate them into terms amenable to scientific inquiry according to the scientific worldview: turn them into "information processing mechanisms" that achieve the value of "maximum adaptation" by solving "the ten problems of [information-processing] culture." It is important to see how far such recent extensions of the myths of scientism move beyond earlier versions, rediscovering humane problems that were once called "meaningless." Taken seriously, Katz's freshly proved values go as far beyond modernism as anyone could ask.

been explained away. First thing you know, I have an identity crisis: I can't find an identity for myself, because everything I look at in "me" is not "mine." I am alienated!

But of course my alienation follows strictly from the definition of my self that I have unthinkingly accepted from the myth. If I see my problem as that of discovering and affirming "my" existence as a discrete and separate entity (on an unacknowledged but powerful physical model of a discrete atom), I have defined myself as *over against* everyone and everything else: my identity, following this definition, is discovered analytically or negatively through discovery of differences. What I am is what everything else is *not*. Self-affirmation in this view is necessarily *other*-negation.[31] Is it any wonder that "I" come to feel threatened in this process? Everything I am can be traced to some material or social cause; all my actions will have chemical accompaniments or antecedents; all my choices will fit statistical patterns; every role I seek will have antecedent causes. Even if I attempt grotesque "gratuitous acts" to express my freedom, I shall find that a given percentage of my contemporaries are doing the same thing for the same social reasons; we can be charted.

At a costume ball at my university last year, a couple arrived dressed as huge condoms. After the ball was over, they wrote a complaint to the student newspaper that nobody had paid sufficient attention: *we* were the most daringly different, but nobody gave us credit for it. Here the search for the self through tearing off the restraints imposed by others ends in a frustrated appeal to the others to recognize what a daring, unique, free person I am.

There are of course many versions of the irrationalist response. If one turns to the arts, for example, and to the beliefs of intellectuals who have been the severest critics of popular American culture, one finds the myth about how the self fulfills itself by relentlessly exploiting its independence and freedom. For at least two hundred years we have grown more and more frenzied in the search for the idiosyncratic, the "innovative," the latest trend: musicians and painters and poets have been urged increasingly to "find your own personal style." In popular mythic talk, this urging early took the form of picturing the true artist

31. Much popular psychology and sociology has owed its success to offering alternatives to this impossible "zero-sum game." David Riesman's *The Lonely Crowd* (New Haven, 1950), for example, made the reader long for a way of being that was not tradition-directed (having no individuality), not "inner-directed" (ignoring the signals of others and obeying only one's moral conditioning), not "other-directed" (totally malleable by social setting), but—ah, release! —autonomous! For an exposition and criticism of the romantic ego, see Eugene Goodheart, *The Cult of the Ego: The Self in Modern Literature* (Chicago, 1968).

as working alone and unappreciated in his garret, developing modes of art that nobody in his time could possibly understand or appreciate. To be ahead of your time often has seemed more important than to be on a road that is going somewhere; to march to the beat of a different drummer is all the direction a man needs, more important than knowing where you are going or actually getting somewhere. In many versions, all institutions and traditions that pretend to speak for or—much worse—to implant any standards of beauty or morality are placed in opposition to the individual who is to discover his truth for himself—a poor thing, perhaps, but his own. Until well into this century, in most versions of the Romantic self (for example, Freud's) the part of the psyche that was socially imposed was essential for survival and thus in a sense accepted. But more recent versions have often seen nothing but evil in any social restraint on the unbridled explorations of the individual self. As Lionel Trilling summarizes the tendency of literature produced by "modern" authors, "all of modern literature prescribes," in the words of Thomas Mann's Clavdia Chauchat, "*se perdre et même . . . se laisser dépérir.*" The end of all modern literature, he says, with considerable exaggeration, is "not merely freedom from the middle class but freedom from society itself. I venture to say that the idea of losing oneself up to the point of self-destruction, of surrendering oneself to experience without regard to self-interest or conventional morality, of escaping wholly from the societal bonds, is an 'element' somewhere in the mind of every modern person who dares to think of what Arnold in his unaffected Victorian way called 'the fulness of spiritual perfection.' "[32]

Trilling is uneasy about what such a literature teaches his students, and with good reason. Many younger readers, educated almost exclusively by it, seem to have swallowed the modernist disjunctions whole: the isolated self is supreme value and society is the villain.

In politics as in art, the self-as-isolate has engaged in futile battle with the ravages of scientism. Many social and political theorists since Hobbes have seen society itself as essentially a collection of such discrete units. Popular versions of the social contract theory always emphasize the essentially negative or defensive posture of the individual units: society is something each unit invents and then puts up with be-

---

32. "On the Teaching of Modern Literature," *Beyond Culture* (New York, 1965), concluding paragraphs. For a vigorous critique of the possessive individualism of modern art, see R. G. Collingwood's *The Principles of Art* (London, 1938), chap. 14. A fine account of what happens to the self in some irrationalist therapy programs is Alan L. Mintz's "Encounter Groups and Other Panaceas," *Commentary* 56 (July 1973): 42–49.

cause it has learned that only by giving up some of its rights can it get the other units to give up rights in return. On those rare occasions when young people these days defend institutions (I live in a dormitory and have watched the process of struggle for community against the slogans of individualism), it is almost always on the social contract model: the isolated individual, by nature absolutely free and autonomous, gives up some of his precious self in exchange for something he wants or needs. In this model, society and institutions are always at best a necessary evil; what is good is only the autonomous self, an entity that is assumed, without proof, to exist. With all of the touting by the under-thirties of community and communes, I never hear anybody admit to what a puny thing, what an unimaginably subhuman thing one's precious self would be if one had not been surrounded by, embedded in, made through other selves in social institutions from birth—literally constituted of other selves who are in turn unthinkable except in matrices of human converse.

We all believe, passionately, in the right of every person to assert and defend his values; about such matters as freedom and equality and justice we are indeed moral absolutists, even those of us who will in the same breath chant, "There are no absolutes."[33] The whole country cries, "Freedom now!"—meaning *"my"* freedom now—but we have little notion of a collectivity of selves that could multiply freedoms rather than simply subtracting from a fixed total.

This irrationalist quest for unlimited individual freedom helps to produce increasing violent conflict, which in turn produces a scientismist backlash, with Skinner and others saying, in effect, "You see what all this nonsense about consciousness and persons and dignity and freedom leads to—an intolerable chaos. Follow us back to rationality, and we will give you an ordered contentment of creatures—our creatures—conditioned to want what they must want if society is to survive."[34]

Even in religion the terms of battle have tended to be set by scientism; the desperately isolated self is not confined to agnostic or atheistic moderns. It can be seen as the battleground of despair and belief in even the most overtly religious figures. The self in Pascal is as much on its

33. See the fine accounts of moral absolutism in a skeptical age in John Passmore's *The Perfectibility of Man* (New York, 1970), especially the final chapter. Michael Polanyi discusses this matter in several works. See esp. *The Tacit Dimension*, pp. 55–63.

34. See the conclusion to *Beyond Freedom and Dignity*, in which Skinner promises the "wonderful possibilities" of a world in which all needs are satisfied, if only we will turn ourselves over to the new technology of behavioral control (pp. 213–14).

own as it was in Descartes, and it is still on its own when Gerard Manley Hopkins, Catholic priest and anguished "believer," tries to wrestle with his moments of despair:

> I taste myself, therefore I am, and when I taste myself I find myself utterly different from everything else whatsoever. . . . And this [my isolation] is much more true when we consider the mind; when I consider my selfbeing, my consciousness and feeling of myself, that taste of myself, of *I* and *me* above and in all things, which is more distinctive than the taste of ale or alum, more distinctive than the smell of walnutleaf or camphor, and is incommunicable by any means to another man (as when I was a child I used to ask myself: What must it be to be someone else?). Nothing else in nature comes near this unspeakable stress of pitch, distinctiveness, and selving, this selfbeing of my own. Nothing explains it or resembles it. . . . searching nature I taste *self* but at one tankard, that of my own being. The development, refinement, condensation of nothing shews any sign of being able to match this to me or give me another taste of it, a taste even resembling it.[35]

It is true that Hopkins had a God to turn to, or at least a sense that such a turning was possible and required. But I think the despair he felt when he found, as he often did, that his God had absconded, was closer in kind to that felt by atheistic irrationalists than the distinction between "believers" and "atheists" suggests. There is, however, one grand difference: when God is removed, even as a possibility, from the world as created by such a self, the one last ground for belief in a genuinely shared discourse is removed. The religious irrationalist could at least hope still to save his soul by communicating with God, and thus he could still hope to save other men from total isolation by converting them. But with God *really* gone—that last buttressing of the meaningful world, that Supreme Truth-teller whose integrity saved Descartes from the notion that the world we construct is a lie told by Satan—belief was left high and dry. The supremely valuable but mysteriously elusive self was free to make whatever discursive worlds it cared to.

And so the stereotyped image of the white-coated, inhuman scientist pursuing his objective truths in the laboratory, carefully ruling out all contamination by human preferences, confronts the long-haired, irrational rebel romantic, desperately affirming his antirational values, shouting his human defiance against the machine, and finally shooting and bombing other men to affirm the dignity of mankind! The atomic

35. From the *Sermons,* as cited by J. Hillis Miller, *The Disappearance of God* (Cambridge, Mass., 1963), p. 271.

self, alienated from God, from history, and from all other men, splits into absolutist embodiments of what is certainly known, as against what is deeply felt.

Descartes thought that he found an indubitable self when he set out to practice systematic doubt on everything that could be doubted. Peeling off the layers, he found a core of awareness of the process of doubt itself, the inescapable consciousness of the mental datum "doubt," even in the moment of most extreme skepticism. But his famous formula for his conclusion that he therefore existed—*cogito, ergo sum; je pense, donc je suis*—renders dramatically the fact that the whole project had been radically social from the beginning. The doubter, as Wittgenstein pointed out, did his doubting in a language that he had not invented. The "I" derived from the experiment already existed in a matrix of other persons before the experiment began; the questions asked and the data discovered even in the most extreme moment were tainted, as it were, with community.

Yet the model of the isolated inquirer has been accepted by increasing numbers of noble doubters—with especially disastrous results once the world no longer found it easy to take Descartes' silent leap from "consciousness of doubt" to the notion of an "I" doubting. But if we want to be skeptical about what has not been proved, surely we ought to be skeptical about the model of inquiry and the isolated inquirer willed to us from that great modern moment. It is surely self-evident (to use Descartes' expression) that the formula should have been *"We* think, therefore *we* are." We discover together that we cannot doubt the process or the value of discovering together; therefore we are.

What happens, then, if we choose to begin with our knowledge that we are essentially creatures made in symbolic exchange, created in the process of sharing intentions, values, meanings; in fact more like each other than different, more valuable in our commonality than in our idiosyncrasies: not, in fact, anything at all when considered separately from our relations? What happens if we think of our selves as essentially participants in a field or process or mode of *being persons together*? If man is essentially a rhetorical animal, in the sense that his nature is discovered and lived only in symbolic process, then the whole world shifts: every usage of words like *I, my, mine, self,* must be reconsidered, because the borderlines between the self and the other have either disappeared or shifted sharply. Yet we seem to be forced to this radical (and old-fashioned) view by modern science itself; we need not rely on any kind of traditionalism—we do not need to fall back, for example, on the notion of God, that word which for moderns obscures a problem by naming an absurd fixity. All we need do is honor what we know about who we are and how we come to be, in language. Once we give up the limiting notions of language and knowledge willed to us by scientism, we can no longer consider adequate any notion of "language as a *means* of communication" or as "one of many forms of conditioning." It is, in recent models, the medium in which selves grow, the social invention through which we make each other and the structures that are our world, the shared product of our efforts to cope with experience.[36]

36. I cannot pretend to be able to summarize where these sciences are or where they are going. But I have turned up a startling number of what in my terms are postmodernist conclusions. Here, for example, is how Jean Piaget, one of the great psychologists of the century, summarizes his splendid book, *Structuralism* (ed. and trans. Chaninah Maschler [New York, 1970]): "It might seem that the foregoing account makes the *subject* disappear to leave only the 'impersonal and general,' but this is to forget that on the plane of knowledge (*as, perhaps, on that of moral and aesthetic values*) the subject's activity calls for a continual 'de-centering' without which he cannot become free from his spontaneous intellectual egocentricity. This 'de-centering' makes the subject enter upon, not so much an already available and therefore external universality, as an uninterrupted process of coordinating and setting in reciprocal relations. It is the latter process which is the true 'generator of structures'" (p. 139). This process sounds very much to me like a rhetoric of assent (for a revealing example of just how rhetorical the study of "the transition from one structure to another" can become, see ibid., pp. 127–28). See also the pioneering work of Lev Semenovich Vygotsky, *Thought and Language* (Cambridge, Mass., 1962), originally published in Russia in 1934, suppressed in 1936, and translated into English only in 1962 (esp. the concluding paragraph). George Kelly explored the ways in which "personal constructs" are made and in turn make selves, limit and free worlds, and unite fact and value: "The psychology of personal constructs is built upon an intellectual model, to be sure, but its application is not . . . limited to that which is ordinarily called intellectual or cognitive. It is also taken to apply to that which is commonly called emotional or affective and to that which has to do with action or conation. The classical threefold division of psychology into cognition, affection, and conation has been completely abandoned" (*The Psychology of Personal Constructs* [New York, 1955], p. 130). A stimulating discussion of what psychologists like Piaget, Vigotsky, and Kelly mean for educators is found in James Britton's *Language and Learning* (London. 1970).

Resisting with difficulty the temptation to cite recent work in ethnology, developmental psychology, philosophical psychology, linguistics, sociology of knowledge, and sociology of language, I mention only *Readings in the Sociology of Language*, ed. Joshua A. Fishman (The Hague, 1968), esp. secs. 1 through 4; Eugene T. Gendlin, *Experiencing and the Creation of Meaning: A Philosophical and Psychological Approach to the Subjective* (New York, 1962); Eric H. Lenneberg, "The Capacity for Language Acquisition," in *The Structure of Language: Readings in the Philosophy of Language*, ed. Jerry A. Fodor and Jerrold J. Katz (Englewood Cliffs, N.J., 1964); and Erving Goffman, *Relations in Public* (New York, 1971).

To put it this way leaves untouched the central metaphysical question, "Who or what made the universe such that it can be apprehended only in a shared language of values?" I am personally interested in that kind of question, and I believe that rhetorical questions pursued honestly will finally lead to a God-term.[37] But it is important to see that we need not rely on any religious doctrine to show how much has been wrong with the dogmas of modernism. It has too often been assumed that to escape modernism one must revive a traditional God-term and "reason down" from it to rules for living; to work thus is to pretend that modernism never happened and that it had no basis for its appeals. But we are working the other way round—looking at the value-ridden facts of man's existence with or without "God." Man is essentially, we are now saying, a self-making-and-remaking, symbol-manipulating creature, an exchanger of information, a communicator, a persuader and manipulator, an inquirer. The terms will differ depending on one's philosophical vocabulary, but what will not vary is the central notion that man's value-embedded symbolic processes are as real as anything we know. Instead of Russell's view of the world vs. man's irrelevant values, we must now deal with a new world that is both found and made in value-exchange. As the pragmatists and phenomenologists

37. See Kenneth Burke's study of "logology" in *The Rhetoric of Religion: Studies in Logology* (Boston, 1961). It is astonishing to see how many professional philosophers and other academics are rediscovering old proofs for the existence of God, and claiming to invent new ones, precisely at the time when the great public has finally heard Nietzsche's pronouncement that God is dead. See for examples Flew and MacIntyre, *New Essays in Philosophical Theology.* For a less systematic but moving version see the account of R. Buckminster Fuller, one of the most popular campus lecturers of the last decade, in *Ideas and Integrities,* ed. Robert W. Marks (Englewood Cliffs, N.J., 1963), pp. 44–45. A good brief bibliography is given in John Hick's *The Existence of God* (New York, 1964).

Many rediscovered proofs for the existence of God do not use the term, and of course the God that is rediscovered does not bring with Him all of the attributes of every traditional notion. In a recent essay Karl R. Popper sets out to prove the reality of "the world of the products of the human mind," including ethical values, social institutions, scientific problems, and theories ("Indeterminism is Not Enough," *Encounter* [April 1973], pp. 20–26). Although Popper says that this world comes into existence only with the first human beings, his way of proving its reality depends in part on the notion that ideas determine minds—his "World III" is real because it acts upon us. Although he proves an open universe in some respects very different from that implied by traditional Gods, it is interesting to see how much similarity there is between his arguments and those found in Augustine's dialogue *On the Free Will,* esp. book II, chap. 3, or in Anselm's *Dialogue on Truth* (the two can be found conveniently juxtaposed, with commentary by the editor, Richard McKeon, in *Selections from Medieval Philosophers,* vol. 1, *From Augustine to Albert the Great* [New York, 1929]).

and Whitehead and many others long ago insisted—with nobody really listening, apparently—we have no reason to see processes and relations and perceptions of quality and value as a less real part of the natural world than atoms or cosmic rays.

## THE PURPOSES OF RHETORIC

It remains only to consider what is perhaps the most significant change made by this redefinition of man as rhetorical animal, what it does to our view of the purpose of trying to change other men's minds. In the scientismist view, you'll remember, the only conceivable purpose of changing minds was to implant our pre-formed views by any available means: force, conditioning, brainwashing, trickery, or at best what Kant calls "wooing." Except in scientific matters, rational persuasion was impossible, because proof was impossible, and persuaders could only propagandize their view of the world.

But if all men make each other in symbolic interchange, then by implication they *should* make each other, and it is an inescapable value in their lives that it is good to do it well—whatever that will mean— and bad to do it badly. If even the most austere, isolated laboratory scientist cannot even claim to exist except as a social self who was made and is still being made in symbolic exchange with others (or the totality of 'the other,' including the symbolically responsive nature that answers his questions), then his very existence depends on the many values he affirms when he respects the truth, refuses to cook his evidence, relies on the traditions and methods taught him by his mentors, and so on. The supreme purpose of persuasion in this view could not be to talk someone else into a preconceived view; rather it must be to engage in mutual inquiry or exploration. In such a world, our rhetorical purpose must always be to perform as well as possible in the same primal symbolic dance which makes us able to dance at all. If it is good for men to attend to each other's reasons—and we all know that it is, because without such attending none of us could come to be and questions about value could not even be asked—it is also good to work for whatever conditions make such mutual inquiry possible. Whatever imposes belief without personal engagement becomes inferior to whatever makes mutual exchange more likely. The purpose of mental change is thus to fulfill one's nature as a creature capable of responding to symbolic offerings. The *process* of inquiry through discourse thus becomes more important than any possible conclusions, and whatever stultifies such fulfillment becomes demonstrably wrong. But this is not quite the same as the popular irrationalist claim that conclusions do not matter, or the favorite dodge of social scientists when their data won't jell: "To raise

questions is more important than to try for answers." The process fulfills itself only when the reasons are as good and the conclusions thus
as solid as the problems and circumstances allow for. Rhetoric is a supremely self-justifying activity for man only when those engaged in it
fully respect the rules and the steps of inquiry. And this holds as much
for a "primitive" priestess persuading with myth, ritual, and omens as
for a modern scientist who knows that his conclusions are at best
tentative.

How then should men change each other's minds? If fact and
value are not implacably separated but inextricably intertwined in man's
nature, we can feel free to seek the answer to our "ought" question by
looking at the facts of what we do and at what we say about persuasion.
Just as all of us knew, in advance of my arguments here, that other
men ought to change their minds when we give them good reasons, we
know now that this is not just a personal preference. The very process
that led men to the modernist dogmas depends for its validity on denying those dogmas.

If a committed doubter says to us that he will not accept the valued fact of man's rhetorical nature, we see now that he cannot avoid
illustrating it as he tries to argue against it: we discuss our doubt together, therefore *we are*. If he chooses to deny the value we are placing
on the fact that this is how we are made, we cannot, it is true, offer him
any easy disproof, in his sense of the word. But we can point out that to
be consistent he must apply his doubt to the value of everything, including every scientific pursuit, every mathematical proof, every thought or
private experience that is in any sense derived from human converse—
every act, in short, except blank silence or suicide. And if he persists,
we have only to ask him, "What are your reasons? Give us good ones
for believing that we should not seek good reasons and attend to them
when they are given." If he offers reasons, we ask him whether we
*should accept* them. Does he feel any argumentative force in them?
If he says yes, he has accepted our premises. If he says no, his direct
challenge to our claims is of course removed, though we may well continue to worry—as in effect I have been doing here—about the intellectual climate that can make his kind of intellectual game seem less
in need of defense than our own.

By this route, as by many another, we are forced to recognize—
though without quite as much anguish as modernist discoveries of
man's "absurd" plight have produced—what looks like an absolute
limitation on our mental powers. Augustine says, "Unless you believe,
you shall not understand." For Aristotle no science can prove its own

first principles, and some principles can be discerned only by the intuitive reason. Gödel proved that no system can prove all the premises it needs. In our rhetorical terms, we can't get anywhere on any problem unless *we agree* on some knowledge for which the best proof is that *we agree* about it. In any formulation, it is just as irrational to shut oneself off from discourse about other men's affirmations of value as to ignore their skeptical doubts about logical proofs or "the facts."

That disputes about values often seem more difficult to resolve than disputes about fact should no longer mislead us; some disputes about what we call fact are harder to resolve than some disputes about more obviously value-laden assertions: (a) Is it a *fact* that space is curved? (b) Would it be *right* for me to conduct an experiment on a group of orphan children who are in my charge, blinding them slowly to observe the effects on their perceptual worlds? Except when we are victimized by dogmatic doubt, it is clearly much easier to settle the second of these questions.

Besides, "all of us here would surely agree that there is something wrong"—note my formula again—about refusing to wrestle with hard questions. So long as we have good reason to know that disputes about values can *sometimes* be debated productively and resolved, we have good reason to tackle any dispute that seems to us, jointly, worth bothering about, no matter how hard it is.

To talk in this way is to leave a lot of questions unanswered. Tomorrow I shall try to give some examples, both of difficult cases when values conflict, and of some forms of warranted assent that are opened up to us through this view of things. If I am right, forms of assent that are often called irrational—assent to religious groups, to dramatic and fictional appeals, to music, to political leaders—are in this view restored to potential intellectual respectability and thus to meaningful debate.

For to make brick without straw or stubble is perhaps an easier labour than to prove morals without a world, and establish a conduct of life without the supposition of anything living or extant besides our immediate fancy and the world of imagination.

Shaftesbury

Until we have understood how we do, in fact, understand each other, all further sociological inquiry will be useless.

Hans Peter Dreitzel

The best course of action is not that course which most quickly, least painfully, least expensively, etc., leads to the gaining of our ends, but *it is the course of action which is supported by the best reasons*. And the best reasons may require us to abandon the aim we actually have set our heart on.

Kurt Baier

All traditions are true, but none of them mean what they say.

Collingwood

A lively and lasting sense of filial duty is more effectually impressed on the mind of a son or daughter by reading *King Lear* than by all the dry volumes of ethics and divinity that ever were written.

Thomas Jefferson

If you would civil your land, first you should civil your speech.

W. H. Auden

# FOUR | Some Warrants of Assent
## with Notes on the Topics of Protest

Rejecting the dogmas of modernism can in itself settle no questions; indeed, for a true believer it can be positively unsettling. For the scientismist who has clung to the dogmas as his last hold on reason in a world gone mad, questioning them will seem just one more failure of nerve. For the irrationalist who has relied on them as his license for unbridled romantic assertion and thoughtless action, the questioning can threaten a return to chains. In one sense a rhetoric of assent attempts merely to be a commonsensical defense of the way we naturally, inescapably, work upon each other, because we are made in rhetoric. But for an age of dogma—and that is what I am calling our open-minded, tolerant time—it will have far more wrenching implications than any one of us can foresee.

If the whole "scene" of the atomic self, isolated in a cold universe, is undermined, the great liberal, critical fiat, "Make up your own mind," no longer quite makes sense. If the self is in fact a kind of value-permeated field in which a value-permeated universe creates and is in turn "processed" by what is really a history of selves in interaction with selves, the handbooks of logical and rhetorical proofs and fallacies must be rewritten.[1] If systematic doubt is to be replaced by systematic assent

1. In a quick check through several elementary handbooks that include lists of fallacies, I find that each author has inevitably committed a fair share of the fallacies he lists, most notably that prop without which all of us would fall, *petitio principii.*

Monroe C. Beardsley's *Thinking Straight* (1950; 3d ed., New York, 1966), one of the best and most widely used handbooks to clear thinking, relies on a model of logical thinking which would preclude much of Beardsley's own argument. He tells us, for example, that argument from analogy is "an unsound form of the inductive argument" (pp. 130–36, 284). But he himself often and inevitably argues from analogy, most notably the analogy of straightness or clean linearity dramatized in his title. Though much of what such books have taught (see, for examples of the best, L. Susan Stebbing, *Thinking to Some Purpose* [Harmondsworth, Middlesex, Eng., 1938]; and Robert H. Thouless, *Straight and Crooked Thinking* [New York, 1932]) must still be learned by every serious student of thought, their almost complete denigration of argument from authority, witnesses, and testimony, and their uncritical divorce of thought and emotion (the latter almost always for them suspect) will have to be revised. They further illustrate the belief that the chief task is seeing through other men's fallacies and confusions: "Analyze the fallacies and confusions in the following passage," Beardsley tells the student again and again. These authors do not dwell on human failures caused by "correct" thought purified of emotion.

Max Black is open about this deficiency: "But what are we to say about the criticism of *feeling?* When is a man justified in expressing hate, indignation, ap-

141

among such selves, the whole history of Western thought begins to shift under one's gaze, and the lines between friends and enemies become blurred. If language is not a means of communication but the source of our being, and if the purpose of rhetoric is not to persuade but to meet other minds in the best possible symbolic exchange—that is, to maintain or improve the "source" itself—then a very great deal that is conventionally said about improving communication begins to look highly questionable. If there is, finally, an inescapable, natural command to "make minds meet," then suddenly a host of commandments that men have said were simply an interesting, perhaps precious but finally indefensible heritage from this or that tradition become genuine imperatives again. If existence is unthinkable without the struggle to make minds meet, everything we value, including the achievement of science and mathematics, depends on this fact which is a value: men ought to attend to whatever good reasons are offered them by other men.

In short, if good reasons apply, many of those views that we have conveniently explained away with this or that form of motivism come flooding back in upon us, demanding a fair hearing. But the question of what is a fair hearing is now more open than any book of rules for clear thinking has ever suggested.

I don't know whether this position—many aspects of it are new to me in the past year, though some are old as the hills—will make me seem a flaming revolutionary or a last-ditch traditionalist. What I do know is that the questioning I have here traced has been for me enormously unsettling, and that the chapter of consequences I turn to now thus seems a deeply unsatisfying though at the same time exhilarating collection of hints and guesses.[2]

---

proval, etc.? These questions, important as they are, take us out of the subject matter of this book into the fields of ethics and aesthetics. They illustrate the limitations of logic" (*Critical Thinking*, 2d ed. [New York, 1952], p. 176). They do indeed, but these books all imply that *here* is how we *think*—and then there are all those other things that somehow get in the way of thinking.

2. In one revision of this lecture I constructed here a twenty-page "answer to objections." Every author ought to go through that exercise, even though the result (self-confirmation) is almost inescapable; only to the degree that we have really tried to face what can be said against us can we claim to pursue something beyond a rhetoric of mere persuasion (see my "Teaching Literary Criticism, 1971," *MMLA*, Spring 1972). The exercise produced for me ten redeemable pages, which then had to be incorporated in revisions of early sections, and ten pages of very dull confirmation, which I could not bring myself to publish. I thus give here only a catalog of short answers: (1) Doesn't all this leave us simply right back where we were, still dependent for all real proof on experts? Will not standards of validation in each field continue to be determined only by those who qualify: in physics by physicists, in baseball by baseball experts? Yes, in a

## The Great Reservoir of Good Reasons

A satisfactory account of good reasons in any one domain of life would necessarily require a sizable book. The repertory of good reasons could never be constructed by any one person, since it would include all good discourse about the grounds of valid discourse in any subject. What I do here should thus be viewed as an invitation to push even further the

---

way. But now we can add value fields that modernism would exclude: in love by lovers, in gastronomy by gourmets, in every kind of value by those who have come to know a good reason from a bad. What is most important, we now can have confidence that there are fields of moral expertise, and that in some questions of rhetoric, life-and-death matters, all mankind becomes potentially the relevant field. (2) Don't your many modern authorities, whom you cite as if to report a single revolutionary movement, in fact disagree with each other greatly? Yes, but the disagreements are not about what I consider essentials; though working on many different problems with many different methods and languages, so that many of them would be shocked to find themselves lumped with the others, they are in fact agreed in the essential matter of casting doubt on one or another of the great Doubts. (3) Doesn't your rhetoric fail to provide what is really needed, a tough philosophical argument for a new epistemology—the grounds of how we know anything, really, and of how we relate knowledge of phenomena to things in themselves? Yes, but I did not set out to build a systematic philosophy, only to undermine confidence in the dogmas and thus restore practical confidence in a process that might, as one product, buttress a variety of philosophies. (4) Isn't your rhetoric in fact just another form of relativism, since it provides no metaphysical grounding, no eternal verities? Yes, in one sense of the word *relativism;* no, in another. (5) Isn't your argument too dependent on citation of authorities, with too little detailed systematic proof of your own? You have offered a "rhetoric of conclusions," but on dozens of crucial matters— the mind-body problem, free will, the relation of theory to practice—any one of your sources would offer more detailed argument for the conclusions. Yes, much of this book is a kind of synthesis of postmodern commonplaces. But I am not as embarrassed as I perhaps should be, because I believe we are all dependent on authorities in this sense. I have cited dozens of sources of proofs which I have had to leave out, and the objection can stand only for the reader who can cite me a list of equally impressive authorities who provide real argument for the modernist case rather than simply assuming it to be self-evident. Use of authority seems a weak way to argue philosophical matters, but of course it is what most of us rely on most of the time, and it is mainly what established modernist dogmas in the first place. Even the genuine prophets of modernism, the fully qualified philosophers, can be seen falling into many of their assumptions because those assumptions were in the air, preached or assumed by "those who seemed expert." See for example Rudolf Carnap's account of how he lost the religious beliefs of his childhood ("Intellectual Autobiography," *Library of Living Philosophers,* ed. Paul A. Schillp, [LaSalle, Ill., 1944]). The account is ridiculous if taken as argument for its conclusions. But Carnap knew that his readers needed no argument supporting such a mental revolution, momentous as it must seem from every perspective except that of modernism. (6) Are these the only objections you can think of? No.

many recent efforts to develop methods of pluralism and manifold logics of inquiry, and to oppose assimilating all proof to a single paradigm.

Classical rhetoric, following Aristotle, distinguished three kinds of proof: (1) substantive arguments about the case to be established; for example, to say that we are not as well prepared for war as our enemy can be a cogent argument for not going to war at this time; (2) "ethical proof"—arguments based on the character of the speaker or his opponent; for example, to say that the king's counselor has lied to you frequently in the past is reason for you to disbelieve his claim that we are not ready to wage war; (3) "emotional proof"—arguments appealing to the special emotions or attitudes of the audience; for example, to argue for peace before a group of middle-aged mothers I will stress "death of our sons" more strongly than I would when speaking to senators.

Almost everyone has agreed with Aristotle that the first kind, if available, is somehow superior as proof to the other two. Example and enthymeme, the rhetorical versions of induction and deduction used in dialectic, are the core of persuasion; and Aristotle often implies that whatever is not valid under one of these heads is very weak proof indeed. And even these as used in rhetoric are inferior to positive proof: "The duty of rhetoric is to deal with such matters as we deliberate upon without arts or systems to guide us"—so far so good—"in the hearing of persons who cannot take in at a glance a complicated argument, or follow a long chain of reasoning."[3] Other and better audiences would clearly be preferred if life could only be managed that way. It should be evident by now that for a rhetoric of assent, these priorities are questioned and perhaps in a sense even reversed; ethical proof—the art of taking in by contagion—now looks much more important.

Aristotle at least knew that practical life required rhetoric and that rhetoric could not be reduced to logic. But many modernists have moved in the contrary direction, not only making logical proof prior but, as we have seen, eliminating all other kinds entirely. The history of

3. My quotations are from the W. Rhys Roberts translation. I am not following Aristotle strictly (*Rhetoric* 1357a and passim) but rather what seems to me the most common Aristotelian tradition. Perhaps I should add, for those who care about such matters and who are therefore likely to wander into a footnote this far along in a book like this, that the rhetoric of assent is not by any means Aristotelian; for my purposes here, Aristotle is much too interested in being scientific. Though I have resisted the temptation to attack him as the first scientismist, there is a sense in which he seems to say: Oh, yes, indeed there *are* many other forms of proof besides the apodictic proof that scientific demonstration affords, and I will deign to give you a book about them; but isn't it, after all, a pity that it cannot all be done with greater rigor.

rhetoric since the seventeenth century could be described as a mounting suspicion and final rejection of ethical and emotional proof and then a progressive narrowing of the range of what is accepted as substantive proof.

To reconstruct our languages according to a rhetoric of assent will be an immense task, as the efforts of the last two decades have shown. The reconstruction will not, if we do it honestly, lead to any comfortable set of rules for clear or straight thinking, though some rules will still be useful for limited cases (presumably physicists will still work at ruling out their emotions and preferences when assessing theories about black holes and quasars, even when they have recognized that they cannot do so in assessing their theories about big bangs and continuous states). It will not even lead to a reconstruction of a clear distinction among the three kinds of classical proof. Emotional and ethical proof will often turn out to be "substantive," and logical proof useless and misleading. But if we recognize that the distinctions will now be hazier than in any traditional rhetoric, it is still useful to discuss our restored reasons under the three traditional heads, substantive or logical, ethical, and emotional. I can only hint, with an example or two in each case, at what a world of reconsiderations we now face.

## VALUE TERMS AND SUBSTANTIVE PROOFS

If what we have said about the potential status of value judgments is true, efforts to establish value through discourse can no longer be dismissed, in Russell's language, as "mere preaching." Values can in some sense be demonstrated.

In classical rhetoric, three kinds of persuasion about values were usually distinguished: judicial or forensic, about the value-ridden facts of guilt or innocence concerning past actions; deliberative, about policy for the future; and demonstrative, praising or blaming persons or institutions in the present.[4] In such a scheme, our modern demonstrations, designed to protest this or that evil or to demand this or that good, take on a special interest. If value can in fact be demonstrated in ways other than by public demonstrations of force or violence, it is also true that extreme public displays of commitment always say something real to anyone seriously inquiring into the values at stake in any conflict. To

4. The best discussion of these kinds is still the source itself: Aristotle, esp. bk. I, chaps. iii–x. For a rhetoric of assent the three types addressed to issues in past, present, and future would, I think, be supplemented by a rhetoric of ultimate values: the rhetoric of sciences and philosophy, inquiring into what was once called "eternal truth." In such a scheme, much music and some literature (for example, poems like Eliot's *Four Quartets* that explicitly address metaphysical or religious truths) would become a "rhetoric of the timeless."

pretend that a display of commitment, even an extreme act of violence, is necessarily unrelated to how we think about such matters is, in our present view, to forget that the way we establish values is the way we establish anything: by earning communal validation through trying them out on other men.

To try them out in simple direct acts of physical protest has become a national habit partly because people seem convinced that they cannot try them out meaningfully in other ways. Thus we once again polarize ourselves, rationalists claiming that demonstrations demonstrate nothing, irrationalists claiming that nothing can be demonstrated without power or violence. The former talk of blind passion, senseless destructiveness, and fascist oppression by self-intoxicated and self-righteous mobs; the latter talk of inhuman and unfeeling machines, of bureaucrats rationalizing the status quo, and of fascist oppression by the entrenched elite. I scarcely expect that anything I say here will transform such groups into mutual inquirers; name-calling, like war, often achieves what we call results, and most men most of the time will probably fail to see the good reasons for rising above their local interests. But those who prefer to use their heads as well as their mouths and bodies need have no shame, if fact-values or valued-facts are accessible to reason.

## Example 1: Finding a Concurring
## Public vs. Getting on the Bandwagon

Modern rhetorics have often listed the bandwagon technique as one fallacious kind of argument. In deciding what I want to believe or do, it is said, I must not be swayed by the fact that everyone's doing it. "Everyone" does a lot of crazy things; fads and fancies fill the air. Clearly the man who respects his mind will make his own decisions and not follow wherever the winds of group assent would carry him.

But of course one man's bandwagon is another man's reasoned consensus. A teacher may find himself arguing against the bandwagon technique in his composition course and then feeling annoyed when students in literature courses refuse to respect what *his* bandwagon says about the importance of literature or of critical thought. "Why should I think Shakespeare is great just because everybody says so?" the student asks, and the liberal teacher says, "Oh, of course you shouldn't; you should make up your own mind"—even while thinking that perhaps something has gone wrong if the weight of generations of thoughtful and sensitive critics counts for absolutely nothing as against the opinion of a green, arrogant, and analphabetic youth.

We should now be able to see (and to seek ways of teaching) that to resist one bandwagon is often to embrace another—possibly but not necessarily one that is older and "better established." The young student cannot make up his own mind about Shakespeare, if by that is meant coming to an opinion about Shakespeare uninfluenced by one tradition or another—even if it is only the tradition of taking TV shows as a standard of dramatic value. And to tell him not to jump on bandwagons because he should think for himself is once again to define his self negatively, as what is left over after all influences have been discounted. No wonder so many of his kind finally tell us, in effect, that whatever bandwagon comes along—Jesus freaks, Devil's Disciples, Hell's Angels, Children of God—is better than no bandwagon at all. After all, we have taught that there's no disputing about taste in bandwagons.

When established universities and their critics have clashed in recent years, the defense has often been in the name of a dispassionate neutrality, while the attackers have claimed, quite rightly, that the universities and colleges are not neutral, that they are defending their own commitments and interests. Professors and administrators have argued, again with justice, that they cannot pursue truth if the truth is prejudged by political or social commitments of the kinds sought by protesting students. And students then have replied—after more or less perfunctory efforts to discuss matters—that "we tried to reason with you, but you wouldn't listen, so we were forced to resort to sit-ins or violence." (The same pattern of argument is heard, needless to say, in national disputes about racial injustice or the Vietnam war or women's rights.) Again and again I've heard people on both sides say, "Well, of course, you can't deal rationally with differences about values." The academic defenders then go on to argue, in an obvious circle, that it is highly important to humanity to preserve institutions which pursue questions in an objective spirit, untainted with values. And the students, having heard the message that values are beyond dispute, grasp the other horn of the false dilemma, and say, "Since according to your own teachings, O my mentors, we cannot hope to deal rationally with our value differences, and since values matter to us more than they do to you, let us then deal with them irrationally: burn it down!" Or words to that effect.

But having examined critically the dogmas of modernism, we can rediscover what never should have been forgotten: that some values are in fact better-grounded than others, and that disputes about them can yield results that *ought* to be accepted by all parties to the dispute, even though they cannot be called certain or positive. A rational protest is possible, in short, about any violation of any value we hold

147

dear. When I enter into the lists, I cannot be sure, it is true, that I will come out unchanged, since my protest may be invalidated—now that I have learned that listening is important—by the reasons offered by my opponents. But I have no good reason to believe, in advance of a conflict, that reasons will prove irrelevant simply because values are at stake. It is not only that most disputes about values turn out, on examination, to be about means and not ends (even the dogmatic modernists admit, most of them, that dispute about means can be rational). It is also that ends are themselves subject to meaningful communal inquiry.

I think, for example, that in pursuing a rhetoric of assent we have at the same time been discoursing about ends and pursuing the grounds for a rationally legitimated protest. Or, to put it another way, *I* have been making what I take to be a reasonable protest against many of the modernist assumptions (and the practices that those assumptions imply) that have been felt to be dehumanizing and soul-destroying by some of the irrationalists who have protested in less discursive ways.

Since I know that I cannot disprove the dogmas in a positivist sense, one way to proceed might have been to organize a sit-in at my university, demanding that all dogmatic modernists be fired. But so long as I believe that the dogmas can and should be tested in another sense, by this kind of discourse, I could never resort to a kind of action that in effect proclaimed reason to be helpless and precluded my discovering how and where I am wrong. A protest, even the most violent protest, becomes legitimated when and only when the affirmations on which it is based are *in fact* (not just in personal conviction) supported by good reasons, good reasons shared or potentially sharable by the community that is relevant.

It is often said, by those who want to defend the rightness of individual protest, that one man plus God makes a majority. The formulation ignores the opposite truth, that one man plus the devil can make a hell on earth. If we are to make our protests not just self-satisfying, not just "sincere," not just desperate and ineffectual last-ditch stands, we must validate them in the courts of communal exchange.

But if there really are such things as good reasons about ends, this is not so difficult a thing as we have often been led to believe. Whenever any person or institution violates the inherent values of free human exchange among persons, imposing upon anyone a diminution of his nature as a rhetorical animal, he is now shown, in this view, to be wrong—not just inconvenient or unpleasant but wrong. There are genuine values, intersubjectively demonstrable, that judge his wrongness. Those same values will of course sit in judgment on any mode of protest against the violation. I am not free to choose whether it is right to silence you because you would silence me: of course it will be wrong to silence you. I may of course be forced to do so in opposing a greater wrong, even knowing that my means are evil, as we had to work at silencing the Nazis once they had set out to use force to silence the rest of us. But as I do so I will know that the justice of my action is determined by whether what *look like* good reasons for the employment of warfare are *in fact* good reasons. And that can only be determined in social or potentially social converse with reasonable men, not in private, isolated, "logical" consultation of my atomic self and its wisdom: as ethical theorists are fond of saying, I must act so that the principles of my conduct are reversible, against myself, universally applicable.[5] Rhetorically speaking, this means that I must have good reason to believe that if my opponent would open his mind to full rhetorical exchange, he would be led, by good reasons, either to come to my view or at least to tolerate it as one reasonable view.

In some such way as this the philosophy of good reasons leads us to a reaffirmation of those central human values that other philosophies and religions have reached by other routes: of tolerance, of justice or fairness, of "democratic" equality of vote in all matters that concern all men equally. Kant once remarked that the result of all his philosophizing was to establish a rational basis for the pious beliefs of his ancestors: the golden rule reappears for him as the categorical imperative, and it reappears in our rhetorical view as the command to pay as much attention to your opponent's reasons as you expect him to pay to yours. This traditionalism of our results doesn't bother me: I revel in it, partly because it is so radical. Here we depend on the obvious and age-old belief that if there is any hope for man it can be found neither in repudiating all past truths nor in repudiating all revolutions. We must select, as always, from old and new by testing in discourse which truths meet circumstances that are always both novel and precedented.

A society cannot exist, the past seems to teach us, unless it can somehow constitute itself as a rhetorical field, as what Dewey called "a public,"[6] and this means that *we* cannot exist without recognizing that

5. The details of argument from "universalizability" are complex; they have been handled similarly (though in varied and seemingly contrasting languages) by many philosophers, from Plato and Aristotle through Kant and Rousseau to many recent "good reason" philosophers (see Appendix B and chap. 3 n. 18).

6. See Dewey's *The Public and Its Problems* (New York, 1927), esp. final chap. The point has of course been made by many sociologists, though in recent years it seems to have become more and more "anthropologized"—see Peter L. Berger and Thomas Luckmann, *The Social Construction of Reality: A Treatise in the Sociology of Knowledge* (Garden City, N.Y., 1966), esp. sec. 2, "Society

*some* of our shared values carry an inescapable weight for all of us. Too often our way of talking about the increasing fragmentation of publics is to throw up our hands: "You can't talk with them because they have gone beyond the pale." In other words, we decide to declare war. Though I hold no great hope that a revitalized rhetoric can ever eliminate "warfare"—lying, trickery, blackmail, and physical persuasions —I think the command upon us is inescapable: we must build new rhetorical communities, we must find a common faith in modes of argument, or every institution we care about will die.

## Example 2: Relevance

Whatever is irrelevant is taken by many students as finally dismissed, without further argument. My files are full, as that rhetorician Joseph McCarthy used to say about the Communist names in his files, of quotations in which students prove that such-and-such an item in the curriculum, say Plato's *Republic,* is bad because irrelevant, and should be replaced by, say, Paul Goodman's *Growing Up Absurd,* or—five years later—Frantz Fanon's *The Wretched of the Earth.* The typical faculty response, not necessarily mistaken but usually ineffective, is to say, "But it *is* relevant, if you only knew. You just don't know what relevance is." To which the good student will say, having been taught to do so, "Relevance is a value term, and conflicts about it are matters of personal choice. If I say Plato is irrelevant, Plato *is* irrelevant to me. I alone know whether I am bored, and if you claim to know better, you are an authoritarian and an elitist, because you claim to speak for a hierarchy of values instead of admitting that you simply prefer Plato to Goodman."

A letter from a student dramatizes the conflict:

> [I'd like to see you] to clear the air regarding the third quarter of Liberal Arts I [last year]. I was highly antagonistic in class, I know, and this had more to do with my own feelings of lack of direction in myself than with any fault in the course, the profes-

---

as Objective Reality." I cannot trace here what seems to be a general infiltration of the social sciences with "the rhetoric of structuralism," according to which— to put it crudely—everything relates to everything else: every belief in a given culture will rely for its credibility on the total structure of beliefs and practices. All societies are in this view rational, in one sense, but no element can be proved outside its context unless, as many structuralists assume, all societies are *au fond* alike, in which case a Supreme Anthropologist could discern a Supreme Public and its Problems, and He could write—that ultimate Lévi-Strauss—an ultimate rhetoric of assent. Lacking such, we can still work with confidence as we assent to more localized publics.

sors, or the University of Chicago. Liberal Arts I got the "frontal attack" though, because of all the "irrelevant" things I was studying it seemed the most irrelevant.

The strange thing now is that in thinking back over what we read, in rereading my papers and also rereading some of the works we studied, I find that while intellectually perhaps I understood them last year, I now understand them in terms of my own experience. In this sense then they have become more than relevant—exciting, intriguing, and positively helpful to me in understanding my own life.

Now what strikes me about this girl's letter is that last year I tried to say all those things to her myself. These documents from the past—this Plato, this Aristotle, this Nietzsche, this Kierkegaard, this Weber, this Shakespeare—all of these, I then said, or perhaps preached, are relevant to a part of you that you have not yet fully discovered. But she, being then involved in radical politics, particularly the women's rights branch called WRAP, felt guilty when she was working on anything that did not relate to the cause *now*. (Her retrospective discoveries, incidentally, were possible only because she had been more *dutiful* than many students; she had done the work even when feeling guilty about it, and hence had the material in some sense available for retrospective revaluation. You won't find the topic "obedience" used favorably in any protest rhetoric, and those of us who see some value in it still must work hard to show its relevance to more popular topics like growth and freedom.)

Relevance is thus a cover word for a variety of real topics about education and what it should be. The students themselves are inevitably ambiguous about it: sometimes they are talking about relevance to "how I feel now"; good education is that education which reveals itself to me right now as vital and alive—as the letter says, "exciting, intriguing, and positively helpful in the present." But sometimes they are talking about relevance to an imagined future—to the triumph of this or that picture of the movement, the revolution, really under the topic of expediency or usefulness.

The tougher revolutionaries sometimes attack their associates for being distracted from the cause by illusions of qualitative improvement in the present: drugs reduce a man's will to fight; enjoyment of literature or music can distract from the future; worry about hurting people is a bourgeois distraction. These defenders of relevance can in fact denigrate every present phenomenon or fact or judgment of quality or feeling as irrelevant to the true picture, that picture of course being a notion of what the future must be. Listen to a publication called

*Fire!* published by the Weatherman branch of SDS (November 21, 1969):

> Since I vamped on the spy pig in the New York Movement Center during the National Action, I've been forced to spend most of my time in hiding. Though I have managed to bomb a lot of shit [I infer, from internal evidence, that this means "use aerosol bombs to scrawl messages on walls," but I'm not sure] and even direct some struggles over these past six weeks, my life in the under has given me a lot of time to think about the needs of our movement coming off of Chicago and now Washington. I've made some decisions and communicated them to the up-front leadership of SDS. Involved in all of this is the Winter National Council Meeting, which will be held December 26–31, place to be announced. . . . One thing that really blew my mind [in Washington] was the incredible number of kids who were paying no attention at all to the Mobe's march and rally. Not just the 10,000 or so kids who trashed up the city Friday and Saturday nights and Sunday morning. There were tens of thousands of others who weren't into violence yet—maybe they weren't sure or were scared—but they knew that standing around looking stupid while some dude told you how beautiful it all was just wasn't where it was at. . . . The new mass movement is taking place in a totally different context—we're moving toward armed struggle in this country. That's what the Chicago action was about, what the South Vietnam Embassy and Justice Department actions in Washington were about, what the wave of bombing over the last month has been about.

> People say what's the point of trashing windows—that won't win the revolution. The criticism seems to come from the left, from a struggle angle that we should be doing more. We should be doing more. . . . But we've got to dig that the criticisms of the Action, of the violence . . . of "terrorism" are coming from the right. . . . They're saying it's a bad thing that Hog Elrod broke his neck. They're saying we shouldn't be moving toward armed struggle.

> The highest level of struggle always defines all the others, puts them in perspective, helps people at the other levels figure out what they're about.

In this branch of the plea for relevance, personal temptations of feeling and morality and justice *now* are attacked as present distractions from the vision of the future that will alone lead to that just future. Note how often the writer here refers to "what it's really about," or to "where it's at." In each case it's "about" the future; "where it's at" is really in the future.

In another article in the same journal, called "Principles, Schminciples," Howie Machtinger begins:

> It is always insightful to point to all the important political questions that confront us, search for "political principles which are at the base of the struggles within SDS," and then facilely quote Mao about unity-struggle-unity. . . . All this avoids what it's all about. Political questions are questions of strategy. Strategy is about winning. . . . So, in America, the central task of the left is the development of a detachment of the international army . . . and moving to armed struggle as soon as possible. For the world revolution is already happening, and every leap in the development of our struggle hastens incredibly the victory of the people of the world. It is in this light that we must look at questions of adventurism [raised by those who want to worry about principles], beating the people, and blah blah blah.

Worry about principles (the topic of what is true or right), and about whether it is bad that a public official was paralyzed (now, in the present) or about whether SDS was in fact responsible is here relegated to blah blah blah: irrelevant, because the *future is now.*

The student revolution has thus come full circle and joined those who were originally its worst enemies: those who willingly corrupt the present in any degree necessary to achieve an imagined future, those vicious establishment constructors of the rat-race who reduce the lives of students and workers to mere means. If we compare what Howie Machtinger, former graduate student at the University of Chicago, says here with what most students were saying two or three years ago in the attacks on the university and its irrelevance, we thus see that what began as a kind of demonstrative rhetoric about intolerable degradations of the quality of life in the present has gradually become a substitute for deliberation about what to do to achieve a desired quality of life in the future.

Such shrill rhetoric can be highly appropriate and even reasonable in showing the world how intolerable a particular degradation feels *in the present.* But as rhetoric about policy, it establishes only the shakiest of claims for any program of action. It is especially weak when the report is not of "how I feel about X now" but of "how I will feel about Y in the future." When a maker of the counterculture echoes that utopian dream of Russell, proclaiming "a new heaven and a new earth, so vast, so marvellous, that the inordinate claims of technical expertise must of necessity withdraw to a subordinate and marginal status in the lives of men," we ought to be able to detect in the desperate inflation of the style that what he is talking about is next to nothing; unlike those who report on "how this present condition makes me feel," such reports on the future and how it will feel are indeed relevant only to a current wish, and it can tell us nothing about anything else. But again we are offered such reports as if they were evidence of what "must of necessity" happen: as if to say, "The revolution is coming as is proved by my demonstrations of violence, or my unbridled statement of feelings, *now*."

In a faculty debate about an "early" sit-in (1966) at the University of Chicago, one faculty member said, "This discussion troubles me: we're being instrumental or utilitarian, in talking of how we can meet the students in what is genuine about their complaint and get them to listen to us about the rest. What we should be doing is trying to feel what they are feeling." Mr. Machtinger and this professor were more or less united in that sit-in. I cannot believe that they are so still, now that Machtinger's branch of the student revolutionary movement has become so cold-bloodedly instrumentalist.[7]

But I find that I cannot think about those conflicts without thinking about and assessing those people as people—as well-meaning or cold-blooded, as trustworthy though misguided, or as self-seeking. And this leads us to another set of topics entirely.

### ETHICAL PROOF AND THE DEMONSTRATION OF VALUE

Many analysts have noted that there is a tremendous reliance in the rhetoric of protest on ethical proof—the character or personal integrity of the speaker—and a relative scarcity of arguments about the subject of dispute. The observation is usually taken as proving the inferiority or inconclusiveness of this rhetoric; as the rhetoric texts have said, "You can't *prove* anything with testimony." But the same can be said for some of the world's great rhetoric, particularly something like the Gospels, which might almost be described as one prolonged piece of ethical proof of the integrity of the hero and of those who told His story. Does this reliance prove the rhetorical inferiority of the Gospels to, say, Hobbes's *Leviathan*?[8]

7. I should note that though I opposed the methods I was united with them in the announced purpose of that early sit-in: to reverse the university's policy of providing class rankings to the Selective Service System. The university changed the policy about one year later, working "through proper channels"; debates are still held about whether the sit-in hastened or slowed that decision, or whether, assuming that it hastened change, the effects justify the choice of means.

8. There are people who would say so, because the Gospels "prove" nothing:

A related point, sometimes confused with use of *ethos,* is that we live in an age of "display rhetoric" (or "demonstrative" or "epideictic" rhetoric, as it appears in the older texts) and that deliberative rhetoric about policy and judicial rhetoric about the past tends to get overwhelmed by demonstrations for values or against evils in the present. Our demonstrations are usually concerned with establishing the iniquity of certain persons or institutions here and now; judgments about guilt in the past, or political judgments about correct policy for the future, tend to be reduced to the demonstrative and to the ethical proof within the demonstrative.

The typical pattern may be that of the Chicago conspiracy trial. The ostensible form of the trial is judicial or forensic: we are met to discuss the legal question of who was to blame for what acts and in what degree on such and such a date in the past. The real form soon becomes demonstrative, working on the question: who are the good guys and who are the bad guys? The *charge* shifts from "You bashed a head" or "You organized a riot" to "You're a dirty subversive." The *response* shifts from "I did not do such and such things" to "You're a pig fascist." There's no need to trace the process by which such countercharges escalate: the very popularity of the word escalate comes these days from the frequency with which debate escalates into polar charges which seem to allow only one honorable reply: further escalation of personal attack. Each side thus provides evidence supporting the other side's claims. One of the problems the modern rhetorician ought to work on is finding techniques for transcending such destructive escalators—running around to another part of the building, as it were, and moving into deliberative or dialectical encounters. Sometimes by attempting to transcend rather than escalate, the participants in even the most heated conflict can suddenly discover topics about which fruitful debate can again take place.

## Example: Sincerity

It is a good general rule that in any protest movement most protesters feel sincere. In my own experience with protesting students, I have

---

but we can grant that they do not prove everything they claim to prove and still recognize just how fatuous such a position turns out to be. Simply imagine how much of our picture of our world and its possibilities would be changed if these writings had never existed. At a bare minimum, the Gospels demonstrate that some men—in fact, many men indeed—have been able to believe these strange beliefs. Their historical weaknesses—even if taken to the extreme of arguing that no such figure as Jesus ever existed—could not entirely destroy their power as a rhetoric for one view of how man can or should live in the world.

known only a few who seemed to be consciously using the protest for merely personal ends, and I suspect that I was wrong even about some of them. The student enters the fray armed with an absolute and justified conviction of his own sincerity, and of the self-evident hypocrisy of the foe. Asked for proof, he may at first be surprised, because he *knows* or *feels* his own sincerity, which makes it self-evident and not in need of proof, that misleading commodity of the hypocrites. The appealing side of this self-validating stance is shown in a long letter I had last year from an excellent student, concluding: "Please write if the spirit moves you to, but whatever it moves you to, do that." Well, if the spirit has moved me and I am following its commands, my sincerity needs no further proof, to *me,* and it will be hard for me to see why it should need proof to you. But if you *want* proof, here it is: I am willing to lay my body on the line. What more could you need? Greater sincerity hath no man, than that he should lay down his life for his cause.

Charged with hypocrisy by the self-evidently sincere demonstrators, the defenders of the university often make the mistake of assuming not only that nothing has been demonstrated but that the demonstrators must be hypocrites. "You cannot be sincere," the argument runs, "because you change your demands from day to day and your logic is bad and you do not always tell the truth." These three charges, *inconsistency, illogicality,* and *lying,* are proof, for many a professor, that you cannot be sincere, since if he were openly inconsistent, illogical, or dishonest, he would certainly take these as signs of his insincerity. And then the professor makes the equally foolish mistake of trying to prove his own sincerity by proving that he has been consistent, logical, and factually accurate.

In that same sit-in, aeons ago, a most able professor of law issued a twenty-page document summarizing the events and issues of several troubled weeks. So far as I could discover, it had no errors of fact or logic in it; it proved, if anything could, that the students had been confused and inconsistent in their demands, illogical in their written arguments, and even willing to distort and suppress facts they obviously knew. But you can predict the reaction of the protesting students: Mr. X has totally ignored the real issues; he has revealed himself as a logic-chopper with no feeling; his cold and inhuman lack of sincerity betrays itself in every line. "He's just not an authentic person," said one very bright graduate student of modern thought. As you would expect, the professors who succeeded in getting through to the students at all did so first by somehow establishing their own sincerity—chiefly by revealing in one way or another that they *felt* as deeply as the students. I myself benefited greatly, I've been told, by the obvious look of deep and self-destructive agony that I carried around with me at the time; it was uncalculated, but it "demonstrated" that I was not a hypocrite even when I opposed the students and assisted in punishing them. I did it with such obvious anguish!

There are of course great dangers for anyone who relies very heavily on ethical proof in plotting his course through today's rhetoric: sincerity is more difficult to check and easier to fake than logicality or consistency, and its presence does not, after all, guarantee very much about the speaker's case. But it is a serious mistake for defenders of institutions to pretend that they are above its appeals, or that the sincerity of a proponent is not in some sense a good reason for his case. We all inevitably rely on our notions of the basic integrity of the rhetor who appeals to us; we all excuse gaps in argumentative cogency if we believe that the speaker or writer is essentially reliable in sharing values we share. And it would be unreasonable not to.

All the art, then, lies in assessing degrees of reliability. In place of easy rules about the irrelevance of sincerity (or of those extensions and multiplications of ethos: testimony, authority, and tradition), we work at developing a "logic" of relative weight. Instead of advising that we "leave such matters to lawyers," as we saw Bertrand Russell doing in *Human Knowledge,* we recognize that the processes developed in the law are codifications of reasonable processes that we follow in every part of our lives, even the scientific. Instead of deploring the public's tendency to vote for candidates on the basis of "image," we work for a discrimination among images.

The fact that politicians have learned to manipulate images, especially on TV, means simply that it is harder to obtain relevant indications of character, not that indications of character are no longer relevant. Mr. Nixon's villainous five o'clock shadow on TV was a poor reason for voting against him in 1964. But my knowledge that President Nixon has lied to me again and again—a knowledge charged with emotion—gives me good reason to mistrust his next words. Nothing could be more irrational than for me to say that since proof is impossible in political matters, especially about value judgments, I will refuse to take emotion-ridden value judgments like *my* image of Nixon, or any other candidate, into account in my political decisions. His ethos is a large part of his capacity as a leader, and I should therefore work hard to refine the process of deciding my view of it.[9]

9. Written in 1971, before Mr. Nixon's reelection, the passage seems strengthened by the Watergate hearings now going on—June 1973. Could we not say that the best single argument about what to expect in Mr. Nixon's administration was his ethos?

Even "sincere body rhetoric" can give good reasons for what it is capable of arguing about: the intensity and direction of a man's concern. It does not give reasons about what should be done, as is dramatized by the uselessness of Bertrand Russell's marches against the bomb in suggesting any practical directions for the control of atomic warfare, or the even greater uselessness of his Stockholm war-crimes trials in establishing real guilt or any direction of action that might remove the horror of the Vietnam war. But even something as quixotic as those trials demonstrates *something*: the fact that such-and-such people see United States policy in Vietnam as properly analogized to the Nazi war crimes. How much weight such demonstration carries will depend largely on their ethos—on who they are and on whether they have lost their credit by demonstrating desperate concern about too many matters or in discrediting ways.

But where, in contemporary education or in books available to the literate public, will I find extensive discussion of such subtle but crucial matters? Except for a few lawyers and lawyers-turned-rhetoricians, like Chaim Perelman, it is hard to find more than ten pages in any one spot on what are often life-and-death matters. Is it any wonder that we have a populace—not a public—who yield up their souls as casually as they buy breakfast cereal? If one mark of an educated man is that he can recognize a good person when he sees one, is it not strange that almost nothing in our enormous program of higher education deals with the question of how it is done?

## "GUT" ISSUES AND EMOTIONAL PROOF

A student at my university once wrote a letter to the editor that revealed just how thoroughly a convinced modernist can divorce evidence and emotion: "I came to Chicago to discover whether life can be proved to be worth living. So far I have found nobody who can prove it. If I find that it can't be proved, I'm going to take a lot of you with me." Aside from whatever personal anguish lies back of such a threat, it could never have been offered if the young man had not fallen for the notion that the *desire* for survival felt by himself and his threatened readers was clearly ruled out as evidence related to his question; it could not deal with the reason side of things, since it is so clearly emotional.

But we do not usually talk this way. We all believe that if someone can show us that our lives are threatened, he has given us good warrant for action. Our ecological anxieties of the past few years have been based precisely on our justified sense that if our lives are threatened we have cause for a response to the threat. It is unqualifiedly reasonable for everyone to want to survive; to talk of such a passion as divorced from reason, just because when it is challenged it can sometimes produce "blind violence," is to fall into the simple division of man's nature that I tried to deal with in my first lecture.

Imagine a scene in Germany, mid–twentieth century:

"For the last time, I plead with you to join me in trying to escape."

"But again I ask, 'Why?' "

"I've already told you. I hear that 'they' have begun gassing us Jews in huge ovens."

"What's your evidence?"

"I was told by C—— who heard it from J—— who had it from . . ."

"Hearsay! I want evidence!"

"Look, have I ever been wrong in such matters?"

The debate is in fact about whether the skeptic will live to hold other debates. Refusal to believe the evidence, such as it was, proved suicidal for millions. Can we say that the study of rhetoric must rule out such extreme cases? I don't see how, except on the grounds that they are inconvenient and difficult. Given the right assumptions about mankind, about Germany, and about the Nazis, anyone in Germany should have been able to conclude, on daily evidence of many kinds (none "conclusive," of course) that atrocities had been committed and that more would be. Has a reasonable rhetoric nothing to do with the study of such assumptions?

This most haunting of examples, dreadfully real, can be matched in form by innumerable choices thrusting themselves at us daily, choices in which there is not adequate evidence for a certain conclusion but in which—often enough—one direction will prove disastrous and the other beneficial. Sometimes a little inquiry will reveal clear and solid ground for decision—here the study of rhetoric can have its clearest triumphs. Sometimes inquiry and thought and intuition can reveal reasons which are very tenuous in themselves but which give some excuse for moving here rather than there. A traditional logical analysis of arguments will not help much in this middle misty ground. But simple common sense and folk wisdom can yield many criteria sounder than mere chance. Sometimes, it is true, one simply has to choose blind—flip a coin or, what is never quite the same thing, trust to intuition or the guidance of the Lord. Until one surrenders to the coin, there is always some sense that *something* in one's mind or heart or gut will help to make the choice right.

## Example 1: Dialysis Machines

The point could be illustrated with any emotional commitment, intense or weak. But it is clearest when death threatens. At present in America, we have a shortage of dialysis machines for people with malfunctioning kidneys. It would seem unreasonable of any kidney patient not to expect equal rights to such machines, since his life is at stake, yet equal rights are not yet in fact possible. The usual conclusion from such inherent conflicts of genuine interests is that reason is impotent in matters of life and death; what we have is a battle of selfish interests in an absurd universe. But we could conclude that when such desperate conflicts occur, we who are "made in symbolic exchange" must work together as symbolically endowed creatures, not as mere animals; there is a moral command built into our natures to explore together for possible ways to remain human in the face of such monstrous and novel problems, as many have done facing similar problems in the past. We must seek topics on the basis of which real and potentially deadly conflicts of interest may be either resolved or, when immediate resolution is impossible, explored without warfare, so that the effort at resolution can continue.

One traditional notion of how to reason about the dialysis machines would be to rely on an elaborate structure of priorities that all men should accept if they would only listen to reason—scientific geniuses first, say, then political leaders, then women and children, or what not. But this arbitrarily circumscribes the circle of relevant judges. Instead, what we are forced to do is what men have in fact done whenever they have managed to avoid warfare or violent revolution: probe together, sometimes intuitively, sometimes discursively, to grounds shared beneath the desperate differences.

There are two main directions available for such probing, each of them better than concluding that moral reasoning is irrelevant, each of them adhered to by a sizable body of moral theorists. The first is based on a kind of social-contract model. If all the kidney victims, for example, were to set out to eliminate each other in armed combat, until there were only enough left for the machines to deal with, it is evident that few if any of the patients would in fact be saved; or if they were to arm themselves against the hospitals and their wicked priorities and calculations, the machines would stop while the hospital officials tried to drive them off, and again everyone's chance of survival would drop to zero. It is thus rational, even according to the most hard-headed of social-contract theories, to submit to some kind of unjust distribution of life, since the probabilities of survival are increased through the very acceptance of what, abstractly considered, is injustice. At the same time it would be unreasonable not to organize politically to elevate dialysis machines higher in national priorities—ahead, say, of moon flight—and if some insensitive soul tells us that we cannot find funds for more machines, because "there is not enough money for both dialysis machines and moon flight," we will feel justified in using every nonviolent means to demonstrate what irrationalities his position entails. (Would a demonstration in which a kidney patient arranged to die before the eyes of the President and public on national TV be an irrational proof, because so emotional?)

Since all men who have thought seriously about moral issues would go with us at least this far, we have already adequate grounds for dismissing the claim that emotional charge and reasoning are incompatible. But our rhetorical approach enables us to follow a second line, since we will also find that most who have thought about it, perhaps all who have really thought about it, will want to go beyond the social-contract model in their actual moral choices if not in their theories. Most of us believe strongly—except insofar as we have been told that we have no solid grounds for the belief—that there is something really wrong about grabbing whatever we can get away with, disregarding other people's needs and values. Like Adiemantus and Glaucon in *The Republic,* we may not be able to answer Thrasymachus' claim that might makes right and that men moderate their pillagings only in order to avoid being pillaged; but we know somehow that each dialysis patient "ought to be fair" to other dialysis patients. And, even more important to my argument here, those of us not immediately threatened by kidney collapse ought to take into account the desperate needs of those who *are*— even if, within the framework of social-contract theories, we can't find any way in which their suffering will reflect obvious harm back upon us. It is not that we can or should stand to one side of those who suffer, and exhort, "Be reasonable." It is that most human beings have some sense that others should be taken into account; they feel guilty when they have failed to do so, unless they can find what we call a rationalization—"He was my enemy," "That tribe is subhuman," "Moral standards and conscience are simply cultural inventions, relative to particular groups." The desperate search for rational explanations when we have followed our motives blindly and hurt others is sometimes cited as evidence that all reason is rationalization. It might just as well be taken as showing that most of us see where the burden of irrationality really lies —on the one who has violated basic communal norms.[10]

10. For a brief account of some of the issues that I abuse so briefly here, see Stuart Hampshire's review of John Rawls's *A Theory of Justice* (*New York Review of Books,* February 24, 1972, pp. 34–39). For our purposes, as apparently

What is true of love of life and fear of death can be true of other passions. In my first lecture I reported on the professor of history who concluded that defense of the university was irrational because professors were simply expressing motives of class interest and personal passions. But we can now see just how superficial such an explaining away is. While it is no doubt true that many professors have come into the "academic racket" for reasons that have nothing to do with love of inquiry or of teaching, and some no doubt from motives they do not understand, it is also true that many come because they once discovered a love of learning and a desire to teach, and they stay mainly for these reasons. Note that I put the good reason here as "love" and "desire"— nobody ever became a good student or professor because learning is a good thing, abstractly considered. "Love of learning" is a phrase that fits neither of the dichotomized columns I constructed earlier (pp. 17–18). It refers to both an emotional drive and, once brought to conscious attention, a defensible value. These assertions cannot be tested easily by anyone who has not experienced the love. To anyone who has, it will be self-evident that such love constitutes a good reason. Sophists can perhaps do no more than wonder why, when the going gets rough, some professors and students do not stop being professors and students;

---

for Mr. Hampshire's, the difference between what he calls the "social contract" theory of Rawls and his own version of "intuitionist" theory is insignificant compared with their agreement in repudiating moral skepticism and expressing confidence that "our moral beliefs have a rational foundation."

My little imaginary rational protest is not intended as more than a fraction of what might be said or done about such a conflict. What I said earlier about the "selves" who find themselves in conflict here could lead us into more interesting reasonable modes of resolving conflicts over who gets saved when some must die. But for now I hope it is enough to illustrate my notion of how topics might be found and explored in discourse and action.

To do justice to the real issues underlying any one public controversy— whether about race, the war, pollution, women's rights, educational reform, or whatever—would obviously require dozens of pages. I suspect that genuine argument of the kind I seek is rarer and rarer these days, but it can still be found—in *The Public Interest*, in *Daedalus*, and more rarely in places like *The Atlantic* and *Harper's*. I cite only one fine example, R. J. Gerber's "Abortion: Parameters for Decision" (*Ethics* 82: 137–54). It is unlikely that every careful reader will be persuaded by him to resist further blanket advocacy of abortion. But every careful reader will be unable after reading to conduct debate about abortion in the standard opposed terms: progressive vs. reactionary, life vs. death, etc. "Any argument that enters the lists on either side should acknowledge the argument on the other side," Mr. Gerber says (p. 148). To do so inevitably forces both sides to a level of encounter on which their real interests and values either join or, if they continue to clash, do so in a genuine engagement.

when the honor disappears or the money dries up, the vocation continues.

What leads us astray, of course, is that motives for doing something are often *not* good reasons for doing it. But any motive, however emotional or "base" or "animal," can become a good reason—not necessarily decisive, but not irrational—simply by entering the consciousness, being weighed, along with other "reasons," and found to be essential or appropriate, no longer accidental, to the decision. Though sexual desire is a poor reason for many decisions (for example, deciding to be a teacher because there will always be delectable young girls around), lack of it becomes one good reason in deciding whom not to marry.[11]

### Example 2: The Pocketbook

Similarly in political choices: desire for economic prosperity—or fear of an empty larder—can be a very good reason for voting for or against a political candidate, once the motive is weighed, found to be relevant, and then compared with other more or less good reasons for the vote. It is not irrational to vote for the candidate who will work for my financial well-being, unless in doing so I violate other reasons on which I put more weight. In fact, it would be irrational not to take a candidate's likely effect on my salary into account, just as it would be irrational not to take his likely effect on war and peace, on the preservation of my personal freedom, and so on. This is not the same, be it said, as arguing that the only rational man is economic man, as some economists seem to suggest. To reduce all choice to economic motives and then to reserve the term *rationality* for the results is as destructive of public reasoning as the position I am countering here.

I read in a student paper the following question and answer, in an interview with a man who is giving much of his life to opposing the Vietnam war:

Q: How can you relate opposition to the war to people outside the academic community?

A: People do not respond only to arguments; people also respond to their interests if it is pointed out to them that their interests are suffering. . . . the common man should know at least two simple facts. One is that the United States has been spending to the tune of $35 billion a year in its war effort in Indochina, and that the economic ills of this country date from— or coincide with—the escalation of the war in Vietnam.[12]

11. To paraphrase Jane Austen on money: A man would be foolish to marry for sexual pleasure alone, but he would be even more foolish to marry without it.

12. *Maroon,* January 29, 1971, p. 1.

The speaker's distinction between "arguments" and what he then goes on to provide seems at first natural to an age that sharply separates knowledge and practice. But the attempt to appeal to the workers' self-interest by teaching them the economic facts about the war would seem to any student of classical rhetoric a clear instance of thoroughly reasonable argument. It is in fact a remarkably cogent argument as it stands, especially when one considers the conditions and standards of newspaper interviewing. The fact that it does not finally clinch the matter for any critical reader says nothing decisive against it; the thoughtful reader will weigh this economic argument against other arguments for and against continuation of the war, and in doing so he will be deliberating, considering the weight he wants to give his economic self-interest in comparison to other interests or motives. But the notion that there is no proper or rational argumentative force in telling a man whose wallet is being pinched that his wallet is being pinched is a very strange notion indeed; if it *is* being pinched, he ought to listen. "YOU ARE BEING ROBBED," says a headline recently used by Ralph Ginsberg to advertise his magazine of advice to consumers—and I find myself weighing my feeling that Ginsberg's warning against commercial "robbery" is sound against the evidence in the ad that it is itself an attempt at sucker-catching. My desire not to be robbed runs like a cool clear rational thread through the whole process of deciding, finally, not to subscribe to this heir to *Eros*.

In short, every desire, every feeling, can become a good reason when called into the court of symbolic exchange. And it requires no psychoanalyst to do the calling, though psychoanalysis is one good model of how a harmony of brain, heart, gut, and gonad can be sought and tested in shared discourse.

It is true that "gut reactions" can be very bad reasons for action. But so can logical proofs. The real art lies always in the proper weighing—and what is proper is a matter finally of shared norms, discovered and applied in the experience of individuals whose very individuality is forged from other selves.

### ART AS THE CHANGING OF MINDS

In the final chapter of Aldous Huxley's *Point Counter Point* (1928) Spandrell concludes that the slow movement of Beethoven's A-Minor Quartet, the *heiliger Dankgesang eines Genesenen an die Gottheit,* "proves all kinds of things—God, the soul, goodness—unescapably. It's the only real proof that exists." But his friend Rampion, who talks and acts like D. H. Lawrence, attacks the music as expressing only "this damned abstract soul," a "kind of cancer." "I don't want your spiritual cancer." And Spandrell begins to doubt what had seemed certain. "It had been a failure. . . . Was the proof, after all, no proof? Did the music refer to nothing outside itself and the idiosyncrasies of its inventor?"

The remainder of the movement satisfies Spandrell's doubts: "The miraculous paradox of external life and eternal repose was musically realized." But Rampion can only whisper, "Almost thou persuadest me. But it's *too* good."

Such talk about a piece of music, with or without Beethoven's kind of caption thanking God for being healed, must strike most true modernists as at best a kind of romantic longing. Irrationalists might, true enough, take it seriously as one among many forlorn appeals by modern man in search of a soul—"hoping it might be so," as Hardy put it hardly more than a decade earlier in "The Oxen." Scientismists must simply scoff at Spandrell's use of the notion of proof; perhaps Huxley means to suggest this by making sure that none of the many True Unbelievers that populate his novel is invited to his final intimate seance.

Music *prove* something? Absurd. Whatever "proves all kinds of things—God, the soul, goodness" of course proves nothing. And the skepticism that almost everyone seems to feel about music would be extended by many to include all the arts; the defining characteristic of art is that it does not argue, is not didactic. "Poetry makes nothing happen." "A poem should not mean but be." "There are no beliefs in poetry, only pseudo-beliefs." "The difference between a novel and a tract is that a novel offers no propositions that ask to be tested for their truth value." "The 'poetic' is a domain entirely different from the domains of discursive speculation or of practical decision and action." Thus to ask what a novel, play, poem, symphony, or painting proves, to ask what good reasons any genuine art work gives for any change of mind, is to commit an absurd confusion of categories.

The position is self-proving, provided we define words like belief and proof in a certain way. Much poetry and most music and graphic art does not depend for its success on truths of the kind thought to be provable or falsifiable in our scientific traditions. I. A. Richards' famous dictum makes sense if we define our terms in his very narrow way: "We need no [scientifically provable or falsifiable] beliefs, and indeed we must have none, if we are to read *King Lear*."

But if I consult my experience instead of modernist abstractions about what art should or should not do, I find myself with a problem: art works change me. Sometimes they seem to be trying to change me and they fail. Sometimes they appear indifferent to what happens to me, but produce great changes anyway. Sometimes, it is true, they produce no discernible change; the more I read, the fewer major changes are produced by any one book. But I can remember—and find that everyone I ask about it can remember—what seem in retrospect epochal transformations. Sometimes they were changes of emotions and fantasies that even modernists will recognize as real—ah, that first pornographic work, at fourteen! and oh, the wonders of Oz, at seven! But if I am right, it is a mistake to think of even these transformations as merely emotional. My conceptual life was simultaneously transformed, the new concepts inseparable from the new joy and guilt in lust, the new longing for impossible magical worlds.

Often enough the transformations were more openly conceptual, though nonetheless emotional. How did a young Mormon boy who had never met a "Negro" become an active member of the NAACP? Not, you can be sure, by knowing any black people or by reading discursive arguments, but by reading works like *Uncle Tom's Cabin* and Lillian Smith's *Strange Fruit,* and by hearing Billie Holiday sing the song of the same name.

In short, by the age of twenty my opinions and emotions were very largely a product—as I know they must be still—of the art I had encountered. And I suspect that most of you could say the same.

I believed, for example, that if I were ever to have the delicious experience of being accosted by a prostitute, what I should do—and it would really prove quite easy—was rescue her (my Sonia!). I believed both that Tess was admirably chaste and that the total sexual freedom of *Brave New World* would be a splendid way to run a world (poor Huxley, the ironies you wasted on that young reader who turned all your sexual satire into bliss). I believed that happiness was to be found in individual isolated striving against tradition and the stupidities of Philistia (*Arrowsmith, Portrait of the Artist,* et al.), or possibly in love (all those marvelous nineteenth-century heroines, starting with my beloved Elizabeth Bennet and ending with Tess, whom *I* would have *saved*), or possibly in the life of the mind (my Socrates!). And I believed that somewhere, somewhere there was a world of bright young people, looking and talking like my picture of Huxley's Londoners and Fitzgerald's cosmopolites, with a bearded Tolstoy or two sitting at the edge of the circle.

But I needn't go on. Except when trying desperately to stave off censorship, hardly anyone has ever claimed that art does not build us and change us in these and other ways. We are what we have consumed; we take in whatever takes us in, and we are forever altered. What *is* often said is one of two things: that the changes are all emotional, non-rational, noncognitive (even the beliefs that are changed are pseudo-beliefs); or that it is pointless or unsophisticated or destructive to judge art works according to the validity or reasonableness of the intellectual changes they may produce.

There is a long tradition of critics opposing these views, from Plato to Kenneth Burke.[13] Plato saw his fellow Greeks being educated by Homer, with minor assistance from other poets, and he concluded that the results were bad. He also concluded, as have most critics in this tradition, that the state should censor works that "argue" for wrong conclusions; I suspect that it is the fear of censorship, which I share, that has made modernists so reluctant to deal with the genuine rhetorical issues that art raises. To ask whether judgments about good and bad art can ever be made according to what is sometimes—I think mistakenly—called content seems to sell us down the river. How can we resist the ever-present demands for censorship, once we have admitted that bad art can have bad effects—can in fact maim and destroy?

But once we see the issue in this form, it becomes clear that it is a false issue: recognizing that a "pure novel" can be bad because it changes minds in ways we deplore is no more in itself an argument for censorship than recognizing that political pamphlets or philosophical works can teach falsehood is ground for censoring *them*. The simple-minded identification of judgment with censorship prevents our seeking the kind of discrimination in art that we often take for granted in argument. When I think of that young man of twenty who was so readily seduced by every offer, I do not wish that a censorship board had protected him from the offers, but that in his education somewhere he could have been led to test the "reasons of art" as energetically as he felt he should the blandishments of advertisements or public orators.

If we believe, as I think we all do, that works of art are in any

13. Burke's literary criticism is a beautiful demonstration of how works of art are in fact "symbolic actions" which "perform attitudes" and produce "identification" between poet and reader, musician and listener, painter and viewer. I wish I could at this point incorporate about five hundred pages of his brilliant discussions of how art serves for maker and receiver as a way of both understanding and coping with the world. But even such a delectable plagiary would not do my job. Performed in Burke's analogical way, his own dance has been strangely unpersuasive to precisely those modernists who would profit from it most: those who are convinced that knowledge is only of what is proved and that proof can only be literal empirical demonstration. What is needed, and what I can only hint at here, is a relatively literal-minded and cautious supplement to his rich analogical probings, showing that even for the man who would be strictly empirical, art must be seen as part of our repertoire of good reasons. Burke's genius is peculiarly resistant to short citation, and it would be absurd to pick out a few essays or chapters for special mention. As one might expect, the woods are full of refutations of Burke based on a quick reading of short and seemingly zany snatches.

sense good or bad for us because they change us in a direction that we consider good or bad (whether that direction is "countercultural," "revolutionary," or "counterrevolutionary"), then we can no longer reasonably take refuge in the easy claim that art has nothing to do with providing good reasons.[14] Unless we want to make the extreme behaviorist claim that all means of change are both ethically and cognitively neutral, provided the "desired" change is achieved, we will find ourselves saying that some art gives good reasons for good changes, some art inadequate or bad reasons for changes that we deplore.

Once we have admitted that art is not "just emotional" or "recreational" or "escapist" or, at best, "beautiful" but rather is of fundamental importance in making and changing our minds (or souls or selves or identities), we are landed in questions that I can certainly not settle in the fringe end of this already frazzled lecture. All I can hope to do is suggest some issues which are reopened once we have seriously questioned the validity of the simple, two-fold division I described in lecture 1, with art necessarily opposed to reason and logic because it is on the side of emotion and faith.

### WHAT ART TEACHES

Suppose we perform a mental experiment. Like the mental experiments of modern science—windowless elevators ascending at the speed of light, for example—this one could never actually be performed. But if we keep our heads screwed on tight, we should still be able to learn something from it.

Imagine a highly intelligent, sensitive adult who had never heard any music but who had—and here is where one impossibility comes in —a complete capacity to "take in" that *heiliger Dankgesang* by Beethoven. I use the ambiguous metaphor of "taking in," aware that no metaphor is finally adequate to what we do to any work—or to

14. In the years since the lectures were given, I detect a rising tide of critical confrontation with one side of this problem, "the morality of art." Reconsiderations of neutralist assumptions can be found on every hand: in debates in *Encounter* and *Commentary* and *The New Yorker* and the literary quarterlies about pornography and violence in literature and film; in demands from Maoists and Freudians and Laingians for a literature or criticism that rejects formalism and deals with the "real substance" of literature; in structuralist rejections of formalism; in Marxist criticism of the synchronic bias of structuralism (for example, Frederic Jameson's excellent work *The Prison-House of Language: A Critical Account of Structuralism and Russian Formalism* (Princeton, 1972). Unfortunately, most of what I see would justify, in its slovenliness, a return to the original revolution against the use of nonliterary standards: if this is what it means to recognize that art changes our minds, then let's go back to impersonal close reading and formal analysis and contemplation of pure forms.

what it does to us. (Literal language is even less adequate. How would complete "mastery" of a work be demonstrated to a behaviorist? The "master" could, if he had the technique, sing or perform or recite or transcribe what he had fully mastered, but even he could not show or prove his feelings about it. And those of us without techniques of performance are even less able to deal literally with what happens when a work *works*.) We master it or appreciate it or enjoy it; it works, hits us hard, carries us away, absorbs or transports us. To me, as to Kenneth Burke, the most nearly adequate metaphors lead here to the notion of identification—I take the work in, or, as phenomenologists say, it enables me to dwell in it. I live the work; it lives its life in me. Its creator and I become, in a part of our lives, indistinguishable as we live the work together.

Choose your own metaphor, then, and apply it to our hero who manages to make the Beethoven his own, becomes as fully involved, is as transported, let us say, as you have been by whatever is the most important art work in your experience. Short of Spandrell's inflated metaphysical speculations, what will this ingenu-turned-sophisticate know at the end that he did not know before?

The experiment can be seen as simply a dramatization of what must have been learned in every person's life before completion of any successful artistic experience. Without art we would not know some things that through art we come to know. My list of six such "cognitions" is no doubt incomplete:

## 1. Shared Patterns of Expectation and Gratification

Most obvious are the innumerable detailed structural relationships that must be perceived before even the simplest fragment of the movement can be experienced: this word, this note, this phrase, this kind of foreshadowing, this rising melodic line, this tempo, this sequence of transformations—each has a meaning that becomes part of the whole. Whether all such meanings are conventional and learned, or (as I believe) some are innate and universal, the repertoire of such "reasons of art" possessed by everyone in a given culture, in advance of any one experience, is immense. Our experimental hero has somehow learned, for example, before or during his listening, how to interpret something like this: "A single violin gave out a long note, then another a sixth above, dropped to the fifth (while the second violin began where the first had started), then leapt to the octave, and hung there suspended through two long beats" (Huxley's words). He knows that there is a sharp contrast between such a rising, tentative, quiet, unaccented line and the firmly accented, more decisive passage that follows after thirty measures. He thus knows in purely formal terms—and in any major musical work the elements of such knowledge are innumerable—a musical analogue to the rough verbal paraphrase that Beethoven writes out when the new passage begins: *"Neue Kraft fühlend"* ("Feeling new power"). Though he knows that the musical experience is far different from any verbal statement about how convalescence feels, he also knows that Beethoven's verbal attributions make sense—a sense that can easily be tested by seeing what happens if radically conflicting verbal labels are applied. If Beethoven had called the whole movement "A Traveller's Curse after Misdirection," our listener would know that something was wrong, just as he would if the second passage were marked "Feeling weaker." I am aware of experiments purporting to show that such attributions are meaningless because listeners do not agree. But the accounts I have seen are so naive about how "votes" can be taken in such matters, and so committed in advance to their conclusions, that they leave me unshaken.

Descriptions of musical forms do vary greatly, but it is within clear limits.[15] In any case, we are not concerned at this point with the

---

15. It should not trouble us that those who have been moved by this profound "argument" cannot agree precisely on how to describe it. For J. W. N. Sullivan the whole movement is a "solemn, pure and profound song of thanksgiving to the Godhead," uttered by a man who during the time of composition was in great spiritual pain: "poor, ill, stone-deaf, wretchedly housed, utterly alone, betrayed and abandoned by the one human being whose love he so desperately and pitifully craved. . . . From this matrix rises the slow movement, the most heart-felt prayer from the most manly soul that has expressed itself in music" (*Beethoven: His Spiritual Development*, [New York, 1944], pp. 244–45). Martin Cooper, considerably less given to sentimental programming and more interested in technical matters, still must talk about it this way: "Serenity in a . . . positive and august sense . . . hymn-like in character. . . . He contrasts a complete archaic, ecclesiastical-sounding hymn—in fact a chorale in five strains . . . —with a completely modern, secular dance-like movement. It is as though Beethoven were aware of two aspects of his recovery. . . . The narrow span of the melody, its rhythmic simplicity . . . and the frequent crossing of the parts combine with harmonic austerity to create the strongest possible impression of remote, other-worldly solemnity. . . . The heavy accents, the wide leaps, the unusual rhythm and the trill [of the section marked *"Neue Kraft fühlend"*] bring the movement in a single bar out of church into the sun, from the stillness of a devout recollection into the tingling activity of the dance, but David's solemn dance of thanksgiving before the Ark" (*Beethoven: The Last Decade* [London: 1970], pp. 362–64). Huxley's own more mystical terms are: "It was the calm of still and rapturous contemplation, not of drowsiness or sleep. It was the serenity of the convalescent who wakes from fever and finds himself born again into a realm of beauty. But the fever was 'the fever called living' and the rebirth was not into this world; the beauty was unearthly, the convalescent serenity was the peace of God. The interweaving of Lydian melodies was heaven. Thirty slow

sharing of verbal knowledge about the experience, but rather with the listener's capacity to take in the musical reasons as a symbolic whole. Such knowledge is essential and important because it gives good reasons for the reconstruction of the experience itself. We cannot be said to have possessed the experience, we have not taken it in, without coming to know these reasons; knowing them, we can answer such questions as why does the "leap to the octave" *follow* the "drop to the fifth" and "Why does the 'strength' *follow* the 'serene prayer'?" We can thus deal with the art of the work consciously, sharing with others good talk about good or bad reasons for the form being what it is.

---

bars had built up heaven, when the character of the music suddenly changed. From being remotely archaic, it became modern [with the '*Neue Kraft fühlend*']. . . . 'He's feeling stronger; but it's not so heavenly' " (chap. 37). All such statements are burdened for me—half-modernist that I am—with a slight air of absurdity, especially when quoted out of context. My point is not that they are adequate or in precise agreement—though they do share a pattern—but that no one can ever hope to talk appropriately about such music without including something about Beethoven's and the listener's sharing of attitudes about life.

My experiment might have been more convincing to some readers if I had performed it with a totally unprogrammed piece of pure music, perhaps one or another of the preludes and fugues in Bach's *Well-Tempered Clavichord*. At one time I swallowed whole the notion that such music was somehow better than any other because totally purified of human content. But it is now clear to me that even then my passions—and not just my love of great technical skill—were engaged. One has only to imagine the effect if some modern dance troupe choreographed an obscene, comic stage rape using a Bach fugue as the music. It could of course be done, and the effect would for everyone be "shocking," "blasphemous"; even those who liked it would speak of its daring or surprising qualities, because everyone knows a kind of meaning in the preludes and fugues that would be violated.

For an impressive treatment of these matters, in terms rather different from mine, see Leonard B. Meyer, *Emotion and Meaning in Music* (Chicago, 1956). His later *Music, the Arts, and Ideas* (Chicago, 1967) touches at many points on issues I have raised throughout these lectures.

*That* music communicates something more than abstract mathematical patterns is a much more general view now, I think, than it was twenty years ago. But *what* it communicates will of course be described in whatever belief-language a writer holds to. For Stravinsky, even in his early period when he was trying to counter the emotional excesses of Wagnerianism, music was "a form of communion with our fellow man—and with the Supreme Being," and in his later years it became more and more overtly a religious act (*Poetics of Music in the Form of Six Lessons* [Cambridge, Mass., 1956], conclusion). For John Cage, a modernist who often claims to produce meaning-free music in which "nothing takes place but sound," the new composing and listening are sometimes given meanings almost as evidently religious: "This psychological turning [giving up traditional musical control and orderings] leads to the world of nature, where, gradually or suddenly, one sees that humanity and nature, not separate, are in this world together" (*Silence* [Middletown, Conn., 1961], p. 8).

This basic experience, which in a work as complex as the Beethoven depends on an incredibly rich cognitive equipment, even if we do not insist that our hero learn musical terms, already goes far beyond what some formalists would want us to say, because it includes knowledge about such matters as how serenity relates to vigor and "new power." And it leads us now much further.

### 2. "The achieve of, the mastery of the thing"

We here move to what knowing the art work teaches through being itself—the good reasons it offers for conclusions beyond its own rich being. For one thing, a human being was able to *do this*. Our imaginary hero now knows that something marvelous is possible that he did not know was possible before. Insofar as he finds the achievement surprising or pre-eminent in its kind, whether pleasant or wonderful or thrilling or provoking (or, for that matter, disgusting or horrifying), he now knows that a fellow creature was capable of this kind of achievement —and it is a kind of achievement even if his emotions are unpleasant. A fellow creature did this, and this fact becomes part of what he knows about human potentiality.

### 3. The Possibility of a New and Special Form of Communication or "Indwelling"

Not only did somebody else make the work, but he, the receiver remade it. He now knows that through an art work one mind can take over or possess another mind. The work has thus given good reason for a radical and incontrovertible claim about human nature and its possibilities: a very elaborate symbolic identification is possible—he's seen it done.

Our experiment again is temporally impossible because in fact no one ever becomes a sane adult without already discovering many forms of indwelling that prove this point—it does not require a Beethoven. Every successful joke, every ghost story, every folk tale shared, every totem pole or landscape painting achieves—or can achieve under the right cultural conditions—this sharing and thus this knowledge. It is only the extraordinary cultural crosscurrents of a time like ours, when we often quite literally are shut out from art works, that could obscure the marvelous powers of art to build stable affirming communities, whether as large as Dickens' millions or as small as the society for the promulgation of Ezra Pound's *Cantos*. And even in our time, when we are told that no values are shared, that all artistic appreciation is relative, every person's daily experience provides many examples of art works successfully shared.

172

## 4. Nonliteral Communication of Elaborate Attitudes

Attitudes can be performed, not simply stated. Beethoven could have said, "I am grateful to God for my convalescence," or, "I thank, thee, God . . ." Instead he wrote a movement for a string quartet.

Since the work has worked for our man, he has experienced a musical version of the attitude of prayerful thanks. Regardless of whether he believes in God or believes that Beethoven believed in God, he now knows that art can be made of an oblique or metaphorical statement of the prayerful attitude. (Every successful metaphor of course proves the same general point.)

## 5. Knowledge of Relative Value of Attitudes

Presumably our hero has encountered many attitudes literally expressed about illness and convalescence. He has heard people say, "It sure feels good to be getting back on my feet," and he has heard others say, "I just don't feel the same since that attack." And he has heard it said that life is absurd; illness, pain, and death the primary reality; health or gladness a momentary illusion in a sea of pain.

But now he has met a kind of elaborate testing or proving of one of the possible attitudes, and it has stood up marvelously well under the testing. The attitude has been danced, and it danced well. It therefore has something to be said for it in a way that would not be true if the results had turned out to be unintentionally ridiculous, pompous, or sentimental.

What this form of proof means can be most clearly seen when the work fails—when the attitude turns out to yield shoddy art. What we mean by sentimentality, for example, is one of the qualities of works based on attitudes that have not survived artistic proof; by definition, presumably, there cannot be a great work of art that suffers from sentimentality—though what is sentimental will vary to some degree from audience to audience.

Here is a poem that strikes me as highly sentimental:

### God

God is a concept
By which we measure
Our pain.
I'll say it again
God is a concept
By which we measure
Our pain.
I don't believe in Magic
I don't believe in I-Ching

I don't believe in the Bible
I don't believe in Tarot
I don't believe in Hitler
I don't believe in Jesus
I don't believe in Kennedy
I don't believe in Buddha
I don't believe in Mantra
I don't believe in Gita
I don't believe in Yoga
I don't believe in Kings
I don't believe in Elvis
I don't believe in Zimmerman
I don't believe in Beatles
I just believe in me,
Yoko and me
And that's reality

The dream is over
What can I say?
The dream is over
Yesterday
I was the dream weaver
But now I'm reborn
I was the walrus
But now I'm John
And so dear friends
You just have to carry on
The dream is over.[16]

Plain silly, of course. The notion that anyone's experience with "the dream" entitles him to this sort of infantile doverbeachism is absurd. John Lennon and Yoko Ono do *not* alone constitute reality—even in the poem itself one finds other bits of reality contradicting the claim: "concepts," "pain," "dear friends," and—presumably—poems and songs and the effort to compose them.

And yet when these feeble words come to us through the music, a new kind of evidence is added. Or rather, since the words were probably never intended to stand alone, we should say that separating them from the music has destroyed their best claim to be taken seriously. As musical lament the verse becomes, for me, moving (as for that same daughter who "yesterday" wept with me over the B-minor Mass), though considerably below Lennon's best. Whether or not we agree with an expressed code, any successful rendition of it places it among the

16. John Lennon, song in record album entitled *John Lennon and the Plastic Band*, Apple Records, 1970–71.

174

artistically viable attitudes. We thus learn from the artistic realization of even such a slight work as this something we would not otherwise know.

Of course it is hard to say precisely what that learning is, which is why critics have found it comfortable to pretend that it is not there. It is difficult to decide whether the proof is ethical (a fellow creature who is admirable because of his artistic skill seems to recommend this attitude with that skill, and I must therefore take it seriously because I must take *him* seriously); or emotional (I find myself moved by the expression of these words, so there must be something here that goes beyond the surface inanity). What has seemed clear to modern critics is that the proof is not logical or substantive in any usual sense. But that surely depends on what we take the substantive case to be. If we shift the emphasis from the absurd explicit statement "I just believe in me, Yoko and me" to the more plausible "You just have to carry on / The dream is over," then even the most case-hardened cynic might have to agree that to "carry on" by writing a good song about how it feels when "the dream is over" constitutes a kind of evidence for the value and possibility of carrying on.

But we needn't go that far if, as I have claimed, we must take ethical and emotional proofs as seriously as any other. Once I have really heard this song, once I have let it work in me, I cannot totally discount it when I make up my mind about what life is like in our time or how one should act when this or that dream is over. Indeed, it has already done part of the job of making up my mind, of *making* my mind, as soon as I have heard it.

Such proving does not require literal song. The music of poetry can provide it too. The doctrines of Ezra Pound's "An Immorality," for example, seem to me almost as absurd as John Lennon's:

> Sing we for love and idleness,
> Naught else is worth the having.
>
> Though I have been in many a land,
> There is naught else in living.
>
> And I would rather have my sweet,
> Though rose-leaves die of grieving,
>
> Than do high deeds in Hungary
> To pass all men's believing.

Just plain false, obviously. There is much else in living; for one thing, poetry is worth the having, even for the speaker. What would Pound say about song or string quartets or prayers of thanksgiving for convalescence or a sound monetary system? A crazy doctrine, appealing

175

*as* doctrine, presumably, only to those who have been annoyed by the opposing oversimplifications of the puritan work ethic.

But somehow the absurdity is removed, or at least made fairly unimportant, when we find the speaker dancing the attitude and dancing it so well. This is surely a genuine way of believing, one must conclude, and the question of what is really worth the having becomes a richer one than it would have been if the same doctrine were offered only in nonmusical terms. The poem raises "love and idleness" in the scale of things worth the having—especially if we count it as in itself a splendid piece of "idleness."

What the poem proves is thus not precisely what it says, and it still seems to me at best a tiny one–thirty-secondths of a truth; perhaps if Pound could write me a great epic or tragedy or satire or comedy performing the same attitude, and take me with him as thoroughly throughout as he does in his short poem, I would be even more shaken in my confidence that the attitude is in itself a bit silly. But of course I don't believe he could do so: the attitude is not capable of surviving the powerful criticism that trying to write a sustained work would provide. In short, the very capacity of an attitude to get itself danced beautifully by a fine artist says something, though it is never easy to determine how much, about the validity of that attitude.

Needless to say, two attitudes that seem contradictory when stated literally can both be "proved"—that is, tested—in this way. Good reasons here do not eliminate conflict, any more than they do in politics, where as we have seen they can yield warrantable assertions in support of what look like, and may actually be, opposing sides. No doubt this is one reason why noncognitive theories of art have seemed so plausible. If the hawk wrote an ode to the joys of sparrow hunting, it could be plausible, but it is surely safer to deny it cognitive value, since the sparrow might compose an equally plausible lyric of suffering.

In granting a kind of cognitive status to the reasons of art, I have opened up issues that I certainly cannot settle here. But I cannot dodge the ultimate issue of whether there is genuine contradiction between works that dance the attitude of total nihilism and works that openly affirm. Many modernists have felt driven by the ultimate absurdity of things to a deliberate pursuit of what does not make sense. Facing the same facts we now face—a world of seemingly contradictory artistic affirmations—they have come to the obvious conclusion that meaninglessness reigns.

But there is one curious limit to the contradictions of artistic reasons that such positions ignore. Consider again the song by Lennon. If it is taken as affirming that the only reality is "Yoko and me," then it is contradicted by any poem that affirms any other reality—including, I suppose, any other couple placing themselves at the solipsistic center. But we concluded that the *song,* in contrast to the *statement,* affirmed that when all other beliefs and dreams fail, "you just have to carry on," as indeed the song itself does carry on. The contradictory of this argument would be a song "concluding" that when all beliefs and dreams fail, you should *not* carry on but give up. But such a belief could not be presented with full coherence in any work of art, because the carrying on of the work itself would always be an open inconsistency. When the would-be nihilist tries to strengthen his argument by weakening his work, turning it into an incoherent bleat, he of course weakens his argument *for us,* because he demonstrates that this attitude somehow doesn't dance well.

Samuel Beckett, for example, has gone about as far as anyone can go in trying to express this ultimate meaninglessness of all activity, including the activity of trying to express meaninglessness, and he has tried to make his works imitate in their very form the chaotic feel of meaninglessness. But insofar as they work for us, they undercut his point—a fact that is not something he has to learn from us: he has stated the problem again and again. In recent years he has been driven by the logic of the case into shorter and shorter works, and lately into what seems to me a tragic near-silence—tragic because the protagonist has chosen a self-destructive fate due to an error of judgment.[17]

Since all art finally affirms something, if only its own value, some attitudes thus dance better than others. As Camus says in *The Rebel,*

In every [artistic] rebellion is to be found the metaphysical demand for unity, the impossibility of capturing it, and the construction of a substitute universe. Rebellion, from this point of view, is a fabricator of universes. . . . The revolutionary spirit, born of total negation, instinctively felt that, as well as refusal, there was also consent to be found in art. . . . No form of art can survive on total denial alone. . . . There is no art that has no signification."[18]

17. The "fallacy of imitative form" was first unmasked, I think, by Yvor Winters—perhaps too aggressively. H. Porter Abbott has discussed Beckett under this concept, trying to remove the blame that the term implies (*The Fiction of Samuel Beckett* [Berkeley, 1973]). See my *A Rhetoric of Irony* (Chicago, 1974), chap. 9.

18. *The Rebel: An Essay on Man in Revolt,* trans. Anthony Bower, (New York, 1956), pp. 254–58. Camus' discussion of what the rebel affirms in revolting often sounds very much like a "rhetoric of assent": "It is for the sake of everyone in the world that the slave asserts himself when he comes to the conclusion that a command has infringed on something in him which does not belong to him alone, but which is common ground where all men—even the man who

## 6. The Value of Some Moments of Life

As our experimental hero listened to the quartet, life was worth living; he can conclude from this that life can (sometimes) be worth living and that this fact-value can be communicated from one person to another.

At this point he does not claim to know that all life is worth living or that the universe is to be accepted or that the existence of God is proved. He is simply recognizing that in the act of dwelling in great art, he knows a kind of self-justifying moment that requires—so far as it goes—no further justification. Regardless of how things may look to him after the event when reflection (or the principles of systematic doubt) enter in, during the moments of reading or looking or listening, when the work is actually *working,* he can never doubt that life is worth living, any more than anyone has ever been able to doubt that life is worth living at the height of a love affair or during orgasm or in the heat of a good tennis match or when looking at a healthy first-born child for the first time.

It is true—again—that a good deal of modern literature has performed the attitude of despairing—many an admirable work, many an engrossing character has *said* that life is meaningless, that all is absurd. According to cognition 4 above, such dancings, when successful, prove at least that the attitude of despair is danceable, up to a point. But as we have just seen, it can be only up to a point. My answer to the problem of contradiction thus applies again here: insofar as the implied claim is that life is meaningless and therefore that nothing is worth doing, such works cannot dance them out completely, because the works themselves are offered as something worth doing; the reader who is transported into them never doubts for a moment, during the experience, that what he and the author are doing together is worth doing. The internal claim that *all* of life is meaningless is thus always self-contradictory in any realized work of art.

This "existential proof" of the value of some moments of life is not quite as trivial as it may at first seem. Think of how many moments of this kind of affirmation the world's art, in all ages and climes, offers to us. Surely the reasons for thinking that life can be (because it has so often been) worth living take on some weight as testimony (now that we have learned to accept testimony as having weight) against

---

insults and oppresses him—have a natural community. . . . When he rebels, a man identifies himself with other men and so surpasses himself, and from this point of view human solidarity is metaphysical" (pp. 16–17).

those who would claim that it is not, or against ourselves when we are in despair.

It might be replied that this argument is simply a restatement of what everyone knows, that life can sometimes be pleasant to some people. Ivan Karamazov, in arguing with Alyosha about the meaninglessness of life, admits that when we are young and full of sap, our pleasure in the "little sticky leaves" makes life feel worth living, but the feeling is an illusion. According to his argument, temporary feelings, whether of joy or despair, cannot affect the essential truth which is that the world is a hideous fraud; the moments of joy are purchased at the cost of infinite suffering, and it is thus dishonest for someone who feels a momentary joy to pretend that it somehow is worth the torture of even one innocent child.

But the argument I am trying to make is not for joy as against pain, and it does not depend on whether one is at a given moment in bliss or anguish. Though I know from experience that it doesn't work very powerfully when offered to myself in a given moment of despair, the question is whether it *ought* to carry any weight at all, even in such moments. We are accustomed to think that whether a moral or metaphysical argument carries weight depends on whether it is persuasive to a particular person in a particular frame of mind. But I am suggesting that the question of whether life has value is a question of fact like any other, and that it is therefore not to be settled according to whether I happen to feel one way or another at this moment or in this decade. I cannot reasonably change my vote from mood to mood, because the fact is that the weight of testimony is mainly on one side of the question. A great majority of the people I most admire—from anonymous African sculptors and musicians to those great egotistical monuments of Western culture like Beethoven or Dickens or Bertrand Russell—have offered me proofs that "to perform life" is possible and worthwhile, even when those proofs contain overt statements saying it is not. Their evidence cannot be shifted according to my moods, or even according to this or that cycle of the cultural stock market: now affirmation is in, now negation.

The evidence is of course not uniform: many of my great witnesses have finally repudiated their testimony in suicide: Virginia Woolf tells me, in her books, that to create and share such performances is valuable, but then she seems to retract her affirmation with suicide. Like everyone else, I am threatened by any act of suicide (except perhaps those which are, like some in Japan, made meaningful by cultural norms which they affirm). When Sylvia Plath or John Berryman or F. O. Matthiessen deliberately leave us, they can seem to say—and sometimes their final written notes do actually state—that the whole thing is intolerable.

Is it an act of disrespect or of supreme respect to reply to these suffering loved ones that their deaths can never mean any more than a local truth: this life has become intolerable, and therefore we know that life is sometimes intolerable? But we also know, from the artistic "remains," that even this life was often not just tolerable but danceable: these beautiful shared semitransparent envelopes—oh my lovely tortured one—cannot be taken back. I know what life can be—not the lives *in* your books but the life *of* your books—because you and your kind have taught me.

If my point here has any validity at all, it will apply to every form of human activity undertaken for its own sake and not for some further good that it will lead to: sharing a joke or piece of "useless" gossip; growing flowers or children or flower children; playing and listening to rock music or jazz or string quartets; discussing whether life has meaning; arguing that it has none; working for practical goals, provided the work is found rewarding in itself. I cannot quite understand why the existence of such moments at every moment of the world's history and in overwhelming numbers should not be thought to carry weight when we are discussing the meaning of life; if the fact of great misery in the world, simultaneous to these moments of joy, is to count in our view of the whole—and it must—surely it is negatively sentimental to ignore the fact of epidemic creativity.[19]

### Stories as Reasons: Explicit Messages

None of this so far—except to some degree cognition 5—depends on any explicit doctrinal content of a work. All works that succeed in any degree, affirmative and negative, true and false, profound and trivial, demonstrate to our ingenuous one at least these six kinds of good reasons that, without art, he would lack or would grasp only in radically

19. A celebrated author interviewed recently by Studs Terkel said, "I can't think of a single good thing that has happened in America in the last ten years." And the interviewer sat there wringing his hands, instead of asking the obvious question, "Including the writing of your books, and their popular response?"

One of the more delicious comedies of the literature of negation is the air it oftens conveys of blithe confidence in the possibility and the importance of communication. Whole magazines are published to prove that nobody ever understands anybody and that true understanding consists in not trying for true understanding. And whole cadres of interpreters attack the notion of interpretation, assuming that their attack can be understood and that it's worth making. All seem to be saying, "Man is essentially alone. Do you not agree?" The old joke about the solipsist who tried to organize a discussion group of solipsists still applies.

different form. The many millions of us, for example, who suddenly found ourselves a few years ago singing the Beatles' "Yellow Submarine" could never have agreed on a single formula for the kind of bouncing communal affirmation we were engaged in. But the song *as shared* both depended on and affirmed at least these six kinds of knowing—all of them unique to man and potentially sharable by all men and women.

As we turn now to look, briefly, at what specific doctrines verbal art works assert, or actually try to prove, we come to more deceptive terrain. To what extent does Malcolm Lowry's *Under the Volcano,* say, give me good reasons for accepting what seems to be its author's unrelievedly bleak, despairing view of man's self-deceiving and inevitably deceived condition? Is there any sense in which *Ulysses* offers me reasons, beyond its mere imposing existence, for joining Mollie as she says "Yes, yes, yes" at the end? Does what happens in *War and Peace* give me any good reason for believing anything that is asserted in it about life, about war, about the elaborate historical doctrines Tolstoy offers? Or, to move to more trivial matters, can Bernard Shaw's *Pygmalion* give me any reason to take seriously what he argues that it was intended to? "But if the play makes the public aware that there are such people as phoneticians, and that they are among the most important people in England at present, it will serve its turn" (from the Preface).

The question I am raising is not whether our seriously held beliefs are necessarily involved in reading any verbal work, however pure. Most critics now would agree that they are.[20] Nor am I asking about the many "little" ways in which a verbal work can properly change my views, even for the most skeptical modernist. Every kind of argument that anyone could ever use in real life might be used in a narrative work, and it could presumably carry as much force one place as another. We can be taught fairly complicated scientific notions in a piece of science fiction, and Tolstoy's introductory essays in *War and Peace* on the theory of history carry at least as much weight, as argument, as when published separately. The question is, do they somehow carry more? *Should* they?

Perhaps no one would deny that narrative embodiment often does in fact strengthen persuasion. Plato warned against dramatizing heroes who embody false values; he knew that when we have fallen in love with a character, we tend (by a kind of ethical proof) to believe what he believes, to fear what he fears, and desire what he desires. There has

20. A point more generally accepted now than when I tried to argue it in *The Rhetoric of Fiction* (Chicago, 1961).

been a lot of critical talk in modern times arguing that to allow this effect is naive, but I doubt that anyone who reads seriously ever escapes it for long, whether in reading "true" works like histories or fictional works. And I know that my students and I discover again and again that we have succumbed to it, and gladly. Like Don Quixote imitating chivalric tasks and Emma Bovary imitating romantic heroines and my freshmen imitating Holden Caulfield and Siddhartha and Yossarian, I find myself trying on for size the attitudes urged upon me by Tolstoy and George Eliot and Faulkner and Bellow, and though my malleability decreases as I grow older, it is only when I haven't been *into* a book that I come out without being changed.

The question is, then, *should* I? It is no good arguing here, as I did in *The Rhetoric of Fiction,* that I can become temporarily a kind of "implied reader" whose beliefs match those of the "implied author," himself in turn a character who may or may not have any direct relationship to the real man who wrote the book. There my problem was how books get themselves read. Here the problem is, What should we let them do to us as we read them?

The answer cannot be as simple as most critics would make it. Troublesome as it is, one can only say, some literary proofs are good reasons and some are not. To make a general rule—either that no change of mind induced merely by vivid dramatic realization should be approved or allowed, or that I should be infinitely malleable— would be as useless as what the scientismist did in outlawing all but scientific proofs from rational discourse. We do in fact make innumerable discriminations when verbal narrative is present, just as we do when no overt verbal content is involved. When the airlines play Muzak tunes at me, to soothe my nerves and "argue" that all is well, I am properly persuaded only to believe that at least one piece of machinery is still functioning, even though the plane I am about to board may be on its last trip. It also tells me something about the airline's opinions of their customers. But even if they could play the *Grosse Fuge* for me, it could not possibly constitute a good reason for expecting a safe flight, though it might properly say something about the quality of life possible as one approaches the end. And similarly, quite precise discriminations matching literary "arguments" to appropriate conclusions are necessary if any of this talk is to make sense when we deal with ideas that works of art openly urge us to accept.

Thus everything depends once again on relating the right reasons to the right conclusions. Don Quixote misread both literature and life, but his mistake was not that he allowed the chivalric books to strengthen his desire to do good in the world. They misled him about *how* to, and about the possibilities in the world for enacting that commitment; with a little more literary sophistication he could have followed the canon's practice (bk. I, chap. 6), consigning some of the books (metaphorically!) to the fire, saving others for casual reading, and preserving some few as constant comparisons and guides. But the knowledge he lacked—though corrigible in experience and therefore genuine knowledge—is not reducible to rules or laws of evidence. It is in large part the kind of know-how that distinguishes the man effective in practical affairs from the bumbler—an art, not a science. But to say this is not, as modernism would say, to take it out of the cognitive domain. Even that part of this knowledge that must always remain tacit is nonetheless knowledge: it is really possible to misread a poem, even though there may be many good ways to avoid misreading.

To attempt to describe those ways would obviously be to write a whole art of criticism, a rhetoric of assent which would match proofs to conclusions, in all the arts, in a way that no one—not even Kenneth Burke—has been able to do. Each of us in fact constructs the fragments of such an art, implicitly and willy-nilly, as he goes through life deciding which artistic works to canonize, which to relegate to pastime, and which to "expurgate" or "ban." And we learn from the experience of many different attitudes the art of counterstatement, of seeking out or constructing ironic cross-lights that protect us from dogmatic or Quixotic errors: we believe in both Dickens and Dante, both the Gospels and Machiavelli, both Beethoven and Bartók, both *Hamlet* and *Rosenkranz and Guildenstern Are Dead.*

But with this obligatory bow to broadmindedness out of the way, I must face briefly the fact that a great deal of the world's narration takes overt stands on precisely the questions raised in these lectures. From Job and Prometheus through Lear and Faust to Molly Bloom and Moses Elkinah Herzog, troubled souls have been shouting and whispering overt *yeses* and *noes* and *maybes* at us. Critics have usually found some way of dealing with such dramatized assertions and denials —some, like Plato, making them the center of their critical task; many, like Aristotle, expelling them from the house of fiction but treating them separately under rhetoric or philosophy or politics. Modernism produced, by its nature as a doubting juggernaut, a new urgency of denial and assertion, and a new kind of problem for critics. As traditional affirmations collapsed, hallelujah choruses became harder and harder to write, and from the romantic period to the present, hundreds of artists have flung questions at the universe and received *yeses* and *noes* in response. In one of his last quartets (op. 135), Beethoven began the final movement with a harsh, interrogative rising melody inscribed

"Muss es sein?" ("must it be?") and went on to an attempt at an answer with a solid, vital affirmation: "Es *muss* sein!" Similar symphonic and poetic and pictorial Odes to Dejection and to Joy—very different in tone from earlier L'Allegro's and Il Penseroso's—have flooded every Western nation, and critics have found themselves retreating, in self-protection, to talk about the irrelevance of conceptual truth to true art.

But despite periodic efforts at objective and formalist criticism (the latest and probably the most extreme being some popular versions of the new criticism in the last three or four decades) many critics have felt impelled to talk about such "conclusions" as seriously as they would if they were found in scripture. But how do you talk about the shout of joyful affirmation, "Hurrah for [Alyosha] Karamazov," that concludes *The Brothers Karamazov,* or the whispered "No" to the universe that Ivan extracts from Alyosha earlier in the book? How do you deal, without falseness or pretentiousness or naïveté, with Ahab's angry quest for meaning behind the inscrutable facelessness of God's symbolic expression, that impersonal white whale? For some the answer is that you ignore the effect of the work on your own religious or metaphysical beliefs, and concentrate on "intrinsic" questions, such as, "Is the conclusion earned or simply asserted?" But even those who in their theory claim to be objectivists can usually be found sneaking their own convictions back into their judgments of the art. It turns out that for some critics, for whom all true art negates or destroys or shocks, every affirmative ending has been unearned—poor Dostoevsky, who persisted in attempting those Christian endings, but whose true convictions *must* have been on the side of Ivan as against Father Zossima and Alyosha, "since all perceptive men know, etc., etc." Melville *must* mean flatly to repudiate Billy Budd's "God bless Captain Vere." For others, there is equally dogmatic insistence on affirmation. For yet others, the greatest art includes both attitudes, but "earns its heavens by passing through hell first."

We can avoid these reductions by remembering that a work of art can give good reasons *only about whatever it is about*—or rather, *about what it is.* The Bible misled men for centuries because its narratives were treated as good reasons for literal conclusions about astronomy, geography, history, medicine, and what not. The higher criticism equally misled the world by turning every biblical question into a true-false test and ignoring the way in which these great stories give us good reasons for conclusions about questions like "Who am I?" or "What is life like for men who try to look beyond the surface awfulness?" or "How should I live in the world, when I see so much evil around me?"

To such questions, simple literal answers, like "Be cheerful, keep smiling" or "Curse God and die" are totally inadequate. Even the most elaborate literal statements, like Aristotle's *Ethics,* will always lack a kind of knowing which the great narratives convey. If I ask, "What is the meaning of life?" or "How should I live my life?" I will feel insulted if you tell me, in good scientism-ese, that my question "is meaningless, because no answer could properly be tested with the criterion of falsifiability," or in good absurdic, that I should stop asking silly questions and simply do as I wish: stop thinking and start living. I will also feel unedified if you give me a statistical study of how men in fact live their lives, how many die of this or that, how many enjoy this or that number of orgasms per week, and so on. But I will not feel insulted if your "answer" runs in any of the following ways:

"There was a man in the land of Uz, whose name was Job; and that man was perfect and upright, and one that feared God, and eschewed evil. . . ."

*And just listen to the terrible things that can happen to a man like that.*

"Happy families are all alike; every unhappy family is unhappy in its own way. Everything was in confusion in the Oblonsky's house. The wife had discovered that the husband was carrying on an intrigue with a French girl. . . ."

*And you would scarcely believe the terrible consequences of all that for Anna Karenina.*

"There was in the days of Herod, the king of Judea, a certain priest named Zacharias, of the course of Abia; and his wife was of the daughters of Aaron, and her name was Elisabeth. And they were both righteous before God, walking in all the commandments and ordinances of the Lord blameless."

*And I tell you all this* "That thou mightest know the certainty of those things wherein thou hast been instructed. . . ."

*There was once a king named Lear who gathered his three daughters and his court about him and said,* "Meantime we shall express our darker purpose. / Give me the map there. Know that we have divided / In three our kingdom; and 'tis our fast intent / To shake all cares and business from our age, / Conferring them on younger strengths while we / Unburthened crawl toward death. . . ."

*And what he learned about life's inner secrets was . . .*

"Mr. Hackett turned the corner and saw, in the failing light, at some little distance, his seat. It seemed to be occupied. This seat, the property very likely of the municipality, or of the public, was of course not his, but he thought of it as his. This was Mr. Hackett's attitude towards things that pleased him. He knew they were not his, but he thought of them as his. He knew they were not his, because they pleased him. . . . Mr. Hackett did not know whether he should go on, or whether he should turn back. Space was open on his right hand, and on his left hand, but he knew that he would never take advantage of this . . ."

*And life went on feeling that way to Mr. Hackett, as it feels to many of us now.*

These "answers" cannot be reduced to literal summary; thematic paraphrase of what the works teach always offends, no matter how sensitively done. It is not just that reduction to easy *yeses* and *noes* reduces their effect, though that is true. It is that any literal statement of message loses the special kind of knowing that the stories offer; even the most blatantly didactic fable by Aesop or allegory by Bunyan loses most of its value when we treat it as if it were a *statement* of its moral rather than a *living out* of how some problems of life can be represented.

We might think, for example, that what is wrong with literal discussions of the Christian Gospels is that they are oversimplified. Instead of reducing their purpose to the easy optimism of some popular American preachers, or the easy pessimism of some Calvinists, we should extract something more subtle: let us say, "The world is perpetually and simultaneously both accursed and redeemed, and there is no redemption except through immense suffering." Or, if that still seems too simple, let us construct the most sensitive book-length theological account we can imagine. Without denigrating such accounts, we can see that they lack something that men know together when, in answer to the question "What is the life of man?" they answer, "There was once in Bethlehem . . ." The only discursive treatises that seem to rival narrative in this kind of adequacy are those which, like Pascal's *Pensées,* make narrative heroes out of their authors. It is the passion of Pascal we read for, the arguments almost becoming characters in his drama.

But it is not only in respect to such large and unmanageable questions that narrative knowledge cannot be replaced with literal statement. J. H. Hexter has recently shown, in "The Rhetoric of History," that there are many quite simple historical questions that can only be answered with a story. Beginning with two questions that look alike— "How did the New York Yankees happen to win the American League pennant in 1939?" and "How did the New York Giants happen to play in the World Series in 1951?"—he shows that the historical truth of the second event, one of the great surprising reversals in the history of baseball, cannot be adequately portrayed without a dramatic narrative, while the first, a clear and easy victory all the way, can be shown fairly well with statistical tables. And he concludes that the rhetoric of narration provides one way of knowing that can never be achieved by "the rhetoric of science": "there may and indeed must be more than one style, one rhetoric, for communicating the things that are both knowable and communicable, and . . . the problem is not that of reducing all styles to one but of carefully investigating what style is appropriate to the particular problems of communication inherent in a particular kind of knowing."[21]

## SAYING YES AND NO IN LITERATURE

There are thus many kinds of questions that only narrative can provide a full answer to: What was it like down town today? How did it happen that the Persians invaded Greece? What is the truth about James Joyce? How can life be lived in the time of Buchenwald?

Most directly pertinent to these lectures are the many modern novels, plays, and poems that overtly grapple with affirmation and negation. Though critics have gone on telling them that they shouldn't, thousands of writers through these two centuries have dramatized the choice between doubt and belief or despair and hope or the nihilistic abyss and a world somehow redeemed. Many of these works can be fully understood only if the reader himself faces the offered choice seriously —they are, as Sheldon Sacks has reminded us, apologues more like *The Book of Job* or *Rasselas* than *Barchester Towers* or *Bleak House*.[22] To some readers the resulting arguments are necessarily heavy, unliterary; literature has no business aspiring to the condition of philosophy

21. *Doing History* (Bloomington, Ind., 1971), p. 76. That we know different things in different ways is now widely recognized, but Isaiah Berlin's plea, made as long ago as 1954, is still pertinent: "The 'logic' of various human studies has been insufficiently examined, and a convincing account of its varieties, with an adequate range of concrete examples drawn from actual practice, is much to be desired" (*Historical Inevitability* [London, 1954], p. 5). I owe the quotation to Charles Wegener.

22. *Fiction and the Shape of Belief*, (Berkeley, 1964), especially the first and last chapters. For the critic who wants to learn how novels work Sacks's claim that *beliefs* work in radically different ways, depending on whether they appear in satires, apologues, or actions, can be liberating: to judge *The Stranger* or *Catch-22* according to standards applicable to either *The Great Gatsby* or *Animal Farm* is an absurdity that can be matched in every book review section every week. Our interest here, however, is still in whether I should allow a given work to change my mind, and for this question the sharp distinction among kinds of work becomes relatively unimportant. A work like *Tom Jones* that Sacks would call an action might very well be, in our terms, more effectively didactic than even the best apologue, because no reader could resist its blandishments; in our view every art work fights for our allegiance—though often with no visible resistance—and the works that do so with open talk about beliefs are only a special case of all narrative argument.

187

or scripture. When James Purdy, for example, wrote a play called *Cracks,* raising explicit questions about the meaning of life, reviewers were generally hostile or uncomprehending. They were baffled because the play cannot even be talked about unless one recognizes that it sets out to ask the question, "Why should we go through the pain of giving birth if it's all going to come to . . . nothing?" and moves toward an affirmative answer that cannot be reduced to literal statement but that is, nevertheless, approached by literal statement within the play: "The world does not come to an end, no matter how great the pain or loss." But they had no vocabulary for dealing with a literature that aspires to be scripture.

It is true that such open-faced statements can be badly done. There are too many novels and movies and poems which seem written to a simple program—either to be the "most shocking picture of the modern condition" or "to show that there *is* hope after all." But this is just to say that we need a criticism that can explain why some cursings of God and shouts of hallelujah succeed and some fail.[23] Such a criticism will not be found in the modernist dodge of divorcing technique or form from "content" and seeing all the art in the former.

One could discuss here a whole host of recent authors, men and women who have tried to cope with the threat of emptiness and negation by writing a kind of secular scripture, demonstrating that it is possible to live for morality or love or art or politics or new religions or revivals of old. For me this postmodern catalog would begin with Albert

23. There have been innumerable critical works about "the literature of despair" and the "literature of faith." I have found especially interesting—though from radically contrasting points of view—J. Hillis Miller, *The Disappearance of God* (Cambridge, Mass., 1963); Robert Martin Adams, *Nil: Episodes in the Literary Conquest of Void During the Nineteenth Century* (New York, 1966); and works by some modern "literary theologians," for example, Nathan A. Scott, *Adversity and Grace* (Chicago, 1968), and *The Wild Prayer of Longing* (New Haven, Conn., 1971); and Amos Wilder, *The New Voice* (New York, 1969). None of these is quite what our present inquiry requires: a rhetoric of art that would rehearse the ways in which artists marshall the "available means of persuasion." Frank Kermode's *The Sense of an Ending* (New York, 1967), a wonderfully stimulating little book, stops short of giving us any way to discriminate among the various "truths about endings" offered by the apocalyptic and millenarian works he describes. How do we decide whether a particular vision of *the end* should be attended to? Kermode does not stay for an answer. John Holloway's *The Victorian Sage* (London, 1953) is a model that might well be pursued in dealing with later authors and with romantic and other Victorian "sages," including novelists and poets, though I would hope for a somewhat richer repertory of reasons than Holloway allowed himself to pursue. The question is, when is a narrative sage a sage and when is he a phony, and how do we decide? Even that fine little book, *The Rhetoric of Fiction,* provides slight help here.

Camus; in my thirties, his portraits of how to "affirm rebellion" sounded in my soul like scripture. Or one could move forward to the more recent Catholic revelations of Flannery O'Connor or W. H. Auden; Protestant explorations of John Updike or Joyce Cary; what might be called Platonic discoveries of William Gaddis (in *The Recognitions,* a sadly neglected novel); the Hebraic rediscoveries in works like Schwarz-Bart's *The Last of the Just* and Malamud's *The Assistant*; or the philosophical, nonsectarian celebrations by Bellow in *Herzog* and *Mr. Sammler's Planet.* In all of these authors the pain of the world is faced so honestly that many readers have misread and attacked them as essentially negative. Words like revelation or celebration disguise the tentativeness, the air of almost embarrassed irony that all of these authors feel they must take when saying to the world, "I do not, cannot accept your superficial despairings about the modernist denuding, because I know some truths that go beyond modernism."

Listen for a moment to the ironic tone of W. H. Auden in a marvelous poem, "The Cave of Nakedness" (part of a long series, *Thanksgiving for a Habitat*), as he talks of the Christian truths he turns to, in his celibate bed, preparing for sleep:

> we retain the right to choose
> our sacred image. (That I often start with sundry
> splendours at sundry times greened after, but always end
> aware of one, the same one, may be of no importance,
> but I hope it is.) . . .
> When I disband from the world,
> and entrust my future to the Gospel Makers,
> I need not fear (not in neutral Austria) being called for
> in the waist of the night by deaf agents, never
> to be heard of on earth again: the assaults I would be spared
> are none of them princely—fire, nightmare, insomnia's
> Vision of Hell, when Nature's wholesome genial fabric
> lies utterly discussed and from a sullen vague
> wafts a contagious stench, her adamant minerals
> all corrupt, each life a worthless iteration
> of the general loathing (to know that, probably,
> its cause is chemical can degrade the panic,
> not stint it). As a rule, with pills to help them, the Holy Four
> exempt my nights from nuisance, and even wake me
> when I would be woken, when, audible here and there
> in the half-dark, members of an avian orchestra
> are already softly noodling, limbering up for
> an overture at sunrise, their effort to express
> in the old convention they inherit that joy in beginning

for which our species was created, and declare it
good.
    We may not be obliged—though it is mannerly—to bless
the Trinity that we are corporal contraptions,
but only a villain will omit to thank Our Lady or
her henwife, Dame Kind, as he, she, or both ensemble
emerge from a private cavity to be reborn,
reneighboured in the Country of Consideration.

Auden's faith is, one suspects, considerably firmer than Pascal's, his Hell of despair certainly no more threatening. But he knows who *we* are, we modernists who know all about a Nature that has been thoroughly "discussed"—analyzed into least chemical parts; every mood, every prayer explicable; every *yea* explained, or explained away. It is as if he must at every point show himself at least as sophisticated as we are—before he can tentatively, smilingly confess that every night and morning he reads the Bible and prays to the one God, in orthodox Trinitarian form, and shyly talks of taking joy in the creation.

You will have noticed how much I myself am troubled by this same awareness, talking about assent to a crowd of sophisticated modernists who, like Samuel Beckett's "unnamable" characters, know that every affirmation and negation can be "invalidated as uttered or sooner or later."[24] Again and again I have caught myself trying to prove to you that I know as much about pain and despair (and about logical analysis and skeptical doubt) as the toughest of you.

So it is that, as I turn now to my final literary example of yea-saying, I am fearful that I will make it seem sentimental in summary, just another example of normanvincentpealism.

How can it make sense to assent to a world, or to any community within that world, when it contains the various holocausts of human history? No literal list of reasons can answer that question—it is as resistant to good reasons of the scientific kind as was Job's lament. To tell the anguished questioner to cheer up because of such and such reasons will always seem somehow impertinent. Even subtle theodicies like Leibniz's seem always vulnerable to the kind of narrative "disproof" offered by Voltaire in *Candide*: now here's a horror, and here's another, and another—do you mean to argue that we can or should assent to *all that*?[25]

24. *The Unnamable* (New York, 1958), p. 1.
25. As bare fact, lists of horrors carry no more weight—though no less—than lists of joys. Each is clearly sentimental if offered as *the* answer to what life is or how it feels. But for many moderns it has seemed not sentimental but tough-minded to assert that disasters are the truth, joys but momentary deception. The position is unanswerable if we think primarily in terms of the future, and if we

But by the same token, crude nihilisms are vulnerable to another kind of narrative disproof—the kind offered by *Paradise Lost* or *The Brothers Karamazov*.[26] To justify the ways of God to man is a subtle business, calling for something more than an exhortation to good cheer, and it is thus not surprising that the best responses in this century to our peculiarly threatening holocausts have been in literary forms that allow evil a "fair hearing."

Among the most moving, for me, have been novels by Jews attempting to find a meaning in Auschwitz—an event that is obviously "unthinkable," "meaningless," "a proof of life's absurdity." How can André Schwarz-Bart and Bernard Malamud and all those others go on writing about such events as if life mattered?

Consider *The Gates of the Forest* by Elie Wiesel.[27] The hero, Gregor, a Hungarian who has endured every imaginable horror in the Nazis' final solution, finds himself, for no discoverable reason, escaped from the holocaust and living in Brooklyn, living in total despair. But the congregation of *hasidim*—that curious fundamentalist Jewish sect to which Gregor has all his life belonged—does not share his despair. They can sing, they can dance—as if nothing had happened. They still expect the Savior who will somehow redeem all the horror. "They sang; and the song gave them life and caused the sap to well up in them and bind them together. Ten times, fifty times, they repeated the same phrase, taken from the Psalms . . . and every time the fire would be renewed again with primordial passion: yes, once God and man were one, then their unity was broken; ever since they have sought each other, pursued each other, and before each other have proclaimed themselves invincible. As long as the song and dance go on, they are."

---

consider death simply a disaster: all men end in disaster. But neither of these views is as self-evident as modernism has taught.

26. Modernists have had to assume that Dostoevsky was more successful in his negative portrayals than in his Christian answers: See for example Peter M. Axthelm, *The Modern Confessional Novel* (New Haven, 1967): "It is characteristic of Dostoevsky and of all modern confessional novelists that the perception achieved by the hero remains ambiguous and elusive, far from the Christian ideal of total absolution and redemption. It is interesting that Dostoevsky's closest approach to such a redemptive vision, the epilogue of *Crime and Punishment,* produces the weakest section of that brilliantly sustained work. Rahv seems justified in his assertion that the epilogue's 'hope and belief play havoc with the imaginative logic of the work.' Ultimately, we must reject the conclusions of that unfortunate addition" (p. 33). Mr. Axthelm, who is trying to move beyond modernist rebellion to an art that will create realities, is mild compared with earlier denigrators of Dostoevsky's Christian values.

27. Trans. Frances Frenaye (New York, 1966).

But "after midnight something unexpected occurred." The rabbi, who has noticed Gregor's total failure to respond, suddenly stops, pales, brings his fist down on the table and asks, "Who can sing in Hungarian?" An old soldier, a bent, shrunken old man, is the only volunteer, and he is shy because the only song he knows is an obscene and blasphemous drinking song. The Rabbi orders him to sing it anyway. Soon they all join him, singing without words.

> The soul has no need of words to sing. The Rebbe glowed with pride and happiness. He had accomplished a miracle.
> Gregor ceased to struggle. He looked on, listened, and opened himself. The song went through him and transported him. . . . So miracles existed.
> The crowd was possessed by joy, a pure joy that every moment made richer, dense and bright. The voices had long ceased to sing; the song was carried now on its own wings, raising breasts, lighting faces, summoning ecstasy, and giving hearts faith. Gregor's lips moved, wishing to sing, to taste joy, to declare that it is man's ally and not his mirage.

(I am aware that out of context and in translation such a passage will strike some of you as unbearably sentimental. But I ask you to ask yourselves why, if it pronounced flat negations in precisely the same style, you would not find that sentimental, too?)

The power of such a wrenching book to make us long for Gregor's final assent is immense, and of course in longing for his assent we are ourselves assenting: it is "wrong" for him to despair, it will be good if he can move beyond despair.

We are made to see that Gregor cannot, yet, give the full assent that the congregation demands. It is not until after further struggle that he can come to his final prayer, reciting "the solemn affirmation, filled with grandeur and serenity. . . . He recited it slowly, concentrating on every sentence, every word, every syllable of praise." The "argument" is complete only because that final affirmation contains within it—as my skeletal account cannot—Gregor's own awareness that Gregor and Wiesel know all that can be said on "the other side." Whether we can ourselves utter a prayer of affirmation, Wiesel's probing moves us irresistibly in that direction, because we find its reasoning good. Unless, of course, like some reviewers, we find it "a tract, not a novel."

### THE HABIT OF NEGATIVE RHETORIC

A recent anthology is called *Anti-Story* (1971). The table of contents runs like this: "Against Mimesis. Against 'Reality.' Against Event.

Against Subject. Against the Middle Range of Experience. Against Analysis. Against Meaning. Against Scale."

At first I thought, naturally enough, that perhaps the editor, Philip Stevick, was trying to say no to something. But then I noticed that every section had a subhead, like this: "Fiction about fiction. The uses of fantasy. The primacy of voice. Fiction in search of something to be about. New forms of extremity. The phenomenal world. Forms of the absurd. The minimal story."

Clearly he could have edited exactly the same anthology under some such heading as "The New Story." With the titles and subtitles reversed, the whole surface would then become affirmative, not in the sense of being optimistic about the world but announcing a program, affirming possibilities.

*"The time has come,"* the title page of another recent book reads, *"to say the things that need to be said about* [that is, *against*] *campus violence, the tyranny of a minority, the crusade of the spoiled children, the parental abdication of responsibility, and the lack of courage, integrity, and wisdom on the part of our educational leaders,* by K. Ross Toole who wrote the famous 'angry' letter that was read by 50,000,000 Americans." Is Toole a yea-sayer or a nay-sayer?

There is a sense, then, in which affirming and denying are rhetorically interchangeable. Every protest implies an affirmative ground for protest; every affirmation implies many negations. (The very word protest at one time meant "attest," as in the expression "I protest my faith in the Lord Jesus Christ.") Illegal protests can be organized in the name of affirming law and order, and faith in justice can be expressed in cries for anarchy. In recent decades the language of affirmation has seemed to be monopolized by "square" or "straight" culture; too many Pollyannas have exhorted us to be cheerful in order to influence people and to keep smiling because it's good business. The easiest way to combat such shoddy goods has been to take a negative pose, with the result that most of the terms available to critics of "mindless America" are, like *mindless,* negative. The popular antithesis of "the establishment" and the "counterculture" suggests that affirmative stands are all on the side of the square or straight culture. Long lists of negative terms are invented to describe the protest-culture; they are seen as *against,* not *for,* as attacking law and order, not asserting justice (or equality), as destroying institutions, not trying to build new ones, as revolutionaries, not as preservers or conservers of values that are negated by present society. The protestors play into this simple yes-no dialectic by the terms they choose for themselves, by the destructive means some

of them use, and by the terms they use to describe society: to read protest literature is to hear nothing but bad about society and institutions;
everything from the family to the university to the law, all traditions,
all customs, are bad because they inhibit man's natural freedom and
creativity. A tactic is good if it has shock value to the enemy, often in
disregard of whether anyone is converted to our side by the shock.
"Reason" is bad because it destroys spontaneity and defends the "mili-
tary-industrial complex." Stability, order, the past are bad; movement,
change, rejection, seeing through accepted truths are good.

Obviously it would get us nowhere simply to substitute a habit
of yea-saying for this habitual protest. But it is clearly implicit in all I
have said that there is a sense in which assent and affirmation are more
fundamental than negation, in both logic and experience. Any of you
who have a two-year-old or seventeen-year-old child may want to deny
this hotly; the *noes* flow fast at a given age. But from birth our primary
movement is toward the world, to grasp it, assenting to and taking in
other selves, new truths, the whole world. Our withdrawals and rejections come always in the light of some affirmation that has been denied
or that is being threatened.[28] If man is essentially a rhetorical animal,
his essential human act is that of making himself into a self, in symbolic communion with his fellows; that is, each of us makes himself or
herself by assenting to and incorporating whoever and whatever represents life at its most immediate and persuasive. Our negatives are
learned as we discover violations of our affirmings.[29]

28. It seems indeed that the mind at birth is already "programmed" to grasp
at and take in the world as meaning, as if on the tacit assumption that "things will
make sense for me if I work to see the sense." One semipopular summary of research on new-born babies describes them as "hypothesis-making and -testing
creatures," creatures who cannot rest until they make sense out of whatever data
comes their way. (See T. G. R. Bower, "Early Learning and Behaviour," *TLS*,
May 7, 1971, pp. 523–24; "The Object in the World of the Infant," *Scientific
American* (October 1971), pp. 30–38; and Jerome Kagan, "Do Infants Think,"
*Scientific American* (March 1972), pp. 74–83.

The many recent discussions of creativity as an inherent drive and of novelty
as an essential need can be interpreted variously, but one thing they seem to mean
is that human beings naturally say yes to whatever novelty offers itself to them
with plausibility; to say no and stand pat is a learned and subordinate though in-
dispensable response. See Frank Barron, *Creative Person and Creative Process*
(New York, 1969), and the bibliography in D. W. Fiske and S. R. Maddi, *Func-
tions of Varied Experience* (Homewood, Ill., 1961).

29. Richard B. Gregg has argued that one chief function served by protestors
and their rhetoric is the "ego-function." Citing the many allusions by protestors
to their struggle for person-hood, and to society's destruction of their true selves,
he concludes that they are proclaiming "their perceptions of ego-deprivation
and their need for self-affirmation" ("The Ego-Function of the Rhetoric of Pro-

## The Habit of Negative Rhetoric

Western culture has from its beginnings developed heroes and saints who have dared to say no: Prometheus defying the gods, Christians saying no to their persecutors, the Protestants saying no to the Catholics, modern scientific saints of scientism saying no to the authority-bound errors of their ancestors, Faust saying no to obedience, artists saying no to tradition, political revolutionaries saying no to various ancient regimes, women saying no to men, blacks saying no to whites, the existentialist rebel saying no to the universe. I don't need to tell you that some of the noblest as well as some of the basest moments in man's history are found in such negations. But we tend to forget that these mythic moments can be treated as either negations or affirmations. All of these saints were saying yes to something. What is more, the truth is not always on the side of the rebel, in spite of what recent rhetoric would tell us; simply to say no when everyone else is saying no is just another form of group compliance, a disguised and therefore feeble yes, and it no more proves moral strength than saying "Fuck you" to an opponent makes one a master of repartee.

We begin to touch here on the edges of religious and metaphysical questions that I have previously skirted. The philosophy of good reasons can be pursued by men of many different faiths, including, I think, by those who deny the existence of God—which is to say, those who affirm some belief that such existence would seem to contradict. But here metaphysical questions enter willy-nilly. Which act *is* prior in "the nature of things," assent or denial? To say yes to the universe is a very different act than to shout no, shaking one's fist in the face of God, as Dr. Rieux does in Camus' *The Plague*. To say yes believing that one is in harmony with a primal yes is very different from even the most courageous yes uttered against the grain of an absurd universe.

We must finally ask ourselves whether a creature made through

---

test," *Philosophy and Rhetoric,* Spring 1971, p. 81). He quotes a manifesto for SCUM, the Society for Cutting Up Men: "the male is a biological accident . . . an incomplete female, a walking abortion. . . . To be male is to be deficient, emotionally limited; maleness is a deficiency disease and males are emotionally crippled" (p. 83). Such negative talk, he is surely right in saying, is equally well described as a disguised affirmation of contrary values. But I think it oversimplifies the case to say as he does that it is in the service of ego-building, almost as if each female was the kind of atomic self I have described, using "women's lib talk" as a kind of private, masturbative ego-trip. Surely the excitement in such statements is a communal excitement: "*We* are somebody. You speak to me of our common enemy, and I assent, I go along with you: we build our egos *together* as we tear men to pieces." For a less sympathetic account of the rhetoric and politics of "consciousness building," see Robert Nisbet, "Radicalism as Therapy," *Encounter,* March 1972, pp. 53–64.

195

assent, a rational animal—that is, a man who can find his "self" only through his communal building of selves, who can find his life, in fact, only by losing himself back into the society of selves that made him— whether such a man can finally withhold assent to the nature of things. The great original choice between being and nothingness was, and eternally is, a fantastic, incomprehensible act of assent rather than de- nial: the universe is, nothingness is not. Whether we choose to call it a choice or not will depend on our religious or philosophical convic- tions, but even the most committed atheist must face, it seems to me, the curious sense in which he cannot avoid complicity in that primal act of affirmation. He can of course choose, as did Kirillov in Dostoev- sky's *The Possessed,* to destroy himself "on principle," but in doing so he cannot escape the domination of the universe, of the way things are. The very efficacy of his chosen weapon will depend on laws he did not make and that are unchangeable by his act. The rightness or wrongness of his act is similarly out of his hands, however "relative" it may be to his particular situation. Thus one cannot escape "the Process" without affirming it. Even to attack it as a trap, one must use a language of real values and imply the primacy of what is attacked.

As Kenneth Burke's Satan puts it in a witty dialogue between God and Satan at the end of *The Rhetoric of Religion*: "In the purely formal sense, then, a person is an entity that can answer yes or no to a com- mand (which in turn implies the distinction between the yes of obedi- ence and the no of disobedience)."[30] Persons find themselves in a uni- verse that is already made and that issues its commands. The assertions have been laid down; the primal assent has been uttered. But as per- sons, they somehow mysteriously can say no, even to truth, and they must choose between the spurious freedom of asserting falsehood and the seeming slavery of assenting to the commands of supreme nature. With their gift of symbolicity, they are divided from the rest of animal creation by the capacity to *say* no—not just in the brute way in which a mule says no by balking, but by constructing elaborate symbolic structures, some of which will belie what they know to be true. Then other men may have to put their *yeses* in the form of denials of these false denials—as I have been putting my "heresies" against the dogmas of modernism. Thus the essential form of human thought and action is ac- ceptance of the proffered gifts while recognizing that in them there are mysterious traps. As the great story has it, man could originally trust every gift offered him by the world except one: the offer of the chance to disobey, to say no and thus to know good and evil. But it was im- possible to live without saying no. The Great Con Man entered the

30. (Boston, 1961), p. 281.

196

picture and taught us all, permanently, that a sucker is born every minute; that life never gives a sucker an even break; that there are, indeed, wooden nickels; that the man who says yes to everything, even to snakes in the garden, ends up being taken in, taken into the circles of hell rather than enfolded in Abraham's bosom.

As Satan continues in Burke's dialogue:

> Could I ask, next: Is there some generative principle in their [mankind's] kind of language, some formal first from which its entire logic might be derived?
>
> The Lord: Indeed there is. We've already considered it somewhat. It's the principle that you would use as your particular sign, were you to be in theory rescinded from the sum total of our identity.
>
> Satan: Milord, the negative! . . .
>
> The Lord: That's it, my lad. And there is a sense in which there are the makings of division even here among *us*. For even pure identity implies the negation of non-identity. So you're always lurking there, my lad, implicitly a No without its Yes, even though (as seen from another angle) the two imply each other.
>
> Satan: Milord, pray do not chide me! Yet, for all my love of negativity, I grant that the negative cannot exist. Anything that exists must, by the same token, be positively what it is.
>
> The Lord: That will apply to *their* negative as well. It will be but a device of language, an *ens rationis* (p. 283).

But you can read the rest of that marvelous book for yourself. I find it significant that Burke felt impelled to move to a mythic form, at the end of his demonstration that the study of the logos as speech leads to faith in the Logos as ground of speech. Because it is in those moments when we move from arguments for or against literal conclusions and express our assents and denials in communal art that our inescapably assenting natures become clearest.

## COMMUNAL AFFIRMATION AND DENIAL

Let us imagine three entirely distinct rhetorical ages. In the first, men and women daily chant from a given celebratory scripture—a scripture that is, like all scripture, full of literal falsehoods about the nature of things, demonstrable errors about astronomy and biology, history and psychology. They join together, these people, every morning and chant the myth of their creation by a loving though mysteriously capricious and awesome and inaccessible Father. They then leave their religious service and move to their daily work, their daily joys and pains. Though they often encounter more pains than joys, they move confirmed in their being, as Martin Buber was fond of saying, by the communal act of saying yes to each other and the Source.

In the second age, inheritors of the first, error-ridden scripture has long since been analyzed and undermined by critical scholars. These people meet communally at most once a week, to hear sermons about how they *ought* to pay more attention to the old scriptures and ignore the vicious underminings of critical scholars. They are not really convinced. They leave church and chapel and face work on Monday morning, work in a society in the first full, exhilarating bloom of an industrial age. Daily they meet with their fellows in commerce, spending great energy in deceiving each other, but in the very deception enjoying a communal affirmation of the importance of what they are doing: they are saying yes to the future, to what Stravinsky once called "that little bastard myth," Progress; and all of their competing, whether moral or immoral, constructive or destructive, is justified because it moves toward a glorious yes somewhere off yonder. In the evenings they may gather together and read from the novels of Dickens, let us say, and they learn, through weeping and laughing together, that all of the troubles which they know surround them, and the daily degradations they commit against each other through their competitions, are somehow transcended by a higher vision of man's affirmations: at least for some people, somewhere, things in fact work out well—in the future. They assent to Dickens' affirmations, even as they find themselves saying no to more and more of the affirmations found in their traditional scriptures.

In the third age the written scriptures have disappeared entirely from the lives of most men, and they have not been replaced by lay-scriptures like Dickens' novels. There is no longer even a semblance of ritual communal affirmation; instead we find three isolated groups, groups who daily say yes to each other only by saying no to the other two. In the first are the believers in scientism. Knowing that in the tools of science are the weapons of truth, they gather daily, in laboratories, history classes, conventions of literary scholars and of biblical exigetes, chanting their *yeses* to the five negative dogmas I have described. Since they see themselves as the last defenders of mind or reason in a world gone mad, their lives are by no means empty of meaning. They have their essential affirmation: "There *is* meaning, found through rigorous and self-sacrificial doubting; and I and my kind are prophets in its service. It is true that our service is mostly laying about us with our swords, destroying the giant weeds other men have planted in the garden of truth. But our faith is secure (even when we write articles to each other questioning it) because securely shared by those entitled to judge."

In the second group in this bronze age are the Philistines who worship daily at the shrine of commercial and industrial progress. Because the scientismists have told them that all values are simply personal preferences, they have faith in nothing but what their own group helps them to affirm: the value of keeping the machine going. They feel attacked from both flanks and they feel resentful and confused, but they do have each other and they do assent daily: every morning, hundreds of millions of them pull themselves out of bed, say their prayers to the God of Functioning by jogging or doing pushups. And they go out *and they function.* At night they watch TV, which gives them further group confirmation, sometimes, that the idols of the marketplace have not been utterly shattered. But they are not joyful—they are even less joyful than the worshipers of scientism. They believe that they *should* say yes, that life *should* be what they think their grandfathers thought it was, a glorious affirmation leading toward a future fulfillment. They are sure that they ought to be cheerful, because *The Reader's Digest* and *U.S. News and World Report* tell them that all is well, and that if you are not cheerful you cannot function, you cannot win friends and influence people, you cannot "succeed and grow rich through persuasion."[31] But meanwhile there are so many enemies to good cheer in the world, so many nay-sayers that must be put down. Just temporarily, for example, we, the affirmers of goodness and reasonableness, are having to kill off a fair body-count daily of wicked nay-sayers over there in Asia; admittedly to kill them is a kind of negation, and it feels somehow uncomfortable to have some of our own boys negated in the process. What is worse, on the left flank there are all the vicious nay-sayers of group three, telling us that we are wicked. Try as we will to read and view only positive things, we are besieged by the future-shocking literature (and even TV fare) provided by the members of group three, the prophets of doom and the purveyors of despair.

Members of group three, the irrationalists or romantics, gather daily to attest the virtue of saying no to the first two groups. Some of them say no by writing literature that Shouts No in Thunder. They produce exposés in the form of novels, plays, movies, and poems, exposés designed to épater those staggering Philistines one last time, to finish them off once and for all. Some of them write attacks on scientism or expose the ultimate doom to be produced by the ultimate engineering Philistine. They read each other's exposés in grief and misery and anger—because they know that the scientismists and Philistines are not really listening.

31. Title of a "rhetoric" displayed in the Notre Dame bookstore at the time of my lectures.

But still they have something: they affirm their own group, they have their religion, they assent to those few good people in the world who have agreed that to refuse assent and work for the great overthrowing, the great No, is the supreme virtue. Some of them finally decide that it is no longer possible to say no loud enough with words: only bombs and guns can state the true horrors of the world created by scientism and Philistine industrialism. But like those who attack in words, those who attack with bombs find that the attacks leave them with more enemies than they had before; the yea-sayers turn on them with ever more resounding and self-righteous *noes*. Soon the very vocabulary of virtue reverses itself; to say louder and louder *noes* to those who are saying no requires stronger and stronger infusions of negative rhetoric, and soon Eldridge Cleaver is praising Huey P. Newton as "the baddest mother-fucker I've ever seen!"

Other splinter parties try to fight scientism and Philistia with desperate *yeses* or less violent but equally desperate *noes*. Flower children poke daisies in gun barrels, turn on (yes!) in order to drop out (no!), rejecting a clear enemy, but being none too clear about what they are attempting to tune in to; they find, in fact, that they are finally as isolated as the traditional hermits who gave up on society and decided to save themselves alone: to try to be a flower child in a world judged crazy can only make one a "crazy." But it is surely significant that these crazies still travel for the most part in groups; they know that they must say yes to somebody.

I have deliberately suggested, quite misleadingly, that the third imaginary age is America today. But America is not divided sharply into three groups or five or twenty-one, and our future will no doubt contain many "consciousnesses" besides "consciousness III." We do move toward the myth, however, insofar as we exclude rational assent, assent with our minds, to institutions, causes, futures, reforms. Our intellectuals "speak truth to power," but, except for those who are said to have "sold out," they have too often forgotten to seek the truths *of* power; our scientists in surprising numbers reject the political order entirely, most recently in the form of repeated suggestions that governments turn over all scientific allocations to scientists who would be absolutely freed of political restraints on what they did with the money. And literary intellectuals often speak even more contemptuously of every "established" institution, affirming instead only the private intuitions of the irrational spirit.

We are a society groping for meaningful affirmation, for intellectually respectable assent. The old faiths seem shattered; men have been told again and again that they must either leap into faith blindly or abandon faith entirely; the mind doubts, the heart may—if it doesn't care about being a bit stupid—affirm. But we know what we know: affirmation, assent to any but the devil's camp is not going to be easy for any man with his eyes open—in the age of Belsen, Dresden, Hiroshima, Vietnam, and the thousands of daily horrors that some members of group three seem almost to enjoy recounting, such clear evidence do they provide about the truth of antitruth, the assertion of negation, the assent to total dissent.

Whatever the truth about this moment, I think that popular negation and affirmation (on both the political right and political left) are conducted on assumptions that are no longer tenable. The predominant mode intellectually and spiritually is shifting toward a postmodernism that may have transcended, at last, the shocks of negation that produced the modern temper. For surprising numbers the burden of proof has been reversed; we are now rejecting a form of rationalism that began with doubt and demanded explicit reasons for every belief and every allegiance. We must now learn to live in a world in which we begin with assent and in which the first question will therefore be, "Why not?" The shift will not be easy to live with for most of us, but it need not be finally threatening except to those who fear that there are no good reasons for saying no.

You may wonder where all this leads in practice. To adumbrate a rhetoric of assent butters no parsnips; nothing in such a rhetoric can in itself tell me how to live, how or whether to vote, what wars to support or protest against, what art works to "take in," or even how to read my daily paper. It gives me no true metaphysic, no religion, no political theory.[32] No one can predict where good reasons will lead as men in

32. A rhetoric of assent does lead, generally but firmly, to important political conclusions. Some of them will seem conservative, at least in our society, though in most societies in the world's history they would be revolutionary enough: traditions of free discourse, of respect for persons, of civil rights, of democratic process become defensible in this view not simply as traditions but as the very conditions for fulfilling man's life as we have defined it. But some of them are radical enough: for example, "capitalist" forms of production and distribution, as now defined, must be discarded, insofar as they depend on systematic deception. An economic system that rewards those who are most willing to corrupt the language in order to "take in" by deception will destroy all hope of a rhetoric that depends on honorable "taking in." As our political life is more and more conducted with the deceptive techniques borrowed from commercial advertising, politicians become less and less interested in an exchange of good reasons; voters become more and more cynical; exposés of corruption become more frequent and less effective; and finally, a point will be reached, if it has not already been passed,

particular rhetorical communities pursue them together; it is implicit in what I have said that no one person or group can ever occupy more than a segment of what must always be a shifting and largely unexplored terrain. The country of the reasonable will always be larger than any of us can traverse.

But there are two major conclusions which can provide bases for all practice. We have found, I think, without falling back on any traditional dogma or depending on any private revelations, a firm public value. And in a world where many claim that there are no shared values, it is no mean practical result to be able to point to one clear value you and I share, in full cognitive respectability: It is always good to maintain and improve the quality of our symbolic exchange with our fellow "selves"—to sharpen our symbolic powers so that we can understand

---

when there is insufficient public trust for democratic processes to work. [Note, August 1973: All of this was written long before the "advertisers" of Watergate were exposed.]

It is thus not just the advertising and political propaganda spawned by capitalism that must go: the whole "liberal" assumption that men are not accountable to their fellows for how they acquire and spend their private fortunes is untenable, if men are inherently accountable to their fellows. The individualism that produced economic liberalism was, as Marx taught, grotesquely destructive of the self and of society: both the exploiters and the exploited become, in such a system of "free enterprise," radically alienated from their "selves," and—what is the same thing—from each other.

I cannot pretend to know what form of economic system could replace the systematic daily corruption we now have, without falling into the systematic suppression of personal dignity that is exacted by the anti-individualism of "Marxist" societies. But it seems clearer and clearer that if we do not find some way to move beyond our inhumane economic system, we will lose what is left of our humane political traditions. This is an issue that goes beyond whether anyone is starving or whether there is economic justice. It is finally a matter of how men are induced by their institutions to treat each other in their daily lives. And it seems to me obvious that our present economic system induces viciousness, deception, and privatization to the point of psychosis. "Weak" forces like tradition, the church, the university, or natural altruism, if any, cannot combat this systematic destructiveness indefinitely.

I am not optimistic about our capacity to find alternatives to repressive forms of communalism; I am simply sure that if repressive capitalism is not radically transformed in democratic ways, it will be radically transformed in totalitarian ways. An open society living by a rhetoric of deception cannot long endure, but I'm afraid that its most likely direction is toward tyranny—that is, toward a complete abandonment of a rhetoric of assent. Needless to say, my own allegiance to such a rhetoric, and to the primal assent that it entails, does not depend on the precise amount of hope I can feel about the future of America, any more than it depends on any hope I can feel about my own future. In the long run, to paraphrase Keynes, we all must assent to death—a truth that leads beyond optimism or pessimism about political systems.

and be understood, "taking in" other selves and thus expanding our own. What we say matters, and it matters how we say it. But the rules for good discourse or clear thinking can no longer be confined to logical prose—we must take in the proofs of personal appeal and commitment, of art and myth and ritual. Though a whole new effort to "purify the language of the tribe" is implicit in the rhetoric of assent, we cannot know in advance of exploration whether the new vocabulary will include or exclude the gestures of yoga and the "nonsense" of Zen along with the propositional analyses of a Wittgenstein.

Perhaps even more important, in a world that talks of the threat of alienation and the loss of community, we have found a community that everyman can assent to: as old as Adam and as new as the morning's newscast, it is the community of those who want to discover good reasons together.

It is not a comfortable community nor a stable one. Even those who join it consciously and systematically, as we all do by talking together here, cannot provide a convenient list of gods and devils, friends and enemies. But at the same time it can give us some ease in whatever subcommunity we have already assented to.

Since rhetoricians are always happy to be bound to time and place, let me conclude with a local application. Like everyone else, I have been fascinated by—and strangely involved in—the recent rhetorical turmoil within the Roman Catholic Church. Some would say that your community is falling apart, torn not by the sharing of good reasons but by the loss of common standards. I suppose it will not help anyone very much for a rhetorician to come along and assert that the good Lord, the Logos in whom we have our being, is on both sides in such battles, that He is in the very process of assent and denial that seems to be tearing you apart.

I have met some rebels in the last four days here who talk as if salvatior will be found if only the Church can be dragged, kicking and screaming, into the twentieth century. Many have been eager to show me that my audiences here will be just as secularized, fully as modernist, as I could find at my own university. Whatever the reasons, good and bad, for turning from traditional Catholic dogmas, I would hope that the turning would not be simply a rerun of the triumph of modernism. To catch up with Bertrand Russell is not enough for a modern Catholic or rebel-Catholic—not if one of the things we know is that beliefs are not disproved simply by asking whether we can prove them in the modernist sense.

In short, it would seem to me a pity if, in fighting the dogmas of premodernism, you were to fall at this late date from the arms of the

Church into the thorns of modernism. I suppose that what I am asking, without being entirely sure that it is possible, is for a leap over modernist battlefields to the postmodern rediscovery that the primal symbolic act is saying yes to processes like the wrenching one in which you are engaged.

# Appendix A | "Self-evidently Absurd" Rhetoric
## Some Pronouncements Reprinted,
## without Comment, by the "Other Side"

TO:   Students and Faculty

FROM:   The Committee of the Council of The University of
Chicago

The following communication was received by registered mail on
the morning of Saturday, March 1, 1969. It is circulated
herewith for your information.

The Committee of the Council                    28 February 1969
c/o Prof. Edward Rosenheim, Jr.
5658 South Blackstone
Chicago, Illinois  60637

Sirs,

A mass meeting of the Committee of 500+ Against Disciplinary
Procedures yesterday passed the following resolution:

"The issue of discipline must be seen in context. The University's maintenance of its authority is designed to protect
what the Kalven Committee calls its 'mission.' This mission
is to produce the skills and specialties--and to inculcate the
political and social orientations--useful to the ruling groups
in society, and to maintain this orientation by any means necessary, including stamping out opposition within the University and oppressing the people of the community surrounding it.

"Students may expect to participate in shaping University policy only so long as they accept this mission, which is defined
by the ruling groups which in fact control the University. If
students do not accept this mission, ipso facto, they are in
opposition to the University's power and authority.

"We therefore demand:

1.  That the recent expulsions be rescinded.
2.  That all cases pending before the disciplinary com-
    mittees be dropped and sentences passed this quarter
    be rescinded.
3.  That the Kalven Committee report be repudiated and
    consigned to oblivion.
4.  That existing disciplinary committees be dissolved."

Failure of the Committee of the Council to respond satisfac-
torily to these demands by Tuesday noon, March 4, will in and
of itself constitute grounds for further militant action.

Steering Committee
Committee of 500+ Against
Disciplinary Procedures
c/o Student Government
Ida Noyes Hall

205

*Appendix A*

There were several statements from the "university side" that were widely redistributed by students. On February 26, 1969, for example, the faculty "spokesman" for the executive committee of the elected faculty council addressed the faculty and students of the University of Chicago as follows:

The following statement was adopted unanimously by the Council of the University Senate on February 25, 1969:

The Council is compelled to take note of continuing acts directed against the privacy and safety of members of the University and against the University's proper conduct of its mission. These acts have included an assault upon the President's house and upon the persons of two members of the University, as well as the invasion of the Quadrangle Club--all of which occurred on February 24, 1969. Moreover, those participating in these acts included a number of persons who had previously been suspended by the University's Disciplinary Committee.

It is increasingly likely that the security of the University can be reestablished only by invoking civil authority --a course that is particularly suitable when, as has occurred, the University's own disciplinary procedures are defied. It is a course which is always open and is entirely appropriate as long as the University lies under the threat of violence and coercion. Before resorting to the civil authorities, the University will seek once again to deal with present disorders through disciplinary means lying in its own jurisdiction. It must be recognized, however, that circumstances--including the refusal of persons concerned to submit to University disciplinary action--may at any time make civil action necessary, and the Council reluctantly accepts this necessity.

In the light of the foregoing facts, the Council of the Senate joins with the Committee of the Council in the following recommendation to the Dean of Students. The behavior of those persons, known to be under suspension by the Disciplinary Committee now sitting, and identified as having participated in the disruptive events of February 24, appropriately calls for immediate expulsion. Accordingly, these persons should be summoned to appear before a University Disciplinary Committee, to be appointed by the Committee of the Council, and there to show cause why they should not be expelled forthwith. Summonses to this action should be issued immediately. Recipients of these summonses should be required to apply for an individual hearing before the Disciplinary Committee, this application to be in writing, sent by registered mail to the Dean of Students of the University. Such responses must be postmarked no later than 5:00 p.m., Thursday, February 27, 1969. Failure so to respond within the time specified should automatically result in expulsion.

## Appendix B | Two-Score and More of Witnesses against the Fact-Value Split

### 1. RECENT PHILOSOPHERS

In analytical philosophy, it is safe to say that what was once almost a settled matter, with "is" questions and "ought" questions clearly distinct, is now practically reversed, with "fusionists" in the ascendancy. See for example Kurt Baier, *The Moral Point of View* (Cornell, 1958), esp. chaps. 1, 5, and 7; and W. D. Hudson, ed., *The Is/Ought Question: A Collection of Papers on the Central Problem in Moral Philosophy* (London, 1969). R. S. Downie and Elizabeth Telfer conclude, in *Respect for Persons* (London, 1969) that the moral principle of respect for persons is not only "universalizable" but "objective" and that specific moral judgments can be judged as true or false (see esp. pp. 148–51). Scarcely a week passes without a new book proving once again that the earlier analytical emotivists were wrong. See also John Rawls, *A Theory of Justice* (Cambridge, Mass., 1971) and two works by Alasdair MacIntyre, *A Short History of Ethics* (London, 1967), esp. chap. 18), and *Against the Self-Images of the Age* (London, 1971), esp. pt. 2 and the chapter entitled "Ought."

Among philosophers of science one finds a similar new climate, ranging from the "early" neglected classic by Wolfgang Köhler, *The Place of Value in a World of Facts* (New York, 1938), which argued that moral and logical "requiredness" are on the same footing, to the Postscript of the second edition of Thomas S. Kuhn's *The Structure of Scientific Revolutions* (Chicago, 1970). Kuhn had not really discovered this aspect of the postmodernist revolution when he wrote his first edition, but now he says, "A number of contemporary philosophers have discovered important contexts in which the normative and the descriptive are inextricably mixed," and he goes on to argue, in section 7, that fact and value are intertwined in all scientific revolutions.

Nelson Goodman, attempting to construct a comprehensive theory of all human symbols, is naturally driven, as was Kenneth Burke in a similar enterprise, to attack the previously reigning dichotomies: "Most of the troubles that have been plaguing us [in thinking about science and aesthetics] can . . . be blamed on the domineering dichotomy between the cognitive and the emotive. On the one side, we put sensation, perception, inference, fact, and truth; on the other, pleasure, pain, interest, satisfaction, disappointment, all brainless affective response, liking and loathing" (*Languages of Art* [Indianapolis, 1968], pp. 247–48; see also p. 262).

Three other philosophers I find convincing—no doubt in part because I already believed: Robert V. Hannaford, "You Ought to Derive 'Ought' from 'Is,' " *Ethics,* vol. 82; Warner Wick, "Three Bases of Objectivity," in *Self, Religion, and Metaphysics,* ed. Gerald E. Myers (New York, 1961); Alan Gewirth, "Categorial Consistency in Ethics," *Philosophical Quarterly* 17 (1967): 289–99; and idem, "Must One Play the Moral Language Game?" *American Philosophical Quarterly* 7 (1970): 107–18.

In the recently founded *Journal of Value Inquiry* (1967—), it seems that almost half of the articles set out to disprove the disjunction of fact and value in some form; see, for example, in vol. 1, essays by Arnold Berleant, J. Prescott Johnson, Joseph Margolis, and George W. Roberts; in vol. 2, essays by John W. Petras and John T. Wilcox; in vol. 3, essays by Ludwig Grünberg, Errol E. Harris, George M. Kren, Henry Margenau, Fredrick Oscanyan, Stephen C. Pepper (reviewing W. H. Werkmeister, *Man and His Values* [Lincoln, Neb., 1967]—a book that examines "values as factual human experiences, and [attempts] to find rationally justified standards for evaluating them"), George Schrader, and George Stack.

## 2. OTHER FIELDS

The fashion in structuralism has dramatized once again how dependent human studies are on finding values in facts (see especially Claude Lévi-Strauss, *The Savage Mind* [Chicago, 1966], esp. chap. 10, "History and Dialectic"). I cannot pretend to have made my way through the complexities of structuralism as a movement. By now it has won adherents in almost every field, and structuralists themselves invariably have difficulty when they try to generalize about structuralists; see, for example, Michael Lane, "The Structuralist Method" and "Structure and Structuralism," in *Structuralism: A Reader* (London, 1970), and Richard Macksey and Eugenio Donato, eds., *The Languages of Criticism and the Sciences of Man* (Baltimore, 1970). Even Piaget, much the most impressive of those I have read, has some trouble when he comes to summarize the social sciences (*Structuralism* [New Yerk, 1970], esp. chap. 6). But I think it is safe to say that all of them would repudiate the fact-value distinction, or at least restrict its application to special cases. And all would in some sense follow Chomsky's claim that some "deep structures"—whether linguistic, social, literary, or political —are universal, provided the investigator goes deep enough. I am often baffled or exasperated by their wild passion for binary generalizations based on what looks like flimsy evidence (see, for example, the brilliant Roland Barthes' *Sur Racine* [Paris, 1963] and *Le Degré Zero de l'écriture* [Paris, 1953]; a translation of the latter is *Writing Degree Zero* [1967]). But in the essentials (as *I* define essentials) they are attacking the right problem: how do you study a creature made by and living in a structure of symbols, when you, the student, are immersed in the same or similar structures?

The structural anthropologists and literary critics are thus in this one respect just one recent manifestation of a form of argument that has been common in anthropology for some decades, though the popularity of cultural relativism obscured what was being said. In the early 1950s, when I was reading Ruth Benedict and concluding from her ambiguities that she proved "all values to be relative to their cultures," many anthropologists would already have agreed with Robert Redfield (summarizing Firth and Kluckhohn) on "the existence of moral values universal in all cultures because necessary conditions for these values are present in all societies" ("Relations of Anthropology to the Social Sciences and to the Humanities," in *Anthropology Today,* ed. A. L. Kroeber [Chicago, 1953], p. 730). But I did not hear about it, and if I had heard, I assume that I would have been unable to take it in; proofs of relativism were more exciting to me at the time.

Recent sociological modes of discovering objective values through "communicative" definitions of man are fully explored in Joshua A. Fishman, ed., *Readings in The Sociology of Language* (Rowley, Mass., 1968; The Hague, 1970). See also Hans Peter Dreitzel, *Recent Sociology, No. 2: Patterns of Communicative Behavior* (Macmillan, 1970); and Reinhard Bendix, "Sociology and the Distrust of Reason," *American Sociological Review* 35 (1970): 831–43. Though sociology is often thought of as the great source of relativism in this century (see Peter L. Berger, "The Perspective of Sociology: Relativizing the Relativizers," in *A Rumor of Angels: Modern Society and the Rediscovery of the Supernatural* [Garden City, N.Y., 1970]), the founding fathers were not all clearly relativists in the sense of considering all value judgments irrational. I am especially impressed by Emile Durkheim's *The Elementary Forms of the Religious Life* (trans. Joseph Ward Swain [London, 1915]), which includes, as its "secondary subject," a brilliant argument for a theory of knowledge that will place logical and moral "necessity" on the same social footing. See especially the Introduction and the Conclusion in which Durkheim tries to show how his sociological approach goes beyond the effort of Kant to place man's moral life on a secure base. "Outside of us," he says, "there is public opinion which judges us; but more than that, since society is also represented inside of us, it sets itself against these revolutionary fancies [that is, any attempt to violate the canons of 'reason' established by human society], even inside of ourselves; we have the feeling that we cannot abandon them if our whole thought is not to cease being really human. This seems to be the origin of the exceptional authority which is inherent in the reason and which makes us accept its suggestions with confidence. . . . The necessity with which the categories are imposed upon us is . . . a special sort of moral necessity which is to the intellectual life what moral obligation is to the will" (pp. 17–18).

Durkheim is often thought of as a positivist, and he can be quoted as supporting at least some of the modernist dogmas. But his insistence on the "reality" of social norms—a reality which is not compromised by the fact that they differ somewhat from society to society—unites fact and value in a way that seems to have been largely ignored until recently. "Thus it is not at all true that between science on the one hand, and morals and religion on the other, there exists that sort of antinomy which has so frequently been admitted, for the two forms of human activity really come from one and the same source" (p. 445). See Georg Henrik von Wright, *Explanation and Understanding* (Ithica, N.Y., 1971): "Some of Durkheim's chief ideas, for example those concerning the *'representations collectives'* of the social consciousness, could be profitably reinterpreted, I think, in the terms of a hermeneutic methodology of understanding" (p. 173)—which is von Wright's way of saying that Durkheim was not a positivist.

For a first-class critique and extension of Durkheim into problems of the credibility and mutual reinforcement of religious beliefs within a society, see Mary Douglas, *Purity and Danger: An Analysis of Concepts of Pollution and Taboo* (London, 1966). Though her extensive bibliography mentions no work of rhetoric, her book might be taken as a guide to how ideas of pollution and purity are made credible —that is, to a rhetoric of religious assent.

Most psychologists of any note have been driven to recognize that they cannot do their work if the distinction between fact and value is rigidly adhered to. I mention some of these in the third lecture, and mention here only the much neglected American, George Kelly (*The Psychology of Personal Constructs* [New York, 1955]), and the famous Jerome Bruner (see, for example, *On Knowing: Essays for the Left Hand* [Cambridge, Mass., 1962], p. 129).

Some historians have recognized that no full history of human events is possible if the fact-value distinction is maintained. R. G. Collingwood in *The Idea of History* (London, 1946) is particularly forceful in defending history against the progressive depredations of what he thinks of as the Cartesian tradition. He sees Vico as attempting to restore history to the domain of cognition by repudiating Descartes' way of dividing the mind and the world, and the mind from the world. "Vico finds this principle [his alternative to Descartes' search for certain grounds for certain knowledge] in the doctrine that *verum et factum convertuntur:* that is, the condition of being able to know anything truly, to understand it as opposed to merely perceiving it, is that the knower himself should have made it. . . . It follows from the *verum-factum* principle that history, which is emphatically something made by the human mind, is especially adapted to an object of human knowledge" (pp. 64–65). See esp. pt. 2, arts. 5–8.

In law one finds in Charles Fried's *An Anatomy of Values: Problems of Personal and Social Choice* (Cambridge, Mass., 1970) a splendidly sustained argument for the claim that some ends (values) are rational (in some sense factual). Fried is especially good in applying his reasons to life and death matters like "kidney banks and life rafts" (see pp. 155–236).

Finally, the split is rejected by any biologist who concludes that organisms are in fact "well designed." From Aristotle to D'Arcy Thompson, biologists have wondered at the general effectiveness of beauty, the sheer engineering "brilliance," of natural forms, and when they have done so they have necessarily, if only for the moment, seen value in fact. It can even be argued that Darwin's notion of the survival of the fittest was a fusion of the *is* and the *good*; the well-formed (as judged by *many* standards) generally survived (one *additional* standard). But the catch-phrase is generally interpreted by moderns as a mere tautology: to be "the fittest" and to survive are identical, in which case there are no real values involved at all, only the one fact: survival. See Stephen Jay Gould, "D'Arcy Thompson and the Science of Form," *New Literary History* 2 (Winter 1971): 229–58.

# Bibliography

The immediate sources for this book are documented in the footnotes, which I have indexed with unusual fulness. Instead of duplicating these references, which are mostly to authors who never use the word rhetoric, I list here mainly authors who are conscious of working in one or another rhetorical tradition, and *only works not previously cited*. I exclude the great theorists before modern times, like Aristotle, Cicero, and Quintilian; they are cited fully in most bibliographies of rhetoric.

Of all the works explicitly about rhetoric that I have not been able to find room for, I most regret those that discuss the rhetoric of recent protest movements. But the bibliography of any one of these —student protest, civil rights, black power, women's liberation, and so on—would more than fill the space available. I also regret having to omit most of the composition and rhetoric texts designed for freshman courses.

Extensive bibliographies of rhetoric can be found in Chaim Perelman, *The New Rhetoric: A Treatise on Argumentation* (Notre Dame, Ind.: University of Notre Dame Press, 1969); James W. Cleary and Frederick W. Haberman, eds., *Rhetoric and Public Address: A Bibliography, 1947–1961* (Madison: University of Wisconsin Press, 1964); Edward P. J. Corbett, *Classical Rhetoric for the Modern Student*, 2d ed. (New York: Oxford University Press, 1965); Daniel Fogarty, *Roots for a New Rhetoric* (New York: Bureau of Publications, Columbia Teachers College, 1959); Joseph Schwartz and John J. Rycenga, eds., *The Province of Rhetoric* (New York: Ronald Press, 1965); and Douglas Ehninger, *Contemporary Rhetoric: A Reader's Coursebook* (Glenview, Ill.: Scott, Foresman, 1972). The *Newsletter* of the Rhetoric Society of America compiles an annual bibliography, "Rhetoric and Books and Articles Relevant to Rhetoric" (see, for example, *Newsletter* for May 1973). Good bibliographies on their special subjects are found in Edward P. J. Corbett, ed., *Rhetorical Analysis of Literary Works* (New York: Oxford University Press, 1969); and Jerome D. Frank, *Persuasion and Healing* (Baltimore: Johns Hopkins University Press, 1961). On style and rhetoric see Richard Bailey and Dolores Burton, eds., *English Stylistics: A Bibliography* (Boston: M.I.T. Press, 1969); Louis T. Milic, ed., *Style and Stylistics: An Analytical Bibliography* (New York: Free Press, 1967); and Harold C. Martin and Richard M. Ohmann, eds., "A Select Bibliography on Style," in *English Institute Essays, 1958* (New York: Columbia University Press, 1959), pp. 192–200.

Alston, R. C., and Rosier, J. L. "Rhetoric and Style: A Bibliographical Guide." *Leeds Studies in English*, n.s., 1 (1967): 137–59.

Apostel, Leo. "Rhétorique, psycho-sociologie et logique." In *La Théorie de l'Argumentation*. Louvain: Éditions Nauwelaerte, 1963.

Baird, Albert Craig. *Rhetoric: A Philosophical Inquiry*. New York: Ronald Press, 1965.

Black, Edwin. *Rhetorical Criticism*. New York: Macmillan, 1965.

Blair, Hugh. *Lectures on Rhetoric and Belles Lettres*. London, 1783.

Booth, T. Y. *The Supreme Organ of the Mind's Self-Ordering Growth*. Logan, Utah: Faculty Association, 1973.

Bosmajian, Haig A., ed. *The Rhetoric of Nonverbal Communication*. Glenview, Ill.: Scott, Foresman, 1970.

Brandt, William J. *The Rhetoric of Argumentation*. Indianapolis, Ind.: Bobbs-Merrill, 1970.

Brockriede, Wayne E. "Dimensions of the Concept of Rhetoric." *Quarterly Journal of Speech* 54 (1966): 33–40.

Brookes, Gerry H. *The Rhetorical Form of Carlyle's* Sartor Resartus. Berkeley: University of California Press, 1972.

Burke, Kenneth. *Attitudes Toward History*. New York: Editorial Publications, 1937. Rev. ed., Los Altos, Calif.: Hermes Publications, 1959.

―――. *Counter-Statement*. Los Altos, Calif.: Hermes Publications, 1931. Rev. ed., 1953.

―――. *Language as Symbolic Action: Essays on Life, Literature, and Method*. Berkeley: University of California Press, 1968.

―――. *The Philosophy of Literary Form: Studies in Symbolic Action*. 2d ed. Baton Rouge, La.: Louisiana State University Press, 1967.

―――. *A Rhetoric of Motives*. New York: George Braziller, 1950.

―――. "Rhetoric Old and New." *Journal of General Education* 5 (1950–51): 203–9.

Campbell, George. *The Philosophy of Rhetoric*. London: W. Strahan, 1776.

Campbell, Karlyn K. "The Ontological Foundations of Rhetorical Theory." *Philosophy and Rhetoric* 3 (1970): 97–108.

Caplan, Harry. *Of Eloquence: Studies in Ancient and Mediaeval Rhetoric*. Edited by Anne King and Helen North. Ithaca, N.Y.: Cornell University Press, 1970.

Clark, Donald Lemen. "The Place of Rhetoric in a Liberal Education." *Quarterly Journal of Speech* 36 (1950): 291–95.

―――. *Rhetoric in Greco-Roman Education*. New York: Columbia University Press, 1957.

Corbett, Edward P. J. "The Rhetoric of the Open Hand and the Rhetoric of the Closed Fist." In *Contemporary Rhetoric*. Edited by Douglas Ehninger. Glenview, Ill.: Scott, Foresman, 1972, pp. 202–10.

Croll, Morris William. *Style, Rhetoric, and Rhythm: Essays by Morris*

*W. Croll.* Edited by J. Max Patrick and others. Princeton, N.J.: Princeton University Press, 1966.

Dorolle, Maurice. *Le raisonnement par analogie.* Bibliothèque de Phillosophie contemporaine. Paris: Presses Universitaires de France, 1949.

Drummond, A. M., ed. *Studies in Rhetoric and Public Speaking, in Honor of James Albert Winans, by Pupils and Colleagues.* New York: Russell and Russell, 1962.

Ehninger, Douglas, and Brockriede, Wayne. *Decision by Debate.* New York: Dodd, Mead, 1963.

Eubanks, Ralph T., and Baker, Virgil L. "Toward an Axiology of Rhetoric." *Quarterly Journal of Speech* 48 (1962): 157–68.

Florescu, Vasile. "Rhetoric and Its Rehabilitation in Contemporary Philosophy." *Philosophy and Rhetoric* 3 (1970): 193–224.

France, Peter. *Rhetoric and Truth in France: Descartes to Diderot.* Oxford: Clarendon Press, 1972.

Friedman, Norman. "The Rhetoric of Logic." *Journal of General Education* 17 (1965–66): 287–94.

Gauthier, David P. *Practical Reasoning: The Structure and Foundations of Prudential and Moral Arguments and Their Exemplification in Discourse.* Oxford: Clarendon Press, 1963.

Genung, John Franklin. *The Practical Elements of Rhetoric.* Boston: Ginn, 1895.

———. *The Working Principles of Rhetoric Examined in Their Literary Relations and Illustrated with Examples.* Boston, Mass.: Ginn, 1900.

Giuliani, Alessandro. *Il Concetto di Prova: Contributo alla Logica Giuridica.* Milan: A. Giuffrè, 1961.

Gouhier, Henri. "La résistance au vrai et le problème cartésien d'une philosophie sans rhétorique." In *Rhetorica e Barocco.* Rome: Fratelli Bocca, 1955.

Hill, Adams Sherman. *The Foundations of Rhetoric.* New York: Harper, 1899.

Hook, Sidney. "The Ethics of Controversy." *New Leader* 37 (February 1954): 12–14.

Hovland, Carl I.; Janis, Irving L.; and Kelley, Harold H. *Communication and Persuasion.* Psychological Studies of Opinion Change. New Haven, Conn.: Yale University Press, 1953.

Howell, Wilbur Samuel. *Eighteenth-Century British Logic and Rhetoric.* Princeton: Princeton University Press, 1971.

Howes, Raymond Floyd. *Historical Studies of Rhetoric and Rhetoricians.* Ithaca, N.Y.: Cornell University Press, 1961.

Hoyt, H. Hudson. "The Field of Rhetoric." *Quarterly Journal of Speech* 9 (1923): 167–80.

Hunt, Everett Lee. "Rhetoric as a Humane Study." *Quarterly Journal of Speech* 41 (1955): 114–17.

215

Johannesen, Richard L., ed. *Ethics and Persuasion: Selected Readings.* New York: Random House, 1966.

Johnstone, Henry W., Jr. "The Relevance of Rhetoric to Philosophy and of Philosophy to Rhetoric." *Quarterly Journal of Speech* 52 (1966): 41–46.

Kennedy, George Alexander. *The Art of Persuasion in Greece.* London: Routledge and Kegan Paul, 1963.

———. *The Art of Rhetoric in the Roman World, 300* B.C.–A.D. *300.* London: Oxford University Press, 1973.

LaDrière, Craig. "Rhetoric as 'Merely Verbal' Art." In *English Institute Essays, 1948.* Edited by D. A. Robertson, Jr. New York: Columbia University Press, 1949, pp. 123–52.

Lanigan, Richard. "Rhetorical Criticism: An Interpretation of Maurice Merleau-Ponty." *Philosophy and Rhetoric* 2 (1969): 61–71.

Loreau, Max. "Pour Situer la Nouvelle Rhétorique." In *La Théorie de l'Argumentation.* Published in honor of Ch. Perelman. Louvain: Éditions Nauwelaerts, 1963, pp. 103–29.

Lundeen, Lyman T. *Risk and Rhetoric in Religion: Whitehead's Theory of Language and the Discourse of Faith.* Philadelphia: Fortress Press, 1972.

McKeon, Richard. "Communication and Community as Philosophy." *Ethics* 63 (1953): 190–206.

———. "Conflict of Values in a Community of Cultures." *Journal of Philosophy* 47 (1950): 197–210.

———. "Dialogue and Controversy in Philosophy." *Philosophy and Phenomenological Research* 17 (1956): 143–63.

———. "Discourse, Demonstration, Verification, and Justification." In *Démonstration, Vérification, Justification.* Paris: Béatrice-Nauwelaerts, 1967.

———. "The Methods of Rhetoric and Philosophy: Invention and Judgment." In *The Classical Tradition: Literary and Historical Studies in Honor of Harry Caplan.* Edited by Luitpold Wallach. Ithaca, N.Y.: Cornell University Press, 1966.

———. "Philosophy and Action." *Ethics* 62 (1952): 79–100.

———. "Philosophy of Communications and the Arts." In *Perspectives in Education, Religion, and the Arts.* Vol. 3 of *Contemporary Philosophic Thought: The International Philosophy Year Conferences at Brockport.* Edited by Howard Keifer and Milton Munitz. Albany, N.Y.: State University of New York Press, 1970.

———. "Poetry and Philosophy in the Twelfth Century: The Renaissance of Rhetoric." *Modern Philology* 53 (1946): 217–34.

———. "Power and the Language of Power." *Ethics* 68 (1958): 98–115.

———. "Rhetoric in the Middle Ages." In *Critics and Criticism:*

*Ancient and Modern.* Edited by R. S. Crane. Chicago: University of Chicago Press, 1952.

———. "Symbols, Myths, and Arguments." In *Symbols and Values: An Initial Study.* Edited by Lyman Bryson et al. New York: Conference on Science, Philosophy, and Religion in Their Relation to the Democratic Way of Life, Inc. (Distributed by Harper and Rowe), 1954.

———. *Thought, Action, and Passion.* Chicago: University of Chicago Press, 1954.

Millioud, Maurice. "La propagation des idées." *Revue Philosophique de la France et de L'Étranger* 69 (1910): 580–600; 70 (1910): 168–91.

Natanson, Maurice. "The Limits of Rhetoric." *Quarterly Journal of Speech* 41 (1955): 133–39.

Needham, Rodney. *Belief, Language, and Experience.* Chicago: University of Chicago Press, 1972.

Newman, John Henry. *An Essay in Aid of A Grammar of Assent.* London, 1870.

Ogden, Charles K., and Richards, I. A. *The Meaning of Meaning: A Study of the Influence of Language upon Thought and of the Science of Symbolism.* London: Kegan Paul, Trench, Trubner, 1923.

Ohmann, Richard. "In Lieu of a New Rhetoric." *College English* 26 (1964): 17–22.

Ong, Walter J. *The Presence of the Word: Some Prolegomena for Cultural and Religious History.* New Haven: Yale University Press, 1967.

———. "The Province of Rhetoric and Poetic." *Modern Schoolman* 19 (1941–42): 24–27.

———. *Rhetoric, Romance, and Technology: Studies in the Interaction of Expression and Culture.* Ithica, N.Y.: Cornell University Press, 1971.

Perelman, Chaim. *The Idea of Justice and the Problem of Argument.* Tr. John Petrie. London: Routledge and Kegan Paul, 1963.

———. "The New Rhetoric: A Theory of Practical Reasoning." In *The Great Ideas Today 1970.* Chicago: Encyclopaedia Britannica, 1970.

———. "The Theoretical Relations of Thought and Action." *Inquiry* 1 (1958): 130–36.

Perelman, Chaim, and Olbrechts-Tyteca, L. "Act and Person in Argument." *Ethics* 61 (1950–51): 251–69.

Richards, I. A. *The Philosophy of Rhetoric.* New York: Oxford University Press, 1936.

Rockas, Leo. *Modes of Rhetoric.* New York: St. Martin's Press, 1964.

Sider, Robert Dick. *Ancient Rhetoric and the Art of Tertullian.* London: Oxford University Press, 1971.

Simmons, James R. "Whitehead's Metaphysic of Persuasion." *Philosophy and Rhetoric* 2 (1969): 72–80.

Steiner, George. *Language and Silence: Essays on Language, Literature, and the Inhuman.* New York: Atheneum, 1967.

Torrence, Donald L. "A Philosophy for Rhetoric from Bertrand Russell." *Quarterly Journal of Speech* 45 (1959): 153–65.

Toulmin, Stephen. *The Uses of Argument.* Cambridge: Cambridge University Press, 1958.

Veatch, Henry B. *Two Logics: The Conflict between Classical and Neo-Analytic Philosophy.* Evanston, Ill.: Northwestern University Press, 1969.

Wallace, Karl Richards. *Francis Bacon on Communication and Rhetoric; or, The Art of Applying Reason to Imagination for the Better Moving of the Will.* Chapel Hill, N.C.: University of North Carolina Press, 1943.

————. "The Philosophical Stance toward Rhetorical Behavior." In *Understanding Discourse: The Speech Act and Rhetorical Action.* Baton Rouge, La.: Louisiana State University Press, 1970.

————. "The Substance of Rhetoric: Good Reasons." *Quarterly Journal of Speech* 49 (1963): 239–49.

Weaver, Richard. *The Ethics of Rhetoric.* Chicago: Regnery, 1953.

White, James B. *The Legal Imagination: Studies in the Nature of Legal Thought and Expression.* Boston: Little, Brown, 1973.

Winterowd, W. Ross. *Rhetoric: A Synthesis.* New York: Holt, Rinehart and Winston, 1968.

# Index

Abbott, H. Porter, 177n17
Abortion, 162n
Absurd, the, 138, 173, 178, 185
Adams, Robert Martin, 188n
*Adversity and Grace* (Scott), 188n
Advertising, 65, 167, 201n; subliminal, 87
Aesop, 186
Aesthetics, 15, 98n
Affirming, 184; in art, 176. *See* Denying
African sculpture, 179
*Against the Self-Images of the Age* (MacIntyre), 207
Agency. *See* Dogmas, five kinds
*Agent, Action, and Reason* (McGowan and Gochnauer), 27n
Aggression, 128
Agreement, as test of knowledge, 118, 120, 125, 148
Ahab, 184
Alchemy, 106, 107
Alienation, 97n, 202n, 203
Altmann, Stuart A., 115n23
Altruism, 202n
America: future of, 202n; today, 200–201
*American Power and the New Mandarins* (Chomsky), 21n13
A-Minor Quartet (Beethoven), 164
Analogy, 98n, 141n; of being, 93
*Analysis of Mind, The* (Russell), 29–30, 51n
*Anatomy of Values, An* (Fried), 65n17, 210
*Animal Farm* (Orwell), 187n22
Animals, symbolic exchange in, 125n
*Anna Karenina* (Tolstoy), 185
Anscombe, G.E.M., 116n
Anselm, 136n
Anshen, Ruth Nanda, x
Anthropology, 12, 16n, 20, 71; and fact-value split, 209
*Anti-Story*, 192
Aquinas, Thomas, 94, 99–100
Architecture, xv
Arendt, Hannah, 97n

Argument, 4. *See also* Good reasons; Reason
Ariely, Yehoshua, 23n
Aristotle, 14, 22n, 31, 44, 48, 66n19, 99–100, 119n, 127n, 138, 144, 144n, 145n, 149n5, 151, 183, 185, 211, 213; *Ethics*, 185
Arnold, Thomas, 2
*Arrowsmith* (Lewis), 166
Art, 98; as achievement, 172; bad, attitudes as sign of, 173–77; as form of knowledge, 169; metaphysic of, 98; neutrality of, rejected, 168n; as providing good reasons, 164–92; as source of assent, 197; as teacher, 168
*Art as Experience* (Dewey), 97n
Arts, atomic self in, 130–31
Assent: degrees of, xiii; with mind, 200; to nature of things, 195–97; primacy of, 194–97; primacy of, in babies, 194n; systematic, xvii. *See also* Affirming; Good reasons
*Assistant, The* (Malamud), 189
Astral projection, 107
Astrology, 48, 107
Astronauts, 26
Atheism, 133
*Atlantic*, 162n
Atomic bomb, 80
Attitudes, 173–77; contradictory, 176
Auden, W. H., 140, 189–90
Augustine, vi, 136n, 138
Austen, Jane, 117–21, 163, 166; *Pride and Prejudice*, 117–21
Authority, 32, 88, 101, 141n, 143n, 157; in science, 109n
*Authority and the Individual* (Russell), 79n25, 81
*Autobiography* (Mill), 56n
*Autobiography of Bertrand Russell*, 46n, 82, 83n
Axthelm, Peter M., 191n26
Ayer, A. J., 114n21; *Language, Truth and Logic*, 64n

Bach, Johann Sebastian, 122–24, 171n; B-minor Mass, 174

# Index

LINCOLN CHRISTIAN UNIVERSITY    130927

CPSIA information can be obtained at www.ICGtesting.com
Printed in the USA
LVOW10s1733101115

461888LV00003B/575/P

3 4711 00225 8848